IN ASSOCIATION WITH

SQA

Hodder Gibson
Model Practice
Papers
WITH ANSWERS

PLUS: Official SQA Specimen Paper &
2014 Past Paper With Answers

National 5
History

2013 Specimen Question Paper,
Model Papers & 2014 Exam

HODDER
GIBSON
AN HACHETTE UK COMPANY

This book contains the official 2013 SQA Specimen Question Paper and 2014 Exam for National 5 History, with associated SQA approved answers modified from the official marking instructions that accompany the paper.

In addition the book contains model practice papers, together with answers, plus study skills advice. These papers, some of which may include a limited number of previously published SQA questions, have been specially commissioned by Hodder Gibson, and have been written by experienced senior teachers and examiners in line with the new National 5 syllabus and assessment outlines, Spring 2013. This is not SQA material but has been devised to provide further practice for National 5 examinations in 2014 and beyond.

Hodder Gibson is grateful to the copyright holders, as credited on the final page of the Answer Section, for permission to use their material. Every effort has been made to trace the copyright holders and to obtain their permission for the use of copyright material. Hodder Gibson will be happy to receive information allowing us to rectify any error or omission in future editions.

Hachette UK's policy is to use papers that are natural, renewable and recyclable products and made from wood grown in sustainable forests. The logging and manufacturing processes are expected to conform to the environmental regulations of the country of origin.

Orders: please contact Bookpoint Ltd, 130 Park Drive, Abingdon, Oxon OX14 4SE. Telephone: (44) 01235 827720. Fax: (44) 01235 400454. Lines are open 9.00–5.00, Monday to Saturday, with a 24-hour message answering service. Visit our website at www.hoddereducation.co.uk. Hodder Gibson can be contacted direct on: Tel: 0141 848 1609; Fax: 0141 889 6315; email: hoddergibson@hodder.co.uk

This collection first published in 2014 by
Hodder Gibson, an imprint of Hodder Education,
An Hachette UK Company
2a Christie Street
Paisley PA1 1NB

BrightRED   Hodder Gibson is grateful to Bright Red Publishing Ltd for collaborative work in preparation of this book and all SQA Past Paper, National 5 and Higher for CfE Model Paper titles 2014.

Specimen Question Paper 2013 and National 5 Exam Paper 2014 © Scottish Qualifications Authority. Answers, Model Question Papers, and Study Skills Section © Hodder Gibson. Model Question Papers creation/compilation, Answers and Study Skills section © John Kerr and Jerry Teale. All rights reserved. Apart from any use permitted under UK copyright law, no part of this publication may be reproduced or transmitted in any form or by any means, electronic or mechanical, including photocopying and recording, or held within any information storage and retrieval system, without permission in writing from the publisher or under licence from the Copyright Licensing Agency Limited. Further details of such licences (for reprographic reproduction) may be obtained from the Copyright Licensing Agency Limited, Saffron House, 6–10 Kirby Street, London EC1N 8TS.

Typeset by PDQ Digital Media Solutions Ltd, Bungay, Suffolk NR35 1BY

Printed in the UK

A catalogue record for this title is available from the British Library

ISBN: 978-1-4718-3707-4

3 2 1

2015 2014

Introduction

Study Skills – what you need to know to pass exams!

Pause for thought

Many students might skip quickly through a page like this. After all, we all know how to revise. Do you really though?

Think about this:

"IF YOU ALWAYS DO WHAT YOU ALWAYS DO, YOU WILL ALWAYS GET WHAT YOU HAVE ALWAYS GOT."

Do you like the grades you get? Do you want to do better? If you get full marks in your assessment, then that's great! Change nothing! This section is just to help you get that little bit better than you already are.

There are two main parts to the advice on offer here. The first part highlights fairly obvious things but which are also very important. The second part makes suggestions about revision that you might not have thought about but which WILL help you.

Part 1

DOH! It's so obvious but …

Start revising in good time

Don't leave it until the last minute – this will make you panic.

Make a revision timetable that sets out work time AND play time.

Sleep and eat!

Obvious really, and very helpful. Avoid arguments or stressful things too – even games that wind you up. You need to be fit, awake and focused!

Know your place!

Make sure you know exactly **WHEN and WHERE** your exams are.

Know your enemy!

Make sure you know what to expect in the exam.

How is the paper structured?

How much time is there for each question?

What types of question are involved?

Which topics seem to come up time and time again?

Which topics are your strongest and which are your weakest?

Are all topics compulsory or are there choices?

Learn by DOING!

There is no substitute for past papers and practice papers – they are simply essential! Tackling this collection of papers and answers is exactly the right thing to be doing as your exams approach.

Part 2

People learn in different ways. Some like low light, some bright. Some like early morning, some like evening / night. Some prefer warm, some prefer cold. But everyone uses their BRAIN and the brain works when it is active. Passive learning – sitting gazing at notes – is the most INEFFICIENT way to learn anything. Below you will find tips and ideas for making your revision more effective and maybe even more enjoyable. What follows gets your brain active, and active learning works!

Activity 1 – Stop and review

Step 1

When you have done no more than 5 minutes of revision reading STOP!

Step 2

Write a heading in your own words which sums up the topic you have been revising.

Step 3

Write a summary of what you have revised in no more than two sentences. Don't fool yourself by saying, "I know it, but I cannot put it into words". That just means you don't know it well enough. If you cannot write your summary, revise that section again, knowing that you must write a summary at the end of it. Many of you will have notebooks full of blue/black ink writing. Many of the pages will not be especially attractive or memorable so try to liven them up a bit with colour as you are reviewing and rewriting. **This is a great memory aid, and memory is the most important thing.**

Activity 2 — Use technology!

Why should everything be written down? Have you thought about "mental" maps, diagrams, cartoons and colour to help you learn? And rather than write down notes, why not record your revision material?

What about having a text message revision session with friends? Keep in touch with them to find out how and what they are revising and share ideas and questions.

Why not make a video diary where you tell the camera what you are doing, what you think you have learned and what you still have to do? No one has to see or hear it, but the process of having to organise your thoughts in a formal way to explain something is a very important learning practice.

Be sure to make use of electronic files. You could begin to summarise your class notes. Your typing might be slow, but it will get faster and the typed notes will be easier to read than the scribbles in your class notes. Try to add different fonts and colours to make your work stand out. You can easily Google relevant pictures, cartoons and diagrams which you can copy and paste to make your work more attractive and **MEMORABLE**.

Activity 3 – This is it. Do this and you will know lots!

Step 1

In this task you must be very honest with yourself! Find the SQA syllabus for your subject (www.sqa.org.uk). Look at how it is broken down into main topics called MANDATORY knowledge. That means stuff you MUST know.

Step 2

BEFORE you do ANY revision on this topic, write a list of everything that you already know about the subject. It might be quite a long list but you only need to write it once. It shows you all the information that is already in your long-term memory so you know what parts you do not need to revise!

Step 3

Pick a chapter or section from your book or revision notes. Choose a fairly large section or a whole chapter to get the most out of this activity.

With a buddy, use Skype, Facetime, Twitter or any other communication you have, to play the game "If this is the answer, what is the question?". For example, if you are revising Geography and the answer you provide is "meander", your buddy would have to make up a question like "What is the word that describes a feature of a river where it flows slowly and bends often from side to side?".

Make up 10 "answers" based on the content of the chapter or section you are using. Give this to your buddy to solve while you solve theirs.

Step 4

Construct a wordsearch of at least 10 X 10 squares. You can make it as big as you like but keep it realistic. Work together with a group of friends. Many apps allow you to make wordsearch puzzles online. The words and phrases can go in any direction and phrases can be split. Your puzzle must only contain facts linked to the topic you are revising. Your task is to find 10 bits of information to hide in your puzzle, but you must not repeat information that you used in Step 3. DO NOT show where the words are. Fill up empty squares with random letters. Remember to keep a note of where your answers are hidden but do not show your friends. When you have a complete puzzle, exchange it with a friend to solve each other's puzzle.

Step 5

Now make up 10 questions (not "answers" this time) based on the same chapter used in the previous two tasks. Again, you must find NEW information that you have not yet used. Now it's getting hard to find that new information! Again, give your questions to a friend to answer.

Step 6

As you have been doing the puzzles, your brain has been actively searching for new information. Now write a NEW LIST that contains only the new information you have discovered when doing the puzzles. Your new list is the one to look at repeatedly for short bursts over the next few days. Try to remember more and more of it without looking at it. After a few days, you should be able to add words from your second list to your first list as you increase the information in your long-term memory.

FINALLY! Be inspired...

Make a list of different revision ideas and beside each one write **THINGS I HAVE** tried, **THINGS I WILL** try and **THINGS I MIGHT** try. Don't be scared of trying something new.

And remember – "FAIL TO PREPARE AND PREPARE TO FAIL!"

National 5 History

The course requirements

The Assignment – how to be successful

The Assignment is an essay written under exam conditions and then sent to the SQA to be marked.

The Assignment counts for 20 marks out of a total of 80 so doing well in it can provide you with a very useful launch pad for future success.

How long does my essay have to be?

There are NO word limits in the Assignment – it is whatever you can write in one hour!

What should I write about?

First, it makes sense to choose a question from the syllabus you are studying, which you can check at: www.sqa.org.uk/sqa/47447.html.

Second, your essay title should be based on a question that allows you to use your evidence to answer the question. You must avoid titles that are just statements such as "The Slave Trade" or "Appeasement". They do not allow you to use information to provide an overall answer to your title question.

Finally, try NOT to make up questions that are too complicated or that ask two questions within the same title.

What is the Resource Sheet?

Your Resource Sheet provides a framework and notes for your essay.

It shows the marker

- that you have researched, selected and organised your information
- that you have thought about your work and reached a decision about the question in your title
- which sources you have used and demonstrates how you have used them.

Your Resource Sheet MUST be sent to the SQA with your finished essay.

Your Resource Sheet should NOT be just a collection of facts, figures and quotes. It should outline the main parts of your essay and remind you what to write.

The Exam Paper

The question paper is made up of three **sections**:

Section 1 – Historical Study: Scottish
Section 2 – Historical Study: British
Section 3 – Historical Study: European and World.

In each **section** you will select **one** part to answer questions on:

Section 1: Historical Study: Scottish

Part A: The Wars of Independence, 1286–1328 ✓
Part B: Mary Queen of Scots, and the Reformation, 1542–1587 ✓
Part C: The Treaty of Union, 1689–1715 ✓
Part D: Migration and Empire, 1830–1939 ✓
Part E: The Era of the Great War, 1910–1928 ✓

Section 2: Historical Study: British

Part A: The Creation of the Medieval Kingdoms, 1066–1406
Part B: War of the Three Kingdoms, 1603–1651
Part C: The Atlantic Slave Trade, 1770–1807 ✓
Part D: Changing Britain, 1760–1900 ✓
Part E: The Making of Modern Britain, 1880–1951 ✓

Section 3: Historical Study: European and World

Part A: The Cross and the Crescent, the Crusades, 1071–1192
Part B: 'Tea and Freedom', the American Revolution, 1774–83 ✓
Part C: USA 1850–1880 ✓
Part D: Hitler and Nazi Germany, 1919–1939 ✓
Part E: Red Flag: Lenin and the Russian Revolution, 1894–1921 ✓
Part F: Mussolini and Fascist Italy, 1919–1939
Part G: Free at Last? Civil Rights in the USA, 1918–1968 ✓
Part H: Appeasement and the Road to War, 1918–1939 ✓
Part I: World War II, 1939–1945 ✓
Part J: The Cold War 1945–1989 ✓

The titles with the tick after them are all included in the model papers.

Answering the Exam Questions

The first rule is simple and is the most important thing that will get you marks:

Answer the question that you are asked, NOT what you would like it to ask.

The Exam paper has 6 types of questions.

TYPE 1 – the **"Describe"** question, worth **5 or 6 marks**.

In this type of question you must describe what happened by using five or six pieces of your own knowledge, known as **recall**. There is no source to help you with information so your answer will be based on your own recall.

TYPE 2 – the **"Explain"** question, worth **5 or 6 marks**.

To be successful with this type of question you must give 5 or 6 reasons why something happened. Once again, there is no source to help you. Use recall that is correct and accurate.

TYPE 3 – the **"To what extent…"** question, worth **8 marks**.

To be successful with this type of question you must write a balanced answer. That means you must decide how important a particular factor was in explaining why something happened. Include at least five pieces of relevant information and give a short conclusion which sums up your answer to the question.

TYPE 4 – the **"How useful…"** question, worth **5 or 6 marks**. This question will ask "Evaluate the usefulness of a source as evidence of …."

Evaluate means **to judge** how good a source is as evidence for finding out about something. The short answer is that it will always be partly useful but it will never be entirely useful in giving all the information you need.

In this type of question it is never enough just to **describe** what is in a source. It might be helpful to base your answer around the following guide questions.

WHO produced the source? Why is the AUTHORSHIP of the source relevant and therefore useful in assessing the value of a source?

WHEN was the source produced and how might that help in the evaluation of the source?

WHY was the source produced? What did the person who produced the source want the readers to think or do or feel because of the information in the source?

WHAT information is in the source and how relevant is that to the question?

WHAT'S NOT THERE? What important information is missing from the source that makes you think the source was not as useful as it could be?

TYPE 5 – the **"Compare"** question, worth **4 marks**

You will always get one question that asks you to compare two sources in your exam. To be successful with this type of question you must make clear connections between sources but do not just describe the two sources.

These questions are easy to spot because they are the only ones that will refer to TWO sources. For this type of question you must say whether you think the sources agree or not and then support your decision by making two comparisons using evidence from the sources.

TYPE 6 – the **"How fully…"** question, worth **5 or 6 marks**.

To be successful with this type of question you must select information from the source which is relevant to the question – usually there will be three points of information in the source for you to use. Use recall that is accurate and relevant to make your answer more balanced. You will never get a source that gives the full story so it is up to you to say that the source PARTLY explains or describes something but there is more information needed to give the full story. That's where you show off your recalled extra knowledge.

Good luck!

Remember that the rewards for passing National 5 History are well worth it! Your pass will help you get the future you want for yourself. In the exam, be confident in your own ability. If you're not sure how to answer a question, trust your instincts and just give it a go anyway. Keep calm and don't panic! GOOD LUCK!

2013 Specimen Question Paper

National
Qualifications
SPECIMEN ONLY

SQ23/N5/01   **History**

Date — Not applicable

Duration — 1 hour and 30 minutes

Total marks — 60

SECTION 1 — SCOTTISH — 20 marks

Attempt ONE part.

SECTION 2 — BRITISH — 20 marks

Attempt ONE part.

SECTION 3 — EUROPEAN AND WORLD — 20 marks

Attempt ONE part.

Before attempting the questions you must check that your answer booklet is for the same subject and level as this question paper.

On the answer booklet, you must clearly identify the question number you are attempting.

Use **blue** or **black** ink.

Before leaving the examination room you must give your answer booklet to the Invigilator. If you do not, you may lose all the marks for this paper.

SECTION 1 — SCOTTISH

SECTION 2 — BRITISH

SECTION 3 — EUROPEAN AND WORLD

SECTION 1 — SCOTTISH — 20 marks

Attempt ONE part

MARKS

Part A — The Wars of Independence, 1286–1328

Attempt the following questions using recalled knowledge and information from the sources where appropriate.

Source A is a letter written by Bishop Fraser of St Andrews to King Edward in October 1290.

Source A

> A rumour has spread among the people that the Maid of Norway has died. The Bishop of Durham, Earl Warenne and I then heard that she has recovered from her sickness but that she is very weak. We have agreed to stay at Perth until we hear definite news about her. We have sent two knights to Orkney to find out exactly what has happened.

1. Evaluate the usefulness of **Source A** as evidence of the succession problem following the death of Alexander III.

   (You may want to comment on who wrote it, when they wrote it, why they wrote it, what they say or what has been missed out.)

   5

2. Describe the role played by William Wallace during the Wars of Independence.

   5

3. Explain the reasons why Robert Bruce was able to take control of Scotland between 1306 and 1313.

   5

Source B is about the Battle of Bannockburn.

Source B

> Bruce's careful preparations for battle were ruined when Edward II moved his army to attack from the east and not from the south. However, this gave the much larger English army no room to move because they were surrounded by marshes and streams. Bruce decided to take advantage of this mistake and to attack them. The English were so jammed together and so tangled up that their leaders struggled to organise any defence and they lost all confidence in Edward II for leading them into this trap.

4. How fully does **Source B** explain why the Scots were able to win the Battle of Bannockburn? (Use **Source B** and recall.)

   5

SECTION 1 — SCOTTISH

Part B – Mary Queen of Scots and the Reformation, 1542–1587

Attempt the following questions using recalled knowledge and information from the sources where appropriate.

Source A is about why the Scots rebelled against Mary of Guise in 1559.

Source A

> After Mary Queen of Scots married in 1558, her mother, Mary of Guise, continued to rule Scotland on behalf of her daughter who was in France. Guise took strong action against Protestants in Scotland, especially after Elizabeth became Queen of England in November of the same year. She made more use of French officials and used more French soldiers to control key strongholds in Scotland. She also demanded a new tax, but the Scottish nobles were determined not to allow that.

1. How fully does **Source A** explain why the Protestant Lords rebelled against Mary of Guise in 1559? (Use **Source A** and recall.) **5**

Source B is Mary Queen of Scots's order to pay ministers of the Church of Scotland, issued in 1566.

Source B

> Because the ministers within Scotland have not been paid for this last year and because I determined that they should be paid in the future, I have, with the advice of my government officials, decided to allocate the sum of £10,000 for their payment. I have also ordered that this sum must be paid in full.

2. Evaluate the usefulness of **Source B** as evidence of Mary Queen of Scots's support for the Church of Scotland in 1566. **5**

   (You may want to comment on who wrote it, when they wrote it, why they wrote it, what they say or what has been missed out.)

3. Describe the effects the murder of Riccio had during the reign of Mary Queen of Scots. **5**

4. Explain the reasons why Mary Queen of Scots was executed in 1587. **5**

SECTION 1 — SCOTTISH

MARKS

Part C – The Treaty of Union, 1689–1715

Attempt the following questions using recalled knowledge and information from the sources where appropriate.

1. Explain the reasons why relations between Scotland and England got worse between 1689 and 1707.

5

Source A is from a letter written in 1707 by a member of the Scottish government.

Source A

> It is impossible to state exactly how much was given to the Duke of Atholl, the Marquis of Tweeddale and the Earls of Roxburghe, Marchmont and Cromartie without revealing exactly how much has been given to everybody else. So far, this has been kept a secret and revealing this information at present would cause embarrassment.

2. Evaluate the usefulness of **Source A** as evidence of why some Scots were persuaded to support the Act of Union.

   (You may want to comment on who wrote it, when they wrote it, why they wrote it, what they say or what has been missed out.)

5

Source B is about some of the arguments used in the debate over the Union.

Source B

> There was very clear opposition to the Union in Scotland and some towns sent petitions against it to Edinburgh. There was a fear that Scotland would lose business to its more powerful neighbour. They would lose the ability to make their own decisions and would be throwing away all that their ancestors had fought so hard to protect. However, opponents of the Union in the Scottish Parliament were not well enough organised to take advantage of this popular opinion.

3. How fully does **Source B** explain the arguments used in the debate over the Union? (Use **Source B** and recall.)

5

4. Describe the main changes to Scotland as a result of the Treaty of Union.

5

SECTION 1 — SCOTTISH

Part D – Migration and Empire, 1830–1939

Attempt the following questions using recalled knowledge and information from the sources where appropriate.

Source A is about why many Irish immigrated to Scotland in the 1840s.

Source A

> Among those who moved to Scotland, the largest group of immigrants came from Ireland. Irish immigration continued steadily until the 1840s. The Irish potato famine of the mid-1840s however led to a sharp increase in this immigration. It led to great poverty and some landlords evicted those who could not pay their rent. Transport costs were cheap, and wages in the west of Scotland continued to be higher than those in Ireland. However, by the end of the 19th century it was not just the Irish who were attracted to Scotland.

1. How fully does **Source A** explain why people moved to Scotland between 1830 and 1939? (Use **Source A** and recall.)   **5**

2. Describe the impact of the Empire on Scotland between 1830 and 1939.   **5**

Source B is from the *Inverness Courier* newspaper, dated 30 May 1838, explaining why poor Scots were able to emigrate in the 19th century.

Source B

> The emigration agent was eagerly awaited by so many poor farmers. They arrived in Inverness promising riches in Australia. Early on the Monday, thousands of Highlanders were seen crowding around the Caledonian Hotel, where the agent was speaking. They were desperate to go and possess the limitless quantity of land in Australia. They could no longer make farming pay here in Scotland. Only the biggest farms could make enough money to support a family.

3. Evaluate the usefulness of **Source B** as evidence of why Scots emigrated from the Highlands between 1830 and 1939.   **5**

    (You may want to comment on who wrote it, when they wrote it, why they wrote it, what they say or what has been missed out.)

4. Explain the reasons why so many Scots were successful in the countries to which they emigrated.   **5**

SECTION 1 — SCOTTISH

Part E – The Era of the Great War, 1910–1928

Attempt the following questions using recalled knowledge and information from the sources where appropriate.

1. Describe the use of new technology during the First World War.

    5

Source A is from the memoirs of Lieutenant George Craik, who fought with the 12th Batallion Highland Light Infantry in 1915.

Source A

> When we arrived at Loos the trenches were in not too bad a state. The problems for commanders were organising supplies and suitable living conditions. The other problem was the disposal of the many dead lying all about. This could only be done under cover of darkness. To venture into no man's land in daylight was instant death.

2. Evaluate the usefulness of **Source A** as evidence of conditions in trenches for soldiers during the First World War.

    5

    (You may want to comment on who wrote it, when they wrote it, why they wrote it, what they say or what has been missed out.)

Source B describes the activities of workers in Glasgow during the War.

Source B

> The Government needed to control the factories to keep the soldiers supplied. However, the Clyde Workers' Committee was formed to campaign against the Munitions Act, which forbade engineers from leaving the works where they were employed. On 25 March 1916, David Kirkwood and other members of the Clyde Workers' Committee were arrested under the Defence of the Realm Act. The men were sentenced to be deported. The Committee's journal, *The Worker*, was prosecuted for an article criticising the war. William Gallacher and John Muir, the editors, were both sent to prison.

3. How fully does **Source B** describe the effects of the war on Scottish industry? (Use **Source B** and recall.)

    5

4. Explain the reasons why women gained the vote in 1919.

    5

SECTION 2 — BRITISH — 20 marks

Attempt ONE part

Part A – The Creation of the Medieval Kingdoms, 1066–1406

Attempt the following questions using recalled knowledge and information from the sources where appropriate.

Source A was written in the 12th century, by a French poet, about chivalry.

Source A

> Many knights are failing to live by the Code of Chivalry. They steal money from churches and rob pilgrims of their possessions. They attack whoever they please and show disrespect to children and the elderly. They speak of honour and bravery when they practice neither. Even though knights have spent years training to be the perfect soldier and role model they often forget their vows.

1. Evaluate the usefulness of **Source A** as evidence of the behaviour of knights in the 12th century.

   (You may want to comment on who wrote it, when they wrote it, why they wrote it, what they say or what has been missed out.)

   6

2. To what extent was the corruption in the legal system the most important problem facing Henry II?

   8

3. Explain the reasons why abbeys and monasteries became more popular in medieval times.

   6

SECTION 2 — BRITISH

MARKS

Part B – War of the Three Kingdoms, 1603–1651

Attempt the following questions using recalled knowledge and information from the sources where appropriate.

Source A is part of Parliament's Petition of Right presented to the king in 1628.

Source A

> (i) No man should be forced to make any gift, loan, donation, tax or similar charge to the Crown without the consent of Parliament.
>
> (ii) No free man should be detained in prison without due cause shown.
>
> (iii) Soldiers and sailors should not be housed upon private citizens without their agreement.
>
> (iv) There should be no military law in times of peace.

1. Evaluate the usefulness of **Source A** as evidence of the poor relations between Crown and Parliament in the reign of King Charles I.

    (You may want to comment on who wrote it, when they wrote it, why they wrote it, what they say or what has been missed out.)

    6

2. To what extent were challenges to royal authority in the 1630s a result of religious differences?

    8

3. Explain the reasons why the Parliamentary forces were able to defeat the Royalist forces at Marston Moor.

    6

SECTION 2 — BRITISH

Part C – The Atlantic Slave Trade, 1770–1807

Attempt the following questions using recalled knowledge and information from the sources where appropriate.

Source A is from a travel memoir by Mungo Park in 1799.

Source A

> There are slave factories near the coast. The African captives are usually secured by putting the right leg of one and the left leg of another into the same pair of fetters. By supporting the fetters with a string, they can just walk, though very slowly. Every four slaves are likewise fastened together by their necks with a strong rope or twisted thongs and at night extra fetters are put on their hands.

1. Evaluate the usefulness of **Source A** as evidence of the treatment of Africans when they were first captured.

   (You may want to comment on who wrote it, when they wrote it, why they wrote it, what they say or what has been missed out.)

   6

2. Explain the reasons why resistance was difficult for slaves on the plantations.

   6

3. To what extent was the success of the abolitionist campaigns due to the work of William Wilberforce?

   8

SECTION 2 — BRITISH

Part D – Changing Britain, 1760–1900

Attempt the following questions using recalled knowledge and information from the sources where appropriate.

1. To what extent were improvements in public health by 1900 brought about by improved medical knowledge?

    8

Source A is from the memoirs of a Scottish railway engineer who worked during the 1840s.

Source A

> We had to build the line to Perth over Lord Seafield's land. Lady Seafield very decidedly told us that she hated railways. "Cheap travel", she said, "brought together such an objectionable variety of people." Lord Seafield said the railway would frighten away the grouse from his moors. "Besides", he went on, "what would become of the men who have for many years been employed to float timber down the River Spey to the sea. Would a railway replace them?"

2. Evaluate the usefulness of **Source A** as evidence of attitudes to the building of railways in 19th century Scotland.

    6

    (You may want to comment on who wrote it, when they wrote it, why they wrote it, what they say or what has been missed out.)

3. Explain the reasons why more people gained the vote by 1867.

    6

SECTION 2 — BRITISH

Part E – The Making of Modern Britain, 1880–1951

Attempt the following questions using recalled knowledge and information from the sources where appropriate.

Source A is from a letter describing conditions in London around 1890 by a campaigner for change.

Source A

> In one cellar a sanitary inspector reports finding a father, mother, three children and four pigs! In another room a missionary found a man ill with smallpox, his wife just recovering from the birth of her eighth child, and the children running about half naked and covered with dirt. Despite efforts of local charities, elsewhere was a poor widow, her three children, and a child who had been dead 13 days.

1. Evaluate the usefulness of **Source A** as evidence of the effects of poverty in Britain around 1900.

    (You may want to comment on who wrote it, when they wrote it, why they wrote it, what they say or what has been missed out.)

    6

2. To what extent were the Liberal Welfare Reforms 1906–14 due to concerns about the increasing popularity of the Labour Party?

    8

3. Explain the reasons why the Labour Government introduced the Welfare State in 1945.

    6

SECTION 3 — EUROPEAN AND WORLD — 20 marks
Attempt ONE part

MARKS

Part A – The Cross and the Crescent: the Crusades, 1071–1192

Attempt the following questions using recalled knowledge and information from the sources where appropriate.

Sources A and **B** describe what happened to Jewish communities during the First Crusade.

Source A

> After only a few weeks of travelling, Peter the Hermit and his followers came upon a Jewish community in Germany. Many of the Crusaders were poor and hungry so they began stealing food and possessions from the Jews. As the Crusaders thought the Jews were the enemy of Christ, most believed they could treat them as they wished. Some forced the Jews to change religion and become Christian. Others, against the orders of Peter the Hermit, slaughtered the Jews.

Source B

> A rumour spread among the Crusaders that whoever killed a Jew would have all their sins forgiven. Immediately Peter the Hermit's army began attacking and killing Jewish men, women and children. Although some Jews tried to fight back they had few weapons and were easily defeated. In the riot that followed, houses were robbed and valuables stolen. Those Jews who survived the massacre were forced to give up their faith and become Christians.

1. Compare the views of **Sources A** and **B** about what happened to Jews during the First Crusade. (Compare the sources overall and/or in detail.) **4**

2. Describe the capture of Nicaea during the First Crusade. **5**

3. Explain the reasons why the Crusaders were able to recapture Jerusalem in 1099. **5**

Source C describes the role of Saladin during the Third Crusade.

Source C

> Saladin was renowned for his knightly virtues which matched those of Richard the Lionheart. When Richard the Lionheart was sick with a fever, Saladin, knowing that he had few supplies, sent him a gift of the best fruits of the land. On another occasion, when Richard's horse had been killed in battle, Saladin sent a fine Arabian horse as a present for his rival. For two years Saladin constantly fought Richard in almost daily combat in attempts to prevent the Crusaders capturing Jerusalem.

4. How fully does **Source C** describe the character of Saladin during the Third Crusade? (Use **Source C** and recall.) **6**

SECTION 3 — EUROPEAN AND WORLD

MARKS

Part B – "Tea and Freedom": the American Revolution, 1774–83

Attempt the following questions using recalled knowledge and information from the sources where appropriate.

1. Explain the reasons why many colonists were unhappy with British rule in 1774.   **5**

Source A is about the American forces which fought against the British army.

Source A

> The Revolutionary War was waged by small armies. The American forces were often led by inefficient, even incompetent, commanders who fought muddled campaigns. The men gathering in Boston were enthusiastic but badly armed and lacking supplies. The American commander, George Washington, could rely on no more than 5,000 regular soldiers. Most men were part-time and served for only a few months. Britain's professional army was larger but not large enough to subdue the Americans.

2. How fully does **Source A** describe the condition of the American army in 1777? (Use **Source A** and recall.)   **6**

Sources B and **C** are about the events of the Battle of Yorktown, 1781.

Source B

> In 1781, Cornwallis moved into Virginia and began to build a base at Yorktown. By late summer, Cornwallis's position at Yorktown was deteriorating fast. While American forces prevented him from moving inland, a large French fleet carrying 3,000 troops had sailed up from the West Indies to join the siege. The fate of Cornwallis was sealed when the French defeated the British fleet in Chesapeake Bay. On 19 October, Cornwallis surrendered his entire army of 7,000 men.

Source C

> To launch his campaign in Virginia, Cornwallis's army carried out raids, harassing the Americans wherever he could. In August 1781, Cornwallis set up camp at Yorktown but this turned out to be a poor position. American troops moved quickly to surround him and keep him there. The British could not help Cornwallis's army to escape or bring in reinforcements.

3. Compare the views of **Sources B** and **C** about the events of the Battle of Yorktown. (Compare the sources overall and/or in detail.)   **4**

4. Describe the events leading up to the British surrender at Saratoga in 1777.   **5**

SECTION 3 — EUROPEAN AND WORLD

Part C – USA 1850–1880

Attempt the following questions using recalled knowledge and information from the sources where appropriate.

1. Describe the effects of westward expansion on American society.

    5

Source A is about the arguments between slave and non-slave states.

Source A

> The Compromise of 1850 was created by Henry Clay and others to deal with the balance between slave and free states. Another issue that further increased tensions was the Kansas-Nebraska Act of 1854. This allowed continued expansion to the west. The real issue occurred in Kansas where pro-slavery people of Missouri began to pour into the state to help force it to be slave. The fight even erupted on the floor of the Senate when anti-slavery campaigner Charles Sumner was beat over the head by South Carolina's Senator Preston Brooks.

2. How fully does **Source A** explain why the Civil War broke out?
   (Use **Source A** and recall.)

    6

3. Explain the reasons why the North was able to defeat the South in the Civil War.

    5

Sources B and **C** are about the treatment of black Americans during Reconstruction.

Source B

> They said that I had committed a great wrong; I had kept a Sunday school which was forbidden. Many school houses were burned down. Hostility was shown to the school teachers like me who taught in schools for blacks. Two school board directors were warned to leave the Board and one of them did. They went at night and gave these warnings. I asked them while they were whipping me what I had done. They said I wanted to make these blacks equal to the white men; that this was a white man's country.

Source C

> The violence that the whites committed was directed not only at black people but anyone who furthered their cause. Teachers became key figures so they were frequently intimidated. These attacks usually took place at night: leaving behind a burning cross they beat, mutilated and murdered. Black Americans were reluctant to resist as they wanted to be seen as peaceful and law-abiding.

4. Compare the views of **Sources B** and **C** about the treatment of black Americans during Reconstruction. (Compare the sources overall and/or in detail.)

    4

SECTION 3 — EUROPEAN AND WORLD

MARKS

Part D – Hitler and Nazi Germany, 1919–1939

Attempt the following questions using recalled knowledge and information from the sources where appropriate.

1. Describe political problems faced by the Weimar Republic between 1919 and 1923.   5

Source A is about the hyper-inflation in Germany in 1923.

Source A

> During 1923, hyper-inflation gripped Germany. On Friday afternoons, workers desperately rushed to the nearest store, where a queue had already formed. It was soul-destroying. When you arrived a pound of sugar cost two million marks but, by the time your turn came, you could only afford a half pound. In the chaos, people pushed prams loaded with money. Life became nightmarish. We were devastated as life savings became worthless.

2. How fully does **Source A** describe the effects of hyper-inflation?   6
   (Use **Source A** and recall.)

3. Explain the reasons why Hitler was able to become Chancellor in 1933.   5

Sources B and **C** are about the Night of the Long Knives.

Source B

> Hitler's courage in taking firm action has made him a hero in the eyes of many Germans. He has won approval and sympathy for the steps he took. People think his action is proof that he wants order and decency in Germany. Reports from different parts of the country are all agreed that people are expressing satisfaction that Hitler has acted against the serious threat posed by Rohm and the SA to Germany and her people.

Source C

> On the morning of 30 June 1934, Rohm and other SA leaders were arrested and eventually shot. Hitler's personal popularity soared as a result of the Night of the Long Knives. Most Germans disliked the corruption of the SA and welcomed the strong action against it. President Hindenburg's telegram to Hitler read: "By your determined action and brave leadership, you have saved the German nation from serious danger."

4. Compare the views of **Sources B** and **C** about the attitude of Germans to the Night of the Long Knives. (Compare the sources overall and/or in detail.)   4

SECTION 3 — EUROPEAN AND WORLD

Part E – Red Flag: Lenin and the Russian Revolution, 1894–1921

Attempt the following questions using recalled knowledge and information from the sources where appropriate.

1. Describe the hardships faced by industrial workers in Russia before 1914.   **5**

Source A is about the outbreak of the 1905 Revolution.

Source A

> By 1905 there was a growing desire to overthrow the repressive government of Nicholas II. There was a great deal of poverty in the cities and the countryside. The revolutionary movement gained strength following Russia's humiliating defeat by Japan. In January an uprising to remove the Tsar began. The non-Russian areas of the empire witnessed violent disturbances. Revolutionary groups became much more organised. They formed a soviet in St Petersburg. A soviet was a type of worker's parliament.

2. How fully does **Source A** explain why there was a revolution in Russia in 1905? (Use **Source A** and recall.)   **6**

3. Explain the reasons why the Bolsheviks were able to seize power in October 1917.

Sources B and **C** describe Trotsky's leadership in the Civil War.   **5**

Source B

> For three years, Trotsky lived on his armoured train travelling to all areas of the front. He covered 65,000 miles during the course of the war, ensuring that the Red Army was well fed and properly armed. He was an inspirational leader and was dedicated to the cause. He made rousing speeches to the troops and raised morale among his men, even when other Bolshevik leaders were not convinced that they would defeat the Whites. Over five million men joined the Red Army of their own free will.

Source C

> Trotsky was appointed Commissar for War in early 1919 and quickly established a reputation as a ruthless leader who used strict discipline and ruled by fear. He forced people to join the Red Army to raise the numbers of troops and introduced 50,000 former Tsarist officers to train the raw recruits. The death penalty was not only used for deserters. When 200 soldiers deserted at Svyazhsk, Trotsky arrived and ordered the execution of one in every ten men in the regiment as a warning to the rest.

4. Compare the views of **Sources B** and **C** about Trotsky's leadership in the Civil War. (Compare the sources overall and/or in detail.)   **4**

SECTION 3 — EUROPEAN AND WORLD

Part F – Mussolini and Fascist Italy, 1919–1939

Attempt the following questions using recalled knowledge and information from the sources where appropriate.

Sources **A** and **B** are about why Mussolini was able to seize power in 1922.

Source A

> The Fascist squads' reputation for ruthless violence had put Mussolini in the position to threaten the government. This he did in what became known as the "March on Rome". Though the government decided to send in the army to stop Mussolini, the king, Victor Emmanuel III, decided instead to give in to Mussolini's demands and appointed him head of a new government.

Source B

> The Socialists and Communists launched an anti-Fascist general strike but the people failed to support them. After the strike, Mussolini decided to seize the government. Mussolini and his followers marched for Rome. Before he resigned, the prime minister called out the army when the Fascists surrounded Rome. However, the pressure proved too much for the Italian king who refused to use the military to squash Mussolini's "march".

1. Compare the views of **Sources A** and **B** about why Mussolini was able to seize power in Italy in 1922. (Compare the sources overall and/or in detail.)   **4**

Source C describes the cult of Il Duce in Fascist Italy.

Source C

> The leadership cult in Fascist Italy started almost as soon as Mussolini came to power in 1922. By the end of 1925, his role as Duce of Fascism and Head of the Government had been secured by changes to the law. The nature of Mussolini's leadership and, above all, the quality of his political judgement, has been hotly debated. Mussolini had undoubted charisma and political intelligence with which to maintain his power over Fascism and the Italian people. However, his main talents lay in the areas of acting and propaganda.

2. How fully does **Source C** describe the cult of Il Duce in Fascist Italy? (Use **Source C** and recall.)   **6**

3. Describe Fascist attempts to rebuild the Italian economy in the 1920s and 1930s.   **5**

4. Explain the reasons why there was so little opposition to Mussolini.   **5**

SECTION 3 — EUROPEAN AND WORLD

MARKS

Part G–Free at Last? Civil Rights in the USA, 1918–1968

Attempt the following questions using recalled knowledge and information from the sources where appropriate.

1. Describe the problems facing black Americans who moved north in the 1920s and 1930s.   **5**

Sources **A** and **B** describe the results of the Montgomery Bus Boycott.

Source A

> Throughout the boycott a young black preacher inspired the black population of Montgomery. His name was Martin Luther King and this was to be his first step towards becoming the leading figure in the Civil Rights Movement. The boycott lasted over a year until eventually the courts decided that segregation on Montgomery's buses was illegal. On its own, the bus boycott only had limited success. Montgomery remained a segregated town. There were still white-only theatres, pool rooms and restaurants.

Source B

> The bus company's services were boycotted by 99% of Montgomery's African Americans for over a year. As a result of the protest, the US Supreme Court announced that Alabama's bus segregation laws were illegal. However, most other facilities and services in Montgomery remained segregated for many years to come. As a result of the boycott, Martin Luther King became involved in the Civil Rights Movement. He went on to become an African American leader who was famous throughout the world.

2. Compare the views of **Sources A** and **B** about the results of the Montgomery Bus Boycott. (Compare the sources overall and/or in detail.)   **4**

3. Explain the reasons why black Americans felt that progress towards civil rights had been made between 1945 and 1964.   **5**

Source C is about the opposition of Malcolm X to non-violent protest.

Source C

> Malcolm X was mistreated in his youth and this gave him a different set of attitudes to Martin Luther King. Later, while in jail, he was influenced by the ideas of Elijah Muhammad who preached hatred of the white race. In his speeches he criticised non-violence. He believed that the support of non-violence was a sign that black people were still living in mental slavery. However, Malcolm X never undertook violent action himself and sometimes prevented it. Instead he often used violent language and threats to frighten the government into action.

4. How fully does **Source C** explain the views of Malcolm X on non-violent protest? (Use **Source C** and recall.)   **6**

SECTION 3 — EUROPEAN AND WORLD

MARKS

Part H – Appeasement and the Road to War, 1918–1939

Attempt the following questions using recalled knowledge and information from the sources where appropriate.

1. Explain the reasons why Hitler wanted to re-arm Germany in the 1930s.
        5

Source A is about Britain's policy of Appeasement in the 1930s.

Source A

> The Great Depression meant that money could not be found for re-armament and the government knew that the British people were totally opposed to war. Chamberlain had been Chancellor before becoming Prime Minister in 1937. He was in favour of personal, face-to-face talks among Europe's leaders and believed he could negotiate directly with Hitler. The British government took the view that Communist Russia was the real threat to peace in the world.

2. How fully does **Source A** explain why Britain followed a policy of Appeasement up to 1937? (Use **Source A** and recall.)
        6

Sources B and **C** describe the Anschluss between Germany and Austria in 1938.

Source B

> It is clear that Anschluss is popular among the Austrian people who are, after all, German in language and culture. Keeping Germany and Austria apart had been one of the more spiteful terms of Versailles and this wrong is now made right. Therefore Europe is likely to benefit from a period of peace and prosperity as Germany moves into a brighter future.

Source C

> Germany has taken over Austria. Any intelligent person can see that an even more powerful Germany is a threat to the peace and stability of Europe. The decision in 1919 to forbid Anschluss had been a very sensible one for limiting the war-like ambitions of Germany. We have permitted Hitler to brutally invade an independent country.

3. Compare the views of **Sources B** and **C** about the Anschluss between Germany and Austria in 1938. (Compare the sources overall and/or in detail.)
        4

4. Describe attempts by Britain and France to avoid war with Germany over the Czech Crisis.
        5

SECTION 3 — EUROPEAN AND WORLD

MARKS

Part I – World War II, 1939–1945

Attempt the following questions using recalled knowledge and information from the sources where appropriate.

1. Explain the reasons why the German army was able to defeat its enemies so quickly between 1939 and 1942.

   5

Sources **A** and **B** are about the work of the French Resistance.

Source A

> For two years the resistance movements of Europe had found it hard to make much of an impression on the might of the German military. However, they had been useful in gathering intelligence for the Allies. The devastating attacks of 1939 to 1941 had given little time for each country to prepare any kind of a secret army to undermine the invaders. German army commanders indicated that the resistance movements were a nuisance, but no more than this.

Source B

> Over the course of the war, the French Resistance scored key victories against the German occupation forces. Resistance members organised themselves in secret to discover French collaborators, kill many ranking Nazi officials, and destroy trains, convoys, and ships used by the German army. These accomplishments carried a heavy price. The Gestapo occasionally carried out bloody revenge attacks on innocent civilians.

2. Compare the views of **Sources A** and **B** about the work of the French Resistance. (Compare the sources overall and/or in detail.)

   4

Source C is about the fall of Berlin.

Source C

> Friday 20 April was Hitler's 56th birthday. The Soviets sent him a birthday present in the form of an artillery barrage right into the heart of the city, while the Western Allies joined in with a massive air raid. The radio announced that Hitler had come out of his safe bomb-proof bunker to talk with the 14-16 year-old boys who had "volunteered" for the "honour" to be accepted into the SS and to die for their Führer in the defence of Berlin. What a cruel lie! These boys did not volunteer, but had no choice, because boys who were found hiding were hanged as traitors by the SS.

3. How fully does **Source C** describe events leading to the fall of Berlin? (Use **Source C** and recall.)

   6

4. Describe the ways in which the Americans were able to defeat Japan in 1945.

   5

SECTION 3 — EUROPEAN AND WORLD

MARKS

Part J – The Cold War, 1945–1989

Attempt the following questions using recalled knowledge and information from the sources where appropriate.

Source A is about the Cuban Missile Crisis.

Source A

> To the American government, placing missiles on Cuba was a war-like act by the Soviets. They believed that the Soviet Union intended to supply a large number of powerful nuclear weapons. The Soviet Union denied any war-like purpose. However, spy photographs proved the offensive purpose of the missiles which were pointed directly at major American cities. It was estimated that within a few minutes of them being fired, 80 million Americans would be dead.

1. How fully does **Source A** explain why the American government took action during the Cuban Missile Crisis? (Use **Source A** and recall.)   6

2. Explain the reasons why the East Germans built the Berlin Wall in 1961.   5

Sources B and **C** are about the tactics of the Vietcong.

Source B

> The Vietcong, or "Charlie" as the Americans called them, were the locally born guerrilla fighters of South Vietnam. The Vietcong consisted of three groups: units of regular soldiers, provincial forces, and part-time guerrillas. The Vietcong generally avoided large-scale attacks on the enemy, but continually harassed their troops and installations. This limited the scale of their casualties to only a handful at a time. They travelled light, carrying basic weapons and few supplies.

Source C

> Our first real battle was in open warfare at the Michelin Rubber Plantation. Thousands of Vietcong launched wave after wave of attacks on our camp. But they had all kinds of Chinese and Russian weapons, such as flamethrowers and rocket launchers. Eventually we counter-attacked and pushed them back. Fortunately, we only lost around seven guys. The Vietcong body count was reported to have been 800, but I thought it was more.

3. Compare the views of **Sources B** and **C** about the tactics used by the Vietcong. (Compare the sources overall and/or in detail.)   4

4. Describe the steps taken to reduce tension between the USA and the USSR between 1968 and 1989.   5

[END OF SPECIMEN QUESTION PAPER]

Page twenty-two

NATIONAL 5

Model Paper 1

Whilst this Model Practice Paper has been specially commissioned by Hodder Gibson for use as practice for the National 5 exams, the key reference documents remain the SQA Specimen Paper 2013 and the SQA Past Paper 2014.

National
Qualifications
MODEL PAPER 1

SQ23/N5/01

History

Duration — 1 hour and 30 minutes

Total marks — 60

SECTION 1 — SCOTTISH — 20 marks

Attempt ONE part.

SECTION 2 — BRITISH — 20 marks

Attempt ONE part.

SECTION 3 — EUROPEAN AND WORLD — 20 marks

Attempt ONE part.

Before attempting the questions you must check that your answer booklet is for the same subject and level as this question paper.

On the answer booklet, you must clearly identify the question number you are attempting.

Use **blue** or **black** ink.

Before leaving the examination room you must give your answer booklet to the Invigilator. If you do not, you may lose all the marks for this paper.

SECTION 1 — SCOTTISH — 20 marks

MARKS

Attempt ONE part

Part A – The Wars of Independence, 1286–1328

Attempt the following questions using recalled knowledge and information from the sources where appropriate.

1. Describe the events between 1286 and 1292 that led to Edward I becoming overlord of Scotland.

    5

Source A explains King Edward's decision to attack Scotland.

Source A

> In 1296 the Scots organised a rebellion against Edward. They rejected his claim to be overlord of Scotland. This was a very dangerous step for Scotland which was less powerful than England. However, Scotland had made an alliance with France to fight against Edward. Angered by these actions, King Edward invaded Scotland and attacked Berwick.

2. How fully does **Source A** explain King Edward's decision to attack Scotland? (Use **Source A** and recall.)

    5

3. Explain the reasons why the leadership of William Wallace was important during the Wars of Independence?

    5

Source B is a description of a Scots raid on Northern England in 1322, written by an English monk.

Source B

> Now after 6th January 1322, when the truce between the kingdoms lapsed, the Scottish army invaded England and marched to Durham and the Scots went forward plundering the country in all directions. One of them raided towards the town of Richmond. The people of Richmond had no defenders and bought off the invaders with a great sum of money.

4. Evaluate the usefulness of **Source B** as evidence showing the tactics used by Robert I to persuade the English to accept him as King of Scots.

    5

    (You may want to comment on who wrote it, when they wrote it, why they wrote it, what they say or what has been missed out.)

SECTION 1 — SCOTTISH

Part B – Mary Queen of Scots and the Reformation, 1542–1587

Attempt the following questions using recalled knowledge and information from the sources where appropriate.

1. Explain the reasons why Henry VIII of England ordered the invasions of Scotland after 1544. **5**

Source A is from a contemporary *History of the Reformation in Scotland* by John Knox.

Source A

> That cruel man, falsely called Archbishop of St Andrews, arrested Walter Myln, a man of old age, and cruelly put him to death by fire in St. Andrews, on 28th April, 1558. That made so many people angry that a new strength of purpose developed amongst the whole people.
>
> On 2nd of May 1559, arrived John Knox from France, who went to Dundee, where he preached the reformed faith amongst them.

2. Evaluate the usefulness of **Source A** as evidence of the growth of Protestantism in Scotland before the Reformation of 1560?

    (You may want to comment on who wrote it, when they wrote it, why they wrote it, what they say or what has been missed out.) **5**

Source B is a comment on how well Mary ruled Scotland.

Source B

> Until Mary allowed her heart to rule her head by marrying Darnley, she had been a successful ruler in Scotland. She had defeated the nobles who challenged her authority and had established a successful government under her half-brother Moray. As a Roman Catholic, her tolerant treatment of Scotland's new Protestant church was ahead of its time.

3. How fully does **Source B** explain how well Mary, Queen of Scots ruled Scotland? (Use **Source B** and recall.) **5**

4. Describe the problems caused by Mary when she was in England. **5**

SECTION 1 — SCOTTISH

Part C – The Treaty of Union, 1689–1715

Attempt the following questions using recalled knowledge and information from the sources where appropriate.

1. Describe what happened during the Worcester affair.   5

Source A is from *History of the Union* (1709) by Daniel Defoe.

Source A

> The people cried out that they were Scotsmen and they would remain Scotsmen. They condemned the word "British" as fit only for the Welsh, who had already been made the subjects of the English. Scotland had always had a famous name in foreign courts, and had enjoyed privileges and honours there for many years. The common people went about the streets crying "no union", and called those negotiators traitors, and threatened them to their faces.

2. Evaluate the usefulness of **Source A** as evidence of the arguments for and against the Treaty of Union?

   (You may want to comment on who wrote it, when they wrote it, why they wrote it, what they say or what has been missed out.)   5

Source B is about the worries that some Scots had about the effects of the Union.

Source B

> Scots feared that, once they lost their independence, they would have little influence over government decisions. Others worried that businesses in Scotland would suffer from competition from English imports. They also thought the money paid to Scotland was a bribe to rich and powerful men—the only way that a Union could be passed.

3. How fully does **Source B** explain the opposition arguments used in the debate over the Union?
   (Use **Source B** and recall.)   5

4. Explain the reasons why many Scots were disappointed by the Act of Union by 1715.   5

SECTION 1 — SCOTTISH

MARKS

Part D – Migration and Empire, 1830–1939

Attempt the following questions using recalled knowledge and information from the sources where appropriate.

1. Explain the reasons why Irish immigrants were attracted to Scotland between 1830 and 1930.

5

Source A is from a newspaper called *The Glasgow Reporter*, 4 March 1846.

Source A

> A mass attack of 300 Irish navvies working near Edinburgh to free two of their companions who had been imprisoned by the police, led to disastrous consequences for themselves and their families. One of the policemen died of his injuries received in the scuffle. A squad of police from Edinburgh then marched to where the Irish navvies were working, set fire to row after row of the Irishmen's huts and beat men, women and children out of the district.

2. Evaluate the usefulness of **Source A** as evidence of the impact of Irish immigration on law and order in Scotland.

   (You may want to comment on who wrote it, when they wrote it, why they wrote it, what they say or what has been missed out.)

5

Source B explains why poor Scots were able to emigrate in the 19th century.

Source B

> Some landlords saw it as in their own interests to encourage poor tenants to seek their fortunes elsewhere. The landlords were willing to pay the full travelling costs, especially to Canada. Landlords often wrote off rent arrears so that the tenants would have some money for their new life and some even bought their cattle which provided the emigrant with some extra help. Glasgow and Edinburgh feared a massive influx of Highlanders and the city authorities made a contribution towards their expenses in emigrating.

3. How fully does **Source B** explain the reasons why so many Scots emigrated during the 19th century?
   (Use **Source B** and recall.)

5

4. Describe ways in which Scots helped to improve the lands to which they emigrated.

5

SECTION 1 — SCOTTISH

Part E – The Era of the Great War, 1910–1928

Attempt the following questions using recalled knowledge and information from the sources where appropriate.

Source A is from Colonel Swinton, an officer who helped develop the tank during the First World War.

Source A

> The immediate purpose of the tank was the destruction of the machine gun which, until the tank appeared, was responsible for more deaths than any other weapon. The tank was the one completely British invention in the war and a great one. It was a great life-saver of infantry. The tank took the place of the artillery bombardment, with more certain results. It also reintroduced the element of surprise in an attack which the artillery bombardment had lost.

1. Evaluate the usefulness of **Source A** as evidence of the use of new technology during the First World War.

    (You may want to comment on who wrote it, when they wrote it, why they wrote it, what they say or what has been missed out.)   5

Source B is about women during World War One.

Source B

> During World War One, many things changed. As men left their jobs to go and fight, their places in industry were increasingly taken by women. Women's most vital work was in munitions factories where they produced weapons and shells. This work was both dirty and dangerous. Women worked on trams and buses to keep the transport system going. With so many men away fighting, women had to take the responsibility of being head of the family.

2. How fully does **Source B** describe the changing role of women during the First World War?
    (Use **Source B** and recall.)   5

3. Describe the economic difficulties faced by Scotland after 1918.   5

4. Explain the reasons why the actions of the militant Suffragettes harmed the campaign for votes for women.   5

SECTION 2 — BRITISH — 20 marks

Attempt ONE part

Part C – The Atlantic Slave Trade, 1770–1807

Attempt the following questions using recalled knowledge and information from the sources where appropriate.

Source A is from a description in 1789 by a former slave, Olaudah Equiano, of his experiences during the Middle Passage.

Source A

> I can now tell of the hardships which cannot be separated from this accursed trade. The wretched conditions below decks were made worse by the chains. The shrieks of women, and the groans of the dying, rendered the whole scene one of unimaginable horror.

1. Evaluate the usefulness of **Source A** as evidence of the treatment of slaves during the Middle Passage.

   (You may want to comment on who wrote it, when they wrote it why they wrote it what they say or what has been missed out.)

   6

2. Describe the effects of the slave trade on African societies.

   5

3. Explain the concerns that people had about the treatment of slaves in the Caribbean.

   5

Sources B and **C** are about the importance of the slave trade for Britain.

Source B

> There were many reasons why it took so long to abolish the slave trade. One reason was that the slave trade had many powerful supporters. Plantation owners and merchants in British ports which relied on the slave trade were well organised and had political influence. They had enough wealth to bribe MPs to support them. They also had the support of King George III. Many people believed that the trade had helped them to make Britain wealthy and prosperous.

Source C

> The Abolitionists faced powerful opposition. The plantation owners allied themselves with important groups to promote the case for slavery and the slave trade. Their case seemed overwhelming. Dozens of British ports and surrounding areas relied on the slave trade. British consumers had become addicted to the products of the slave trade, most notably sugar. The Atlantic slave trade represented a large amount of British trade and seemed vital to the continuing prosperity of Britain and the Caribbean Islands.

4. Compare the views in **Sources B** and **C** about the reasons why the slave trade continued in Britain throughout the 18th century.
   (Compare the sources overall and/or in detail.)

   4

SECTION 2 — BRITISH

Part D – Changing Britain, 1760–1900

Attempt the following questions using recalled knowledge and information from the sources where appropriate.

1. Explain the reasons why the health of the British population improved in the 19th century. **5**

Source **A** was written by a visitor to a cotton mill in Bolton, Lancashire in 1847.

Source A

> The factory people are better clothed and fed than many other working class people. I found the mill to be a large building and very clean. The working rooms were spacious and well ventilated. There were many windows in each room. This left me wondering if there was a window tax to pay. I observed that great care had been taken to put guards on dangerous machinery. I was told accidents in the factory were very rare and were caused by stupidity or negligence by the worker. However, accidents did occur.

2. Evaluate the usefulness of **Source A** as evidence about working conditions in cotton mills in the 19th century. **6**

   (You may want to comment on who wrote it, when they wrote it, why they wrote it, what they say or what has been missed out.)

3. Describe the impact of new technology on coal mining in the 19th century. **5**

Sources **B** and **C** explain the rise of the Chartist movement.

Source B

> Many working people had supported the 1832 Reform Act in the belief that this would be a first step towards wider democracy. They were angry at the Whig government's failure to deliver. Also, these were hard times; trade was poor, wages were low and faced further cuts and there was fury over the new Poor Law which established the workhouse system. This led to an increased demand for revolutionary change in society which found an outlet in Chartism. This was also a time when, following the repeal of the anti-trade union Combination Acts, working people were becoming more confident in forming their own organisations.

Source C

> The Great Reform Act of 1832 gave the vote to male householders who owned property which meant that more middle class men benefited. Only one man in every five had the vote in England this caused fury among many members of the working class who had expected to be given the vote. Two years later parliament passed the Poor Law Amendment Act which introduced the hated workhouses. This combined with the case of the Tolpuddle Martyrs created a working class backlash which gave rise to the Chartist movement.

4. Compare the views in **Sources B** and **C** on the reasons for the rise of the Chartist movement. **4**
   (Compare the sources overall and/or in detail.)

SECTION 2 — BRITISH

Part E – The Making of Modern Britain, 1880–1951

Attempt the following questions using recalled knowledge and information from the sources where appropriate.

Source A is from a speech by Lloyd George, a leading Liberal MP in 1906.

Source A

> What are some of the causes of poverty? There is the fact that a man's earnings are not enough to maintain himself and his family. There is the inability to obtain employment for economic reasons. There is the inability of men to work owing to sickness, old age or lack of physical stamina or vitality. Then there is the most fertile cause of all – a man's own habits such as drinking and gambling.

1. Evaluate the usefulness of **Source A** as evidence about the causes of poverty in the early 20th century.

   (You may want to comment on who wrote it, when they wrote it, why they wrote it, what they say or what has been missed out.)

   6

Sources B and **C** describe the impact of the Liberal social reforms.

Source B

> The Liberal social reforms were in no sense a welfare state. They were not intended as a comprehensive system of welfare provision. Rather, they involved targeting certain small areas of the problem of poverty. Those not included continued to need a safety net. The poor law was less important but still necessary.

Source C

> All the Liberal reforms offered levels of support that were only designed to support the poor, not free them from poverty. They helped to insure certain types of workers against sickness and unemployment. Some people were freed from having to seek poor relief but living on 5 shillings a week in old age was almost impossible.

2. Compare the views in **Sources B** and **C** as evidence about the impact of the Liberal reforms.
   (Compare the sources overall and/or in detail.)

   4

3. Describe the impact of the Blitz on people's attitude towards poverty.

   5

4. Explain the reasons why the Beveridge Report was popular with so many people.

   5

SECTION 3 — EUROPEAN AND WORLD — 20 marks

Attempt ONE part

Part B – "Tea and Freedom,": the American Revolution, 1774–1783

Attempt the following questions using recalled knowledge and information from the sources where appropriate.

1. Describe the Boston Tea Party and the British government's response to it.   **6**

Source A is from a letter written by the leaders of the 13 colonies when they met in May 1775.

Source A

> On the 19th day of April, General Gage sent out a large detachment of his army who made an unprovoked attack on the inhabitants of the town of Lexington. They murdered eight of the inhabitants and wounded many others. The troops then proceeded to the town of Concord, where they cruelly slaughtered several people and wounded many more, until they were forced to retreat by a group of brave colonists suddenly assembled to repel this cruel aggression.

2. Evaluate the usefulness of **Source A** as evidence about what happened at Lexington and Concord in April 1775.   **6**

   (You may want to comment on who wrote it, when they wrote it, why they wrote it, what they say or what has been missed out.)

3. To what extent did the involvement of foreign countries cause difficulties for Britain in the War of Independence?   **8**

SECTION 3 — EUROPEAN AND WORLD

Part C – USA, 1850–1880

Attempt the following questions using recalled knowledge and information from the sources where appropriate.

1. Explain the reasons why tensions existed between Native Americans and white settlers.

   6

Source A is from George Ogden's diary in which he describes the impact of Reconstruction on black Americans in the South.

Source A

> My first impression of the South was shock at the shabby conditions of the living quarters that many black Americans still lived in. I was dismayed their life had shown no improvement. Initially I was puzzled why so many black Americans remained in the South, still working for their old masters, when they could move freely. Congress passed many laws. However, it always struck me as worrying that some white Americans felt justified in lynching and using violence against a black American. At first I found it strange that the white and black Americans did not work together in the field or elsewhere.

2. Evaluate the usefulness of **Source A** as attitudes towards Reconstruction in the South.

   (You may want to comment on who wrote it, when they wrote it, why they wrote it, what they say or what has been missed out.)

   6

3. To what extent did differing attitudes to the union bring about the Civil War?

   8

SECTION 3 — EUROPEAN AND WORLD

Part D – Hitler and Nazi Germany, 1919–1939

Attempt the following questions using recalled knowledge and information from the sources where appropriate.

1. Explain the reasons why the Spartacist Revolt failed.   **6**

Source A is from the memories of Sebastian Haffner who lived in Germany in 1918. They were published in 2002.

Source A

> Although November 1918 meant the end of the war, I recall no sense of joy. There was only confusion as men returned from the Front. On Saturday the papers announced the Kaiser's abdication. On Sunday, I heard shots fired in the streets of Berlin. During the whole war I hadn't heard a single shot, yet now the war was over they began shooting. I felt uneasy. On November 11th, I saw the newspaper headline "Armistice Signed". I turned to stone. I felt my whole world had collapsed.

2. Evaluate the usefulness of **Source A** as evidence about Germany at the end of the First World War.   **6**

    (You may want to comment on who wrote it, when they wrote, it why they wrote it, what they say or what has been missed out.)

3. To what extent was Hitler's success in 1933 due to violence and intimidation?   **8**

SECTION 3 — EUROPEAN AND WORLD

Part E – Red Flag: Lenin and the Russian Revolution, 1894–1921

Attempt the following questions using recalled knowledge and information from the sources where appropriate.

1. Explain the reasons why the Orthodox Church was important in Tsarist Russia.

   6

2. To what extent was defeat in the Russo-Japanese war the main cause of the 1905 Revolution?

   8

Source A is from a letter by the leader of the Provisional Government to his parents on 3 July 1917.

Source A

> Without doubt, the country is heading for chaos. We are facing famine, defeat at the front and the collapse of law and order in the cities. There will be wars in the countryside as desperate refugees from the cities fight each other for food and land.

3. Evaluate the usefulness of **Source A** as evidence of the problems facing the Provisional Government.

   (You may want to comment on who wrote it, when they wrote it, why they wrote it, what they say or what has been missed.)

   6

SECTION 3 — EUROPEAN AND WORLD

Part G – Free at Last? Civil Rights in the USA, 1918–1968

Attempt the following questions using recalled knowledge and information from the sources where appropriate.

1. Describe the problems facing European immigrants to the USA in the 1920s.   **6**

Source A is from a speech made in 1954 by the Grand Dragon of the Federated Klans of Alabama.

Source A

> The Klan don't hate nobody! In fact, the Klan is the black man's best friend. He should behave himself and not allow himself to be fooled by the lies of Northerners. Then he will reap the rewards of hard work, instead of the disappointments of chasing unrealistic dreams!

2. Evaluate the usefulness of **Source A** as evidence of attitudes towards black Americans in the Southern states at the time of the Civil Rights Movement.   **6**

   (You may want to comment on who wrote it, when they wrote it, why they wrote it, what they say or what has been missed out.)

3. To what extent was the growth of the Civil Rights Movement due to the experience of black Americans in the Second World War?   **8**

SECTION 3 — EUROPEAN AND WORLD

Part H – Appeasement and the Road to War, 1918–1939

Attempt the following questions using recalled knowledge and information from the sources where appropriate.

1. Describe the ways in which Britain appeased Germany between 1933 and 1936.   **6**

Source A is from a report by the British ambassador to Germany, August 1938.

Source A

> No matter how badly the Germans behave, we must also condemn Czechoslovakia. No one has much faith in the Czech government's honesty or even their ability to do the right thing over the Sudetenland. We must not blame the Germans for preparing their army because they are convinced that the Czechs want to start a war as soon as possible so they can drag Britain and France into it.

2. Evaluate the usefulness of **Source A** as evidence of Britain's attitude to Czechoslovakia in 1938.   **6**

   (You may want to comment on who wrote it, when they wrote it, why they wrote it, what they say or what has been missed out.)

3. To what extent was fear of bombing the main reason why the people of Europe wanted to avoid war during the 1930s?   **8**

SECTION 3 — EUROPEAN AND WORLD

MARKS

Part I – World War II, 1939–1945

Attempt the following questions using recalled knowledge and information from the sources where appropriate.

1. To what extent was sea power the main reason for American success in the war with Japan 1941–1945?

8

Source A was written by a member of US President Truman's government in 1945.

Source A

> Using the atomic bomb was a mistake. Conventional bombing was increasingly effective. Using this barbarous weapon on Hiroshima and Nagasaki was of no real help in our war against Japan. The Japanese were already defeated and ready to surrender. The effectiveness of our sea blockade had brought them to their knees. It was all a dreadful waste of life.

2. Evaluate the usefulness of **Source A** as evidence of attitudes towards the atomic bombing of Japan.

   (You may want to comment on who wrote it, when they wrote it, why they wrote it, what they say or what has been missed out.)

6

3. Explain the reasons why Germany was finally defeated in 1945.

6

SECTION 3 — EUROPEAN AND WORLD

MARKS

Part J – The Cold War, 1945–1989

Attempt the following questions using recalled knowledge and information from the sources where appropriate.

1. To what extent was the Cold War caused by mutual suspicion between the USA and the USSR?

   8

2. Describe the ways in which people showed their opposition to the war in Vietnam.

   6

Source A is from a speech by President Leonid Brezhnev in 1976.

Source A

> We are attempting to follow the path of peaceful co-existence. We are trying to bring about lasting peace to reduce, and in the longer term to eliminate, the danger of another world war. This is the main element of our policy towards the capitalist states. It may be noticed that considerable progress in this area has been achieved in the last five years.

3. Evaluate the usefulness of **Source A** as evidence of the Soviet attitude towards détente.

   (You may want to comment on who wrote it, when they wrote it, why they wrote it, what they say or what has been missed out.)

   6

Model Paper 2

Whilst this Model Practice Paper has been specially commissioned by Hodder Gibson for use as practice for the National 5 exams, the key reference documents remain the SQA Specimen Paper 2013 and the SQA Past Paper 2014.

 HODDER GIBSON
LEARN MORE

National Qualifications MODEL PAPER 2

SQ23/N5/01

History

Duration — 1 hour and 30 minutes

Total marks — 60

SECTION 1 — SCOTTISH — 20 marks

Attempt ONE part.

SECTION 2 — BRITISH — 20 marks

Attempt ONE part.

SECTION 3 — EUROPEAN AND WORLD — 20 marks

Attempt ONE part.

Before attempting the questions you must check that your answer booklet is for the same subject and level as this question paper.

On the answer booklet, you must clearly identify the question number you are attempting.

Use **blue** or **black** ink.

Before leaving the examination room you must give your answer booklet to the Invigilator. If you do not, you may lose all the marks for this paper.

SECTION 1 — SCOTTISH
PARTS

SECTION 2 — BRITISH
PARTS

SECTION 3 — EUROPEAN AND WORLD
PARTS

SECTION 1 — SCOTTISH — 20 marks

Attempt ONE part

Part A – The Wars of Independence, 1286–1328

Attempt the following questions using recalled knowledge and information from the sources where appropriate.

1. Explain the reasons why the Scots asked King Edward of England to help them after the death of King Alexander III.   **5**

2. Describe the events that led to the defeat and capture of King John Balliol.   **5**

Source A was written by the English chronicler, Walter of Guisborough in 1298.

Source A

> On one side of a little hill close to Falkirk, the Scots placed their soldiers in four round circles with their pikes held outwards at an angle. Between these circles, which are called schiltrons, were the archers and behind them was the cavalry. When our men attacked, the Scots horsemen fled without striking a sword's blow.

3. Evaluate the usefulness of **Source A** as evidence of what happened at the Battle of Falkirk.   **5**

    (You may want to comment on who wrote it, when they wrote it, why they wrote it, what they say or what has been missed out.)

Source B explains why Bruce was not fully accepted as King of Scots until 1328.

Source B

> It took almost twenty-two years of fighting before Bruce was accepted as King of Scots. He had to force many Scots to abandon King John Balliol, and others to reject the claims of Edward II as overlord. Bruce emphasised his own royal blood to justify his claim and his victory at Bannockburn as a sign of God's approval. However, he was unable to change the mind of Edward II.

4. How fully does **Source B** explain the reasons why it took so long for Robert the Bruce to be accepted as King of Scots?   **5**
    (Use **Source B** and recall.)

SECTION 1 — SCOTTISH

Part B – Mary Queen of Scots and the Reformation, 1542–1587

Attempt the following questions using recalled knowledge and information from the sources where appropriate.

1. Describe the events which led to the assassination of Cardinal Beaton at St Andrews in 1546.   **5**

Source A is from a book by F. Mignet called *The History of Mary, Queen of Scots*, published in 1851.

Source A

> Mary's actions before and after the murder are quite sufficient to convince us that she was involved in the murder plot. Her journey to Glasgow took place at a time when she was openly expressing her distrust and hatred of Darnley. She persuaded him to come with her to Edinburgh. Kirk o' Field was selected as the most convenient place to commit the crime. On the evening before the murder she removed from the house all the furniture of any value that it contained.

2. Evaluate the usefulness of **Source A** as evidence of the involvement of Mary, Queen of Scots, in the death of Darnley.

    (You may want to comment on who wrote it, when they wrote it, why they wrote it, what they say or what has been missed out.)   **5**

3. Explain the reasons why events surrounding Queen Mary's marriage to Bothwell led to her downfall.   **5**

Source B describes Mary's involvement in the Babington Plot in 1585.

Source B

> Mary enjoyed the excitement of plotting and sending coded letters hidden in a beer keg to Babington. Elizabeth's men knew about the plot from the beginning because they had a spy in Mary's household. The end came when Mary sent a letter enthusiastically approving the assassination of Elizabeth. When the letter was decoded, the spy drew a gallows on the letter.

4. How fully does **Source B** explain Mary's involvement in the Babington Plot in 1585? (Compare the sources overall and/or in detail.)   **5**

SECTION 1 — SCOTTISH

Part C – The Treaty of Union, 1689–1715

Attempt the following questions using recalled knowledge and information from the sources where appropriate.

1. Explain the reasons why there was bad feeling between Scotland and England over the Worcester incident.   **5**

Source A is from a report by Daniel Defoe, an English spy sent to Scotland in 1706.

Source A

> I had not been in Edinburgh for long when I heard a great noise and, looking out, I saw a terrible mob coming up the High Street led by a drummer. They were shouting and swearing and crying out "all Scotland will stand together!", "No Union! No Union!", "English dogs" and things like that.

2. Evaluate the usefulness of **Source A** as evidence about Scottish attitudes to the Union.

   (You may want to comment on who wrote it, when they wrote it, why they wrote it, what they say or what has been missed out.)   **5**

3. Describe how the passing of the Act of Union helped the Jacobite Cause.   **5**

Source B was written about the effects of the Union on Scotland.

Source B

> Now that their Parliament is gone, the Scottish nobles and gentlemen spend their time and consequently their money in England. The Union has opened the door to English manufacturers and ruined Scottish ones. Their cattle are sent to England, but money is spent there too. The troops raised in Scotland are in English service and Scotland receives no money from them either.

4. How fully does **Source B** explain the effects of the Union on Scotland?
   (Use **Source B** and recall.)   **5**

SECTION 1 — SCOTTISH

Part D – Migration and Empire, 1830–1939

Attempt the following questions using recalled knowledge and information from the sources where appropriate.

1. Describe the "pull" factors, which led many Irish people to leave for Scotland after 1830.

   5

2. Explain the reasons why so many Scots disliked Irish immigrants.

   5

Source A is from Angus Nicholson, Canada's Special Immigration Agent in the Highlands of Scotland. It was written in 1875.

Source A

> All the competing Emigration Agencies are still at work as actively as ever. The New Zealand and Australian authorities are particularly alert, the streets of every town and village being always well covered with their posters offering free passages to emigrants. It is extremely difficult for us to attract emigrants when these territories are offering free passages while we expect the emigrants to pay their own fares to Canada.

3. Evaluate the usefulness of **Source A** as evidence about the reasons for Scottish emigration.

   (You may want to comment on who wrote it, when they wrote it, why they wrote it, what they say or what has been missed out.)

   5

Source B is about the impact of the Scots on the British Empire.

Source B

> Two countries more than any other have been moulded by the Scots: Canada and Australia. Though numbering only one fifteenth of the population, Scots dominated the government and controlled the fur trade, the educational institutions and the banks. Australia saw similar manipulation by Scots, John Macarthur introducing the Merino sheep and considered to be the founder of Australia's sheep industry.

4. How fully does **Source B** illustrate the impact of Scots emigrants on the British Empire?
   (Use **Source B** and recall.)

   5

SECTION 1 — SCOTTISH

Part E – The Era of the Great War, 1910–1928

Attempt the following questions using recalled knowledge and information from the sources where appropriate.

1. Explain the reasons why large numbers of Scots volunteered to fight during the war.   **5**

2. Describe how conscientious objectors were treated during the First World War.   **5**

Source A was written by a modern historian.

Source A

> By 1923, 14.3 percent of workers in Scotland were out of work compared with 11.6 per cent in the United Kingdom as a whole. It was also a different kind of unemployment from the short, irregular lay-offs which had marked the years before 1914. After the war it was long-term unemployment and it affected the skilled more than the unskilled. The huge demand for labour in wartime manufacturing had gone.

3. How fully does **Source A** show the effect of the war on the Scottish economy between 1914 and 1928?
   (Use **Source A** and recall.)

Source B is an extract from *Women's Suffrage*, written by a Suffragist, Milicent Fawcett, in 1912.

Source B

> The Women's Social and Political Union had not attracted any public notice until 1905. By adopting new and startling methods they succeeded in drawing a large amount of public attention to the cause of votes for women. However many campaigners viewed these methods with disgust. They believed the lawful and peaceful action would prove more effective in the long run as a way of converting the public and government to believe in women's suffrage.

4. Evaluate the usefulness of **Source B** as evidence of the contribution of the Suffragettes to the extension of female suffrage.

   (You may want to comment on who wrote it, when they wrote it, why they wrote it, what they say or what has been missed out.)   **5**

SECTION 2 — BRITISH — 20 marks

Attempt ONE part

Part C – The Atlantic Slave Trade, 1770–1807

Attempt the following questions using recalled knowledge and information from the sources where appropriate.

Source A was written by a modern historian in 1997.

Source A

> Most slaves in the West Indies were involved in the production of sugar which was hard, heavy work. The life of the slave on the plantation was controlled by strict slave laws, or codes. Some slaves, however, refused to accept their circumstances and attempted to escape or plotted revolt. Those who escaped would be hunted down. Slave owners lived in constant fear of a revolt by their slaves. Slave risings took place throughout the colonies but very few had effective leadership and they were soon crushed by the better armed and organised whites.

1. Evaluate the usefulness of **Source A** as evidence about why resistance was difficult for slaves on the plantations.

   (You may want to comment on who wrote it, when they wrote it, why they wrote it, what they say or what has been missed out.)   **6**

2. To what extent was the abolitionist movement important in bringing about the end of the slave trade?   **8**

3. Explain the reasons why the need for the slave trade declined in Britain by the late 18th century.   **6**

SECTION 2 — BRITISH

Part D – Changing Britain, 1760–1900

Attempt the following questions using recalled knowledge and information from the sources where appropriate.

1. To what extent were improvements in health in Britain's towns due to better sanitation? **8**

2. Describe the impact of the growth of the railway network on the British economy. **6**

Source A was written by a modern historian.

Source A

> The Radical War broke out in the spring of 1820, when workers in Glasgow and surrounding towns attempted a rebellion. Many weavers, whose pay had been falling, supported the call to strike. Radical notices were posted in Glasgow calling on people to revolt. Only a few workers actually took up arms. One group of armed Radicals, led by James Wilson, marched on Glasgow. They found no support there and went home. Wilson was arrested and put on trial.

3. Evaluate the usefulness of **Source A** for investigating the importance of the Radical Movement in Scotland in 1820.

   (You may want to comment on who wrote it, when they wrote it, why they wrote it, what they say or what has been missed out.) **6**

SECTION 2 — BRITISH

Part E – The Making of Modern Britain, 1880–1951

Attempt the following questions using recalled knowledge and information from the sources where appropriate.

Source A is by the Aberdeen association for Improving the Conditions of the Poor. It was written in the late 19th century.

Source A

> Our aims are to encourage, in every available way, the efforts of the poor to live sober lives and to discourage idleness. In general, we want to help those who are sober and hardworking but who through illness or accident are in danger of being plunged into poverty. These are the only people who deserve our help.

1. Evaluate the usefulness of **Source A** as evidence of attitudes to the poor at the end of the 19th century.

   (You may want to comment on who wrote it, when they wrote it, why they wrote it, what they say or what has been missed out.)

   6

2. Explain the reasons why the Second World War changed people's attitudes towards welfare reform.

   6

3. To what extent was free health care the main reason why people welcomed the Labour reforms?

   8

SECTION 3 — EUROPEAN AND WORLD — 20 marks

MARKS

Attempt ONE part

Part B – "Tea and Freedom,": the American Revolution, 1774–1783

Attempt the following questions using recalled knowledge and information from the sources where appropriate.

1. Describe what happened during the Gaspée incident in 1772.

5

Source A describes the Battle of Bunker Hill

Source A

> In June 1775, General Howe was ordered to re-capture the high ground known as Bunker Hill which had been occupied by the colonists. On the morning of 17th June, the British navy opened fire on the colonists' positions, but their shells fell short. They then charged the hill on three occasions in order to drive the American forces away.

2. How fully does **Source A** describe what happened at the Battle of Bunker Hill? (Use **Source A** and recall.)

5

Sources B and **C** are about the defeat of British forces, led by General Cornwallis, at Yorktown.

Source B

> In 1781, Cornwallis moved into Virginia and began to build a base at Yorktown. By late summer, Cornwallis's position at Yorktown was deteriorating fast. While American forces prevented him from moving inland, a large French fleet carrying 3,000 troops had sailed up from the West Indies to join the siege. The fate of Cornwallis was sealed when the French defeated the British fleet in Chesapeake Bay. On October 19 Cornwallis surrendered his entire army of 7,000 men.

Source C

> To launch his campaign in Virginia, Cornwallis's army carried out raids, harassing the Americans wherever he could. In August 1781, Cornwallis set up camp at Yorktown but this turned out to be a poor position. American troops moved quickly to surround him and keep him there. The British could not help Cornwallis's army to escape or bring in reinforcements. In September, the French defeated the British fleet in a naval battle near Yorktown, giving the allies control over the sea in the area.

3. Compare the views in **Sources B** and **C** about the reasons for the defeat of the forces led by Cornwallis at Yorktown. (Compare the sources overall and/or in detail.)

4

4. Explain the reasons why the colonists were able to achieve victory in their war against the British by 1783.

6

SECTION 3 — EUROPEAN AND WORLD

Part C – USA, 1850–1880

Attempt the following questions using recalled knowledge and information from the sources where appropriate.

1. Describe the effects of the westward expansion of Mormons.   **5**

Source A is about the events at Fort Sumter in April, 1861.

Source A

> Lincoln sent a naval expedition to supply Fort Sumter with food. Unwilling to permit this, the Confederates opened fire on the fort on April 12th, before the ships arrived. After holding out for 34 hours, Major Robert Anderson and his men surrendered. The attack started an outburst of patriotic fever in the North. America's civil war had begun.

2. How fully does **Source A** explain the outbreak of the Civil War?   **6**
    (Use **Source A** and recall.)

3. Explain how important a problem the restrictions of the Black Codes were for Black Americans in the South after 1865.   **5**

Source B is from George Ogden's diary in which he describes the impact of Reconstruction.

Source B

> My first impression of the South was shock at the shabby conditions of the living quarters that many Black Americans still lived in. I was dismayed their life had shown no improvement. Initially I was puzzled why so many Black Americans remained in the South, still working for their old masters, when they could move freely. Congress passed many laws. However, it always struck me as worrying that some White Americans felt justified in lynching and using violence against a Black American. At first I found it strange that the White and Black Americans did not work together in the field or elsewhere.

Source C is from a history textbook and describes life during Reconstruction.

Source C

> Freed black slaves had gained their freedom but because they were too poor, many stayed in the South. The 1875 Civil Rights Act was the last government attempt to improve conditions for black people, but it had little effect in the South. Black churches and Freedmen's Bureaus made education more available for black Americans so the percentage of illiteracy went down. In effect, black people came nowhere near attaining social acceptance, with many white Americans remaining fearful and hostile, encouraging little interaction. Secret organisations were set up to terrorise black people.

4. Compare the views in **Sources B** and **C** about the effects of Reconstruction in the South.   **4**
    (Compare the sources overall and/or in detail.)

SECTION 3 — EUROPEAN AND WORLD

Part D – Hitler and Nazi Germany, 1919–1939

Attempt the following questions using recalled knowledge and information from the sources where appropriate.

1. Describe the effects of the Paris Peace Settlement on Germany.   **5**

2. Explain the reasons why Hitler was able to increase his control over Germany in 1933/34.   **5**

Source A explains the reasons why Germans supported the Nazis.

Source A

> The most important thing for me was that I had personally to choose between a future Communist Germany or a future National Socialist Germany. My mother saw an SA parade on the streets of Heidelburg. The sight of their discipline in a time of chaos won her over even though she had never read a Nazi pamphlet.

3. How fully does **Source A** explain the reasons why Germans supported the Nazi Party in the 1930s?
    (Use **Source A** and recall.)   **6**

Source B was written by a member of the League of German Maidens.

Source B

> We had to be present for meetings with local leaders and businessmen. We had to attend events relating to health and well-being. Our week-ends were crammed full with camps and sporting activities. It was fun in a way. We certainly had a lot of exercise, but it had a bad effect on my school work. None of this was going to help me to get a good career in the future.

Source C is by a modern historian.

Source C

> Many young Germans enjoyed the emphasis on activity and sport. However, those who had wanted to achieve academic success were frustrated and resentful at the amount of time spent on outdoor activities. Girls in particular felt that their education was being downgraded and their future prospects were being limited.

4. Compare the views in **Sources B** and **C** on the effects of Nazi policies on young people.
    (Compare the sources overall and/or in detail.)   **4**

SECTION 3 — EUROPEAN AND WORLD

Part E – Red Flag: Lenin and the Russian Revolution, 1894–1921

Attempt the following questions using recalled knowledge and information from the sources where appropriate.

Source A explains the treatment of national minorities in the Russian Empire.

Source A

> The diversity of the Empire made it difficult to govern. Many minorities resented the policy of Russification. It made non-Russians use the Russian language instead of their own. Russian style clothes were to be worn and Russian customs were to be adopted. Russian officials were put in to run regional government in non-Russian parts of the Empire like Poland, Latvia and Finland. When Poles complained they were treated as second class citizens, they were told to change and become Russian citizens.

1. How fully does **Source A** explain the reasons why national minorities disliked the policy of Russification?
   (Use **Source A** and recall.)   **6**

2. Explain the reasons why the Tsar was able to remain in power following the 1905 revolution.   **5**

3. Describe Lenin's return to Russia in April 1917.   **5**

Sources B and **C** discuss the reasons for the success of the October Revolution.

Source B

> The Bolsheviks were a small group of extremists who were able to seize power for themselves. They did not have the support of Russian people. There was nothing inevitable about this. The Bolsheviks simply took advantage of the chaos brought about by the First World War. The revolution was a skillfully led military operation with little popular involvement resulting in a dictatorship being imposed on the Russian people

Source C

> In the months leading up to the revolution Bolshevik demands for Peace, Bread and Land won them massive support from workers and peasants. Lenin succeeded because he spoke for the ordinary people. The October revolution was a popular rising which was guided by the Bolsheviks. The events of October 1917 were the next stage of an inevitable process driven by a desire for greater justice for the downtrodden people of the world.

4. Compare the views in **Sources B** and **C** as evidence about the reasons for the Bolshevik success in October 1917.
   (Compare the sources overall and/or in detail.)   **4**

SECTION 3 — EUROPEAN AND WORLD

MARKS

Part G – Free at Last? Civil Rights in the USA, 1918–1968

Attempt the following questions using recalled knowledge and information from the sources where appropriate.

1. Describe the activities of the Ku Klux Klan in the 1920s and 1930s.   **5**

2. Explain the reasons for the growth of the Civil Rights Movement after World War II.   **5**

Sources A and **B** describe the results of the Montgomery Bus Boycott.

Source A

> Throughout the boycott a young black preacher inspired the black population of Montgomery. His name was Martin Luther King and this was to be his first step towards becoming the leading figure in the Civil Rights Movement. The boycott lasted over a year until eventually the courts decided that segregation on Montgomery's buses was illegal. On its own the bus boycott only had limited success. Montgomery remained a segregated town. There were still white-only theatres, pool rooms and restaurants.

Source B

> The bus company's services were boycotted by 99% of Montgomery's African Americans for over a year. As a result of the protest, the US Supreme Court announced that Alabama's bus segregation laws were illegal. However, most other facilities and services in Montgomery remained segregated for many years to come. As a result of the boycott, Martin Luther King became involved in the Civil Rights Movement. He went on to become an African American leader who was famous throughout the world.

3. Compare the views in **Sources A** and **B** about the results of the Montgomery Bus Boycott.
   (Compare the sources overall and/or in detail.)   **4**

Source C explains why Malcolm X opposed non-violent protest.

Source C

> Malcolm X was mistreated in his youth and this gave him a different set of attitudes to Martin Luther King. Later, while in jail, he was influenced by the ideas of Elijah Muhammad who preached hatred of the white race. In his speeches he criticised non-violence. He believed that the support of non-violence was a sign that black people were still living in mental slavery. However, Malcolm X never undertook violent action himself and sometimes prevented it. Instead he often used violent language and threats to frighten the government into action

4. How fully does **Source C** explain the reasons why Malcolm X opposed non-violent protest?
   (Use **Source C** and recall.)   **6**

SECTION 3 — EUROPEAN AND WORLD

Part H – Appeasement and the Road to War, 1918–1939

Attempt the following questions using recalled knowledge and information from the sources where appropriate.

Source A explains why Britain and France were worried about Germany's actions.

Source A

> From 1933 onwards it looked as if Germany's policies were beginning to change. As soon as he could, Hitler removed the German representatives from the Disarmament Conference in Geneva. Hitler was working hard to create an image of strong leadership among his own people and most of them supported him when Germany gave up her membership of the League of Nations. Germany's non-aggression treaty with Poland meant that France lost a valuable ally in Eastern Europe. In 1935 Germany announced the creation of an air force and navy.

1. How fully does **Source A** describe the worries Britain and France had about Germany's actions by 1936?
   (Use **Source A** and recall.)   **6**

2. Explain the reasons why Germany wanted to expand its territories between 1933 and 1938.   **5**

Sources B and **C** are about the Germans in the Sudetenland, Czechoslovakia.

Source B

> Germany's justification for interfering in Czechoslovakia was that the Sudetenland wanted to return to the German Fatherland. Ever since 1919 the Sudeten Germans had resented being part of the new state of Czechoslovakia which was based on the medieval kingdom of Bohemia. The German government claimed that the Germans in Czechoslovakia had suffered constant persecution because they were an ethnic minority.

Source C

> Sudeten German unrest grew only after the economic depression began in the early 1930s. Germany seemed to be the only country whose economy was improving. Although they shared the same language and culture, the Sudetenland had never been part of Germany. Since 1919, the Sudeten Germans had been treated with respect in Czechoslovakia because they had contributed greatly to the nation's wealth.

3. Compare the views of **Sources B** and **C** about the Germans living in Czechoslovakia. (Compare the sources overall and/or in detail.)   **4**

4. Describe the events in 1939 that led to the outbreak of war between Britain and Germany.

SECTION 3 — EUROPEAN AND WORLD

MARKS

Part I – World War II, 1939–1945

Attempt the following questions using recalled knowledge and information from the sources where appropriate.

1. Explain the reasons why German forces were so successful in the early years of the war.

5

Source A is about the activities of the French Resistance.

Source A

> For two years the resistance movements of Europe had found it hard to make much of an impression on the might of the German military. However, they had been useful in gathering intelligence for the Allies. The devastating attacks of 1939 to 1941 had given little time for each country to prepare any kind of a secret army to undermine the invaders. Resistance members organised themselves in secret to discover French collaborators, kill many ranking Nazi officials, and destroy trains, convoys, and ships used by the German army.

2. How fully does **Source A** explain how effective resistance groups were in Nazi occupied Europe?
(Use **Source A** and recall.)

6

3. Describe the difficulties faced by the allies in planning and carrying out the Normandy landings.

5

Source B was written by a member of US President Truman's government in 1945.

Source B

> Using the atomic bomb was a mistake. Conventional bombing was increasingly effective. Using this barbarous weapon on Hiroshima and Nagasaki was of no real help in our war against Japan. The Japanese were already defeated and ready to surrender. The effectiveness of our sea blockade had brought them to their knees. It was all a dreadful waste of life.

Source C was written by an Allied prisoner of the Japanese after the Second World War.

Source C

> There is no doubt in my mind or the other prisoners' that using the atomic bomb was justified. The bomb saved the lives of thousands of prisoners as well as the Allied servicemen who would have had to invade Japan. Make no mistake, the Japanese government had decided to fight on to the last man. Listen to the emperor's speeches if you don't believe me. I have no doubt Hiroshima and Nagasaki made them surrender sooner.

4. Compare the views of **Source B** and **C** about the use of the atomic bomb on Japan.
(Compare the sources overall and/or in detail.)

4

SECTION 3 — EUROPEAN AND WORLD

MARKS

Part J – The Cold War, 1945–1989

Attempt the following questions using recalled knowledge and information from the sources where appropriate.

1. Describe the events which led to the formation of the Warsaw Pact in 1955.   **5**

Sources **A** and **B** are about the Cuban Missile Crisis.

Source A

> Under Fidel Castro, Cuba was a proud example of a Communist country and was a role model to other countries. Khrushchev had the idea of installing a small number of nuclear missiles on Cuba without letting the USA know until it was too late to stop them. Khrushchev said they only wanted to keep the Americans from invading Cuba. He stated they had no desire to start a war.

Source B

> To the American government, placing missiles on Cuba was a warlike act by the Soviets. They believed that the Soviet Union intended to supply a large number of powerful nuclear weapons. Spy photographs proved the offensive purpose of the missiles which were pointed directly at major American cities. It was estimated that within a few minutes of them being fired, 80 million Americans would be dead.

2. Compare the views in **Sources A** and **B** about the Soviet Union's actions during the Cuban Missile Crisis.   **4**
   (Compare the sources overall and/or in detail.)

Source **C** explains why the United States became involved in a war in Vietnam.

Source C

> In its early stages, the war in Vietnam had nothing to do with the USA. American involvement began when it was asked by its ally, France, for assistance. France was fighting to regain control over its former colony. The Americans agreed. They disapproved of French colonialism, but feared Communism more. They believed that they could establish a friendly government in South Vietnam, under the leadership of President Diem. By the early 1960s an increase in Vietcong attacks in South Vietnam led to a fear that a civil war was developing.

3. How fully does **Source C** explain the reasons why America became involved in a full scale war in Vietnam by 1964?   **6**
   (Use **Source C** and recall.)

4. Explain the reasons why a crisis developed in Berlin in 1961.   **5**

Model Paper 3

Whilst this Model Practice Paper has been specially commissioned by Hodder Gibson for use as practice for the National 5 exams, the key reference documents remain the SQA Specimen Paper 2013 and the SQA Past Paper 2014.

National
Qualifications
MODEL PAPER 3

SQ23/N5/01

History

Duration — 1 hour and 30 minutes

Total marks — 60

SECTION 1 — SCOTTISH — 20 marks

Attempt ONE part.

SECTION 2 — BRITISH — 20 marks

Attempt ONE part.

SECTION 3 — EUROPEAN AND WORLD — 20 marks

Attempt ONE part.

Before attempting the questions you must check that your answer booklet is for the same subject and level as this question paper.

On the answer booklet, you must clearly identify the question number you are attempting.

Use **blue** or **black** ink.

Before leaving the examination room you must give your answer booklet to the Invigilator. If you do not, you may lose all the marks for this paper.

SECTION 1 — SCOTTISH
PARTS

SECTION 2 — BRITISH
PARTS

SECTION 3 — EUROPEAN AND WORLD
PARTS

SECTION 1 — SCOTTISH — 20 marks
Attempt ONE part

Part A – The Wars of Independence, 1286–1328

Attempt the following questions using recalled knowledge and information from the sources where appropriate.

Sources A and **B** are about who should be the next King of Scots.

Source A

> John Balliol said he had the strongest right to be King of Scots. He argued this was because he was descended from the eldest daughter in the family of David, Earl of Huntingdon, the brother of King William the Lion. Balliol said it did not matter that he was a generation younger than Bruce because the feudal law of primogeniture always supported the eldest line of a family.

Source B

> Robert Bruce was determined that he was to be the next King of Scots. He said that Imperial Law supported him because he was one generation closer to the Earl of Huntingdon's family than Balliol. Bruce argued that the feudal law of primogeniture did not apply to kingdoms. He argued that it did not matter that Balliol was descended from the eldest of Earl David's daughters.

1. Compare the views in **Sources A** and **B** about who should be the next King of Scots. (Compare the sources overall and/or in detail.)   **4**

2. Explain the reasons why Balliol was a failure as King of Scots.   **5**

Source C describes the Battle of Stirling Bridge.

Source C

> The Scots allowed as many of the English to cross the bridge as they could hope to defeat, and then, having blocked the bridge, they slaughtered all who had crossed over. Among those who perished was Cressingham. De Warenne escaped with difficulty and with a small following.

3. How fully does **Source C** explain what happened at the Battle of Stirling Bridge? (Use **Source C** and recall.)   **6**

4. Describe how Robert Bruce made all the Scots accept him as King.   **5**

SECTION 1 — SCOTTISH

Part B – Mary Queen of Scots and the Reformation, 1542–1587

Attempt the following questions using recalled knowledge and information from the sources where appropriate.

Source A explains why King Henry VIII interfered in Scotland after 1542.

Source A

> King James V of Scots died in 1542, only eight days after the birth of his daughter Mary. King Henry VIII of England immediately realised the benefits of marrying the young Queen Mary to his son. It would also end French influence in Scotland and bring about an end to centuries of warfare between Scotland and England. The most recent war had contributed to the early death of James V. Henry VIII also saw an opportunity to spread Protestantism north of the border.

1. How fully does **Source A** explain the reasons why King Henry VIII interfered in Scotland after 1542?
   (Use **Source A** and recall.)   6

2. Describe the problems that Mary, Queen of Scots faced when she arrived in Scotland in 1561.   5

Sources B and **C** describe what happened in Scotland after Mary, Queen of Scots, fled to England.

Source B

> Queen Mary's supporters fought for several years after she fled to England. They hoped that the tribunal Elizabeth held in England would lead to their Queen's return. When this failed, one of Mary's supporters assassinated the Regent Moray. A year later, his replacement, the Earl of Lennox, was killed in a skirmish. The capture of Edinburgh Castle in 1573 removed Mary's last power base in Scotland.

Source C

> Mary's support in Scotland was undermined in 1569 when her Governor, Châtelherault and his deputy, the Earl of Argyll, changed sides. Nevertheless, her supporters killed both the Regent Moray and his successor. In 1573, after a few years of fighting, the Regent Morton finally persuaded most of Mary's supporters to recognise his authority. A few months later, Edinburgh Castle was forced to surrender.

3. Compare the views in **Sources B** and **C** about what happened in Scotland after Mary, Queen of Scots, fled to England.
   (Compare the sources overall and/or in detail.)   4

4. Explain the reasons why Queen Elizabeth kept Mary, Queen of Scots, in prison for so long.   5

SECTION 1 — SCOTTISH

Part C – The Treaty of Union, 1689–1715

Attempt the following questions using recalled knowledge and information from the sources where appropriate.

Source A explains why so many Scots decided to invest in the Darien Scheme.

Source A

> After the Union of the Crowns, the Scots became aware that the prosperity of their country depended on farming which suffered from bad weather and poor soil. In fact, very little was done to improve Scottish farming for another fifty years. Scottish overseas trade was limited and it did not make huge amounts of money for the country. The Scots thought that England's prosperity came from its overseas trade with its colonies. William Paterson promised them a colony where "trade will increase and money will make money".

1. How fully does **Source A** show why the Scots invested in the Darien Scheme? (Use **Source A** and recall.)   **6**

Sources B and **C** are about why some Scots suggested a Union.

Source B

> Queen Anne had always wanted a union between her two kingdoms. A number of Scots supported the idea believing that trading with England's colonies would make Scotland a wealthier country. Many English people worried that a union would make England poorer. England's frequent wars with France annoyed the Scots because Scotland's trade with France was badly affected. The Scottish "Act of Security" offered England a shared monarch in return for access to its colonies.

Source C

> Bad feelings between Scotland and England erupted into a crisis when Anne became Queen in 1702. The Scots were angry because the ban from trading with England's colonies stopped them from increasing their wealth, especially since they blamed England for the failure of Darien. In 1703, they demanded access to England's colonies in return for sharing a monarch. Then they passed the Wine Act to reduce the bad effects of England's wars against France on Scotland's trade.

2. Compare the views in **Sources B** and **C** about why some Scots suggested a Union. (Compare the sources overall and/or in detail.)   **4**

3. Describe how Queen Anne's government won support for the Act of Union.   **5**

4. Explain the reasons why support for the Jacobites grew between 1707 and 1715.   **5**

SECTION 1 — SCOTTISH

Part D – Migration and Empire, 1830–1939

Attempt the following questions using recalled knowledge and information from the sources where appropriate.

1. Describe the "push" factors, which led many Irish to emigrate after 1830.   **5**

Source A explains why the Catholic Church was important for many Irish immigrants in the 19th century.

Source A

> The Irish immigrants were not very well-off and the native Scots often did not welcome them. The church gave them a place to worship and a sense of security. Immigrants knew that they could be baptised, married and buried according to their religion. The priests usually spoke Irish so there was someone to whom they could explain their problems. Over time a number of Catholic churches were established in the west of Scotland. The church became a centre of social life and gave the immigrants an opportunity to meet their fellow countrymen.

2. How fully does **Source A** explain the importance of the Catholic Church to many Irish immigrants in the 19th century?
    (Use **Source A** and recall.)   **6**

3. Explain the reasons why so many Scots emigrated between 1830 and 1900.   **5**

Sources B and **C** are about the experiences of Scottish emigrants.

Source B

> I feel that everything the agent told me about this country has turned out to be false and I dearly wish to return home. I am very much dissatisfied with the poor quality of the land which will never be of much use. The nearest town is two days' journey away and my daughter and I suffer a great deal from loneliness.

Source C

> I have already prepared 14 acres of good land and, if I am spared, I shall have 40 ready next year. I got a splendid horse and a good cow and a calf, plenty milk and butter, plenty to eat of everything. Our wee community is doing well and our fellow immigrants have already built a church and a school-house. There is not a better place in the whole world.

4. Compare the views in **Sources B** and **C** about the experiences of Scottish emigrants.
    (Compare the sources overall and/or in detail.)   **4**

SECTION 1 — SCOTTISH

Part E – The Era of the Great War, 1910–1928

Attempt the following questions using recalled knowledge and information from the sources where appropriate.

Source A is about the recruitment campaign to the armed forces in 1914.

Source A

> At first the outbreak of war was exciting. The opportunity to go on an adventure with your pals in a kilted uniform was too good to miss. There were more Scots volunteers in proportion to the size of the population than any other area of the UK. The possibilities of facing serious injury or death were put aside. War hysteria also played a part. The War Propaganda Bureau told stories of Belgian babies being bayoneted and nurses and nuns being raped by German soldiers.

1. How fully does **Source A** explain why so many Scots volunteered for the armed forces in 1914?
    (Use **Source A** and recall.)   **6**

2. Describe the impact of war on the lives of women in Scotland.   **5**

3. Explain the reasons for the decline of heavy industry after World War I.   **5**

Source B was written by William Gallacher, a Glasgow Trade Union leader in 1919.

Source B

> A socialist rising was expected and it should have taken place. The workers were ready and able to carry it out. The mistake we made on Friday 31st January was marching to the centre of Glasgow. If we had gone to the barracks at Maryhill we could easily have persuaded the soldiers to support us and Clydeside would have been in our hands.

Source C was written by a modern historian.

Source C

> The government was worried about the loyalty of the police and armed forces in Glasgow. Had the government understood the situation better they could have saved themselves and the country a lot of bother. The leaders of the movement had no real support for their plans. The day after their protest in George Square the strikers went to the football just as they always did.

4. Compare the views in **Sources B** and **C** about what happened on Clydeside in 1919.
    (Compare the sources overall and/or in detail.)   **4**

SECTION 2 — BRITISH — 20 marks

Attempt ONE part

Part C – The Atlantic Slave Trade, 1770–1807

Attempt the following questions using recalled knowledge and information from the sources where appropriate.

Source A was written by a modern historian, describing the treatment of slaves on the middle passage.

Source A

> Troublesome slaves were kept in chains and only let on the deck a few at a time for exercise. To keep the slaves as healthy as possible the crew would whip them to make them dance during exercise time. In desperation some slaves tried to jump overboard. Many slaves died during the middle passage from harsh treatment, poor food and disease. So did many of the crew.

1. Evaluate the usefulness of **Source A** as evidence of how slaves were treated on the middle passage.

   (You may want to comment on who wrote it, when they wrote it, why they wrote it, what they say or what has been missed out.)   **6**

2. Explain the reasons for the success of British ports involved in the slave trade.   **6**

3. To what extent was the case of the Zong important to the growth of the abolitionist campaign?   **8**

SECTION 2 — BRITISH

Part D – Changing Britain, 1760–1900

Attempt the following questions using recalled knowledge and information from the sources where appropriate.

1. Explain the reasons for poor health in British cities at the start of the 19th century.   6

Source A is from the *New Statistical Account* for the parish of Lochwinnoch, 1846.

Source A

> The population has increased rapidly since 1791. The chief reason for this was the building of cotton mills and the boost this gave to every other kind of business. The cotton mill employees can afford to live and dress well. A new mill stands on the banks of the River Calder. It employs 345 workers. Those employed in the mills work twelve hours a day, five days a week, and nine hours on Saturdays. The high temperatures in the mills weaken the body and damage the workers' health.

2. Evaluate the usefulness of **Source A** for investigating how improvements in technology in the textile industry affected the Scottish people.

   (You may want to comment on who wrote it, when they wrote it, why they wrote it, what they say or what has been missed out.)   6

3. To what extent did the Radicals pose a serious threat to order in Scotland in 1820?   8

SECTION 2 — BRITISH

Part E – The Making of Modern Britain, 1880–1951

Attempt the following questions using recalled knowledge and information from the sources where appropriate.

1. Explain the reasons why Liberals introduced reforms to support children and the elderly.

    6

Source A is taken from a speech made by Winston Churchill before the 1945 election.

Source A

> Here in old England we do not like to have every aspect of our lives organized for us. Let us leave Labour's welfare reformers to their unrealistic dreams. Let us make sure that the home to which the soldiers return is blessed with modest but solid prosperity but that Britons remain free to plan their lives for themselves and for those they love

2. Evaluate the usefulness of **Source A** as evidence of attitudes towards welfare reform after the Second World War.

    (You may want to comment on who wrote it, when they wrote it, why they wrote it, what they say or what has been missed out.)

    6

3. To what extent was the experience of rationing important in changing attitudes to poverty by 1945?

    8

SECTION 3 — EUROPEAN AND WORLD — 20 marks
Attempt ONE part

MARKS

Part B – "Tea and Freedom,": the American Revolution, 1774–1783

Attempt the following questions using recalled knowledge and information from the sources where appropriate.

Source A explains why many colonists were unhappy with British rule by 1774.

Source A

> The writer Thomas Paine was firmly opposed to British rule. In January 1776, he published a cleverly written pamphlet called "Common Sense". In it, he argued that the British government was abusing the rights of the American people and many colonists were persuaded by his arguments. The answer, Paine believed, was independence. Paine's ideas were very popular and 150,000 pamphlets were sold. The King's rejection of the Olive Branch Petition also moved many colonists towards independence, as did news that the British were hiring mercenary soldiers from Germany to help them control the colonies.

1. How fully does **Source A** explain the reasons why many colonists had turned against British rule by 1776?
    (Use **Source A** and recall.)   5

Source B is from the trial of a British officer which followed the Boston Massacre in 1770.

Source B

> One of my soldiers received a severe blow with a stick, which caused him to fire his weapon accidentally. There followed a general attack on my men by a great number of heavy clubs. At this point our lives were in imminent danger and three or four of my soldiers fired, claiming that they heard an order to shoot. I can assure you that I gave no such order.

2. Evaluate the usefulness of **Source B** as evidence of why the Boston Massacre took place?   5

    (You may want to comment on who wrote it, when they wrote it, why they wrote it, what they say or what has been missed out.)

3. Describe the ways in which foreign countries helped the colonists in the war against the British.   5

4. Explain the reasons why some colonists remained loyal to Britain during the War of Independence.   5

SECTION 3 — EUROPEAN AND WORLD

Part C – USA, 1850–1880

Attempt the following questions using recalled knowledge and information from the sources where appropriate.

Source A explains why there was tension between the whites and Native Americans.

Source A

> Professional hunters like "Buffalo Bill" were hired to shoot the buffalo to provide meat for settlers and railway workers. They crossed the sacred land of the Native Americans to do this. The white settlers also shot the buffalo for sport which offended the Sioux. Relations between the whites and Native Americans grew more and more tense.

1. How fully does **Source A** explain the causes of tension between whites and Native Americans?
    (Use **Source A** and recall.)   5

2. Explain the reasons why many people in the North were opposed to slavery.   5

3. Describe the aims of the Republican Party in 1860.   5

Source B was written by the historian Janet Riehecky in her book *The Abolition of Slavery*, published in 2002.

Source B

> A secret terrorist organisation called the Ku Klux Klan was formed in 1866. Their main objective was to maintain white supremacy. They did this by taking steps to prevent black Americans from voting. The Klan wore hooded robes to maintain their anonymity and intimidate their victims. They used burning crosses to frighten victims. Most importantly they attacked and murdered black Americans, sometimes by lynching. They burned down their homes and churches. Schools were a particular target to prevent black Americans from becoming literate.

4. Evaluate the usefulness of **Source B** as evidence about the effects of the Ku Klux Klan's tactics on black Americans.   5

    (You may want to comment on who wrote it, when they wrote it, why they wrote it, what they say or what has been missed out.)

SECTION 3 — EUROPEAN AND WORLD

MARKS

Part D – Hitler and Nazi Germany, 1919–1939

Attempt the following questions using recalled knowledge and information from the sources where appropriate.

1. Describe the events of the Beer Hall Putsch.

5

Source A explains why many Germans disliked the Weimar Republic by the mid 1920s.

Source A

> The system of elections for the Reichstag meant no one party ever won a majority of seats. Germany, therefore, had a series of coalition governments which some people believed made the government weak. Many Germans felt the parties were too busy arguing amongst each other to solve the country's problems. Any success the government achieved was quickly forgotten.

2. How fully does **Source A** explain the reasons why the Weimar government was so unpopular by the mid 1920s?
   (Use **Source A** and recall.)

5

3. Explain the reasons why it was so difficult to oppose the Nazi government after 1933.

5

Source B was written by historians J. F. Corkery and R. C. F. Stone in *Weimar Germany and the Third Reich*, published in 1980.

Source B

> Government organisation of the workers gave opportunity for brainwashing them. In 1935 the Labour Service was established. This meant that every male between the ages of 18 and 25 had to do six months in public work camps. Camp discipline was semi-military. Camp leaders were given ranks. Men drilled with spades instead of rifles. The Labour Service was an opportunity to spread Nazi propaganda, building upon that already provided by the schools and Hitler Youth. Workers were urged to regard themselves as 'soldiers of work'.

4. Evaluate the usefulness of **Source B** as evidence about militarism in Nazi Germany.

5

   (You may want to comment on who wrote it, when they wrote it, why they wrote it, what they say or what has been missed out.)

SECTION 3 — EUROPEAN AND WORLD

Part E – Red Flag: Lenin and the Russian Revolution, 1894–1921

Attempt the following questions using recalled knowledge and information from the sources where appropriate.

Source A is from *History of the Russian Revolution* by Leon Trotsky, written in 1932.

Source A

> Nicholas II was unreliable and not to be trusted. He kept his gentlest smiles and kindest words for officials whom he planned to dismiss. He drew back with distaste from anyone gifted or capable. He only felt relaxed among very average and unimaginative people such as so-called holy men— people who could not show up his stupidity.

1. Evaluate the usefulness of **Source A** as evidence about Nicholas II.

   (You may want to comment on who wrote it, when they wrote it, why they wrote it, what they say or what has been missed out.)   **5**

2. Describe the events of Bloody Sunday in January 1905.   **5**

3. Explain the reasons why the Russian people were so discontented by February 1917.   **5**

Source B explains why the Bolsheviks were able to stay in power in Russia in 1917–1918.

Source B

> The successful seizure of power in Petrograd was only a beginning. Almost immediately the Congress of Soviets pleased the peasants by declaring that landlords' rights to property were abolished so that the land could be redistributed. A new Bolshevik Cabinet, Sovnarkom, was set up and given authority to pass new laws. In November, the Bolsheviks allowed the long-awaited elections to the Constitutional Assembly to be held; over 47 million Russians, including many peasants, voted. In December, Sovnarkom created a new secret police, the Cheka, to wipe out any counter-revolutionary activity.

4. How fully does **Source B** explain why the Bolsheviks were able to stay in power in Russia in 1917–1918?
   (Use **Source B** and recall.)   **5**

SECTION 3 — EUROPEAN AND WORLD

Part G – Free at Last? Civil Rights in the USA, 1918–1968

Attempt the following questions using recalled knowledge and information from the sources where appropriate.

1. Describe the impact of the Jim Crow laws on the lives of black Americans.   **5**

Source A is from a statement made by President Kennedy in May 1963.

Source A

> I think that the situation in Birmingham will be peacefully settled in the next 24 hours. Quite obviously the situation was damaging the reputation of Birmingham and the United States. It seems to me that the best way to prevent that kind of serious damage is to take steps to provide equal treatment for all of our citizens. That is the best remedy in this case and other cases.

2. Evaluate the usefulness of **Source A** as evidence of the effects of the Civil Rights protest in Birmingham.

    (You may want to comment on who wrote it, when they wrote it, why they wrote it, what they say or what has been missed out.)   **5**

Source B is about the march on Washington in 1963.

Source B

> More than thirty Freedom Trains and 2000 Freedom Buses were hired to take marchers to the capital city. Marchers assembled in front of the Lincoln Memorial in the capital city of the USA. Many of the marchers were African Americans, but about 20 per cent of the crowd was made up of white marchers who were demonstrating their support for the Civil Rights Movement. The demonstration was peaceful and orderly.

3. How fully does **Source B** explain the reasons why the march on Washington was important for the Civil Rights Movement?
    (Use **Source B** and recall.)   **5**

4. Explain the reasons for the riots by black Americans in northern cities in the late 1960s.   **5**

SECTION 3 — EUROPEAN AND WORLD

MARKS

Part H – Appeasement and the Road to War, 1918–1939

Attempt the following questions using recalled knowledge and information from the sources where appropriate.

Source A is from one of the school textbooks introduced by the Nazis in 1934.

Source A

> For many centuries the Germans have protected Europe from the dangers of the east. It was German blood that defended Europe from Slav invaders and proved the superiority of our race. It is important that the Aryan race remains pure to fulfill its historic sacred mission to dominate inferior peoples and spread German culture and civilisation wherever possible.

1. Evaluate the usefulness of **Source A** as evidence of Nazi ideas on race.

   (You may want to comment on who wrote it, when they wrote it, why they wrote it, what they say or what has been missed out.)   5

Source B explains why Hitler wanted to rearm Germany in the 1930s.

Source B

> Hitler claimed that Germany alone was forced to leave herself defenceless as part of the punishment dictated by her enemies in 1919. He never missed an opportunity to attack the Treaty of Versailles. Hitler further stated that Germany was surrounded by hostile countries whose main purpose was to keep her in a weakened position and this could no longer be tolerated. A strong Germany would not only restore the balance of power in Europe but was also necessary to safeguard European civilisation against the threat from the east.

2. How fully does **Source B** explain the reasons why Hitler wanted to rearm Germany in the 1930s?   5
   (Use **Source B** and recall.)

3. Explain the reasons by Britain followed a policy of appeasement in the 1930s.   5

4. Describe the events that led to the takeover of Czechoslovakia.   5

SECTION 3 — EUROPEAN AND WORLD

Part I – World War II, 1939–1945

Attempt the following questions using recalled knowledge and information from the sources where appropriate.

Source A is from a diary journal kept by General Erwin Rommel, leader of the 7th Panzer Division. In this excerpt, he describes the action on May 14 as he leads a tank attack against French forces.

Source A

> The tanks now rolled in a long column through the line of fortifications and on towards the first houses, which had been set alight by our fire. Our artillery was dropping heavy harassing fire on villages and the road far ahead of the regiment. Gradually the speed increased. We crossed the railway line and then swung north to the main road which was soon reached. Civilians and French troops, their faces distorted with terror, lay huddled in the ditches. We passed refugee columns, the carts abandoned by their owners, who had fled in panic into the fields. On we went, at a steady speed, towards our objective. We were through the Maginot Line!

1. Evaluate the usefulness of **Source A** as evidence of Blitzkreig tactics used by Germany in 1940.

   (You may want to comment on who wrote it, when they wrote it, why they wrote it, what they say or what has been missed out.)   **5**

2. Describe the problems facing ordinary people living in occupied Europe.   **5**

Source B is about the activities of the Dutch underground resistance groups in Nazi occupied Europe.

Source B

> Underground resistance groups were organized to serve a variety of functions including the rescue and sheltering of Jews and other persecuted individuals. Underground cells were involved in the manufacture of false papers or acted as couriers of secret documents to countries outside of the Netherlands to assist Allied war efforts. It is estimated that over fifty to sixty thousand individuals were directly involved in underground activities with hundreds of thousands more offering assistance.

3. How fully does **Source B** describe the activities of resistance groups in Nazi occupied Europe?
   (Use **Source B** and recall.)   **5**

4. Explain the reasons why America was able to defeat Japan by 1945.   **5**

SECTION 3 — EUROPEAN AND WORLD

MARKS

Part J – The Cold War, 1945–1989

Attempt the following questions using recalled knowledge and information from the sources where appropriate.

Source A explains why there was a crisis in Berlin in 1961.

Source A

> By 1960 the situation in East Berlin was very dangerous. A new East German labour law, which stopped workers from going on strike, had led to growing unrest in the factories. The East German government's reforms of agriculture had led to shortages of food and higher prices. All of this led to a massive increase in the numbers of refugees fleeing to the West. At a meeting of the Warsaw Pact states, Khrushchev had been informed about the situation. In the six months up to June 1961, 103,000 East Germans had fled through Berlin. The decision to act was taken.

1. How fully does **Source A** explain the reasons why there was a crisis in Berlin in 1961? (Use **Source A** and recall.)　　5

2. Describe the part played by the USSR in the Cuban Missile Crisis.　　5

3. Explain the reasons why most Americans were opposed to the war in Vietnam by 1970.　　5

Source B is from a speech to the American people by President Reagan in March 1983.

Source B

> Our efforts to rebuild America's forces began two years ago. For twenty years the Soviet Union has been accumulating enormous military might. They didn't stop building their forces, even when they had more than enough to defend themselves. They haven't stopped now. I know that all of you want peace, and so do I. However, the freeze on building nuclear weapons would make us less, not more, secure and would increase the risk of war.

4. Evaluate the usefulness of **Source B** as evidence of why the process of détente had come to a halt by the early 1980s.

   (You may want to comment on who wrote it, when they wrote it, why they wrote it, what they say or what has been missed out.)　　5

NATIONAL 5

2014

National
Qualifications
2014

X737/75/01

History

WEDNESDAY, 7 MAY
9:00 AM – 10:30 AM

Total marks — 60

SECTION 1 — SCOTTISH CONTEXTS — 20 marks

Attempt ONE part.

SECTION 2 — BRITISH CONTEXTS — 20 marks

Attempt ONE part.

SECTION 3 — EUROPEAN AND WORLD CONTEXTS — 20 marks

Attempt ONE part.

Write your answers clearly in the answer booklet provided. In the answer booklet, you must clearly identify the question number you are attempting.

Use **blue** or **black** ink.

Before leaving the examination room you must give your answer booklet to the Invigilator; if you do not, you may lose all the marks for this paper.

SECTION 1 — SCOTTISH CONTEXTS

PARTS

SECTION 2 — BRITISH CONTEXTS

PARTS

SECTION 3 — EUROPEAN AND WORLD CONTEXTS

PARTS

SECTION 1 — SCOTTISH CONTEXTS — 20 marks   MARKS

Part A — The Wars of Independence, 1286–1328

Attempt the following questions using recalled knowledge and information from the sources where appropriate.

1. Explain the reasons why Edward I was able to become involved in Scottish affairs between 1286 and 1292.   5

2. Describe what happened at the Battle of Stirling Bridge in 1297.   5

Source A is from the chronicle of Walter of Guisborough, written in 1306.

Source A

> Robert the Bruce wanted to be king of Scotland but feared Lord John Comyn would stop him. He lured him to a meeting in Greyfriars Church in Dumfries to deal with business concerning them both. Comyn suspected nothing and they greeted each other in a friendly way. Suddenly Bruce accused Comyn of telling lies about him to the king of England. He struck him with his sword and marched out.

3. Evaluate the usefulness of **Source A** as evidence of Bruce's actions in 1306.   5

    (You may want to comment on who wrote it, when they wrote it, why they wrote it, what they say or what has been missed out.)

Source B describes how Bruce established himself as king of an independent Scotland.

Source B

> After Bannockburn, Bruce's parliament agreed that Scots nobles who had not made peace with him would lose their lands in Scotland. Bruce gave this forfeited land to his own supporters. The Douglases benefited greatly from this. Scots nobles would no longer be allowed to have English estates so their loyalties would not be divided. Bruce also backed his brother's campaign in Ireland to continue to challenge English rule. He continued to raid the north of England to put pressure on Edward to recognise him as king of an independent nation.

4. How fully does **Source B** describe how Bruce established himself as king of an independent Scotland after the Battle of Bannockburn? (Use **Source B** and recall.)   5

[Now go to SECTION 2 starting on *Page eight*]

SECTION 1 — SCOTTISH CONTEXTS — 20 marks

MARKS

Part B — Mary Queen of Scots and the Scottish Reformation, 1542–1587

Attempt the following questions using recalled knowledge and information from the sources where appropriate.

1. Describe the events which led Mary, Queen of Scots, to move to France in 1548.   **5**

Source A is about the growth of Protestantism in Scotland.

Source A

> The Protestant form of worship meant that people could participate much more in services. The Bible was available in English, not Latin; therefore people who could not read Latin could still understand it. Only churchmen and a few others could understand Latin. A conflict between Catholics and Protestants was developing in Scotland for various reasons. Some people began to criticise the Catholic Church because of its great wealth. Local priests were resented for charging people for christening their children. This was a ceremony people would not dare go without.

2. How fully does **Source A** explain the reasons for the growth in the Protestant religion in Scotland? (Use **Source A** and recall.)   **5**

Source B is from a sermon written in the 1560s by John Knox.

Source B

> In 1563 there was a great famine in Scotland. But in the north of the country, where Mary had travelled before harvest time, the famine was hardest with great suffering. Many people died. Thus did God punish the many sins of our wicked Queen and her followers. The excessive celebrations and huge feasts in the palace and in the country provoked God into this action.

3. Evaluate the usefulness of **Source B** as evidence of Protestant attitudes towards Mary, Queen of Scots, during her reign in Scotland.   **5**

    (You may want to comment on who wrote it, when they wrote it, why they wrote it, what they say or what has been missed out.)

4. Explain the reasons why Riccio became unpopular with Darnley and the Scottish nobles.   **5**

[Now go to SECTION 2 starting on *Page eight*]

SECTION 1 — SCOTTISH CONTEXTS — 20 marks

MARKS

Part C — The Treaty of Union, 1689–1715

Attempt the following questions using recalled knowledge and information from the sources where appropriate.

1. Describe the worsening relations between Scotland and England between 1689 and 1705.   **5**

Source A is from a leaflet written by Andrew Fletcher in 1706.

Source A

> Let me explain my opposition to Union. Scotland needs to keep its own separate law and church. They cannot be governed and supported by a Parliament in London. If the Scots agree to these interests being controlled by a single Parliament they will surrender control to the English. The Scots deserve no pity if they surrender their interests to a Parliament where the English will have a vast majority.

2. Evaluate the usefulness of **Source A** as evidence of the arguments used by Scots against the Union.   **5**

    (You may want to comment on who wrote it, when they wrote it, why they wrote it, what they say or what has been missed out.)

Source B is about the Treaty of Union.

Source B

> I could give you some account of the many advantages we will obtain by a union with England. By this union we will all have access to all the advantages of trade that the English enjoy at the moment. We will be able to improve our wealth which will be for the benefit of the whole island. We will have our liberty, our property and our religion secured. Scotland will be under the protection of one sovereign and one Parliament of Great Britain.

3. How fully does **Source B** explain the arguments used by Scots in favour of the Union? (Use **Source B** and recall.)   **5**

4. Explain the reasons why many Scots participated in the Jacobite rebellion of 1715.   **5**

[Now go to SECTION 2 starting on *Page eight*]

SECTION 1 — SCOTTISH CONTEXTS — 20 marks   MARKS

Part D — Migration and Empire, 1830–1939

Attempt the following questions using recalled knowledge and information from the sources where appropriate.

1. Explain the reasons why many Scots resented immigrants between 1830 and 1939.   5

2. Describe the assistance given to Scots to help them to emigrate to the Empire.   5

Source A describes the career of a Scots emigrant to Australia in the 19th century.

Source A

> Alexander Spark left Elgin for lack of local opportunities. With a good education and some inherited money he applied for a land grant in Australia. He settled in Sydney. Within three years he was a leading member of the business community, prominent in banking and by 1840 owned £40,000 of land. He became the local agent for a variety of companies including shipping, banks and the Australian Gas company. Scottish Agents in Australia handled the interests of many Scots who invested money in Australian businesses without ever leaving Scotland.

3. How fully does Source A describe the contribution of Scots to their new countries? (Use Source A and recall.)   5

Source B is from a memoir by Mary Contini, about her Italian grandparents who emigrated to Scotland in the early 20th century.

Source B

> When my grandparents visited other Italian families, invariably the conversation turned to the price of potatoes. The price they paid was important because so many of them made their living selling fish and chips. The unfamiliar ideas of banks and debt worried them and made them work even harder. Their shops were open long hours and the whole family helped serve customers. This helped their shops become the focus of social life in many communities.

4. Evaluate the usefulness of Source B as evidence of the ways immigrants fitted in to Scottish society.   5

   (You may want to comment on who wrote it, when they wrote it, why they wrote it, what they say or what has been missed out.)

[Now go to SECTION 2 starting on *Page eight*]

SECTION 1 — SCOTTISH CONTEXTS — 20 marks

MARKS

Part E — The Era of the Great War, 1910–1928

Attempt the following questions using recalled knowledge and information from the sources where appropriate.

1. Describe the use of new technology on the Western Front.

5

Source A is from the memoirs of David Lloyd George who was in charge of the Ministry of Munitions in 1915.

Source A

> The courage of the women engaged in these factories has never been sufficiently recognised. They had to work under conditions of real danger to life. What some of them probably dreaded more was horrible disfigurement — for one of the risks of the shell filling factories was toxic jaundice resulting from TNT poisoning. The poor girls were nicknamed "canaries". They were quite proud of this. They had earned it in the path of duty.

2. Evaluate the usefulness of **Source A** as evidence of the impact of the Great War on Scottish women.

   (You may want to comment on who wrote it, when they wrote it, why they wrote it, what they say or what has been missed out.)

5

Source B is about the treatment of conscientious objectors.

Source B

> Men who refused to enlist in the army had to face military discipline. Some were sentenced to death for refusing orders although the sentence was always reduced if the "conchie" still refused to give in. Many refused non-combatant duty on the grounds that it simply released another man to kill. Special prisons and work camps were opened up in addition to ordinary prisons to which many objectors were sent. Twenty-four objectors died while detained at these work camps.

3. How fully does **Source B** describe how conscientious objectors were treated during the Great War? (Use **Source B** and recall.)

5

4. Explain the reasons why heavy industry declined in Scotland after the Great War.

5

[Now go to SECTION 2 starting on *Page eight*]

SECTION 2 — BRITISH CONTEXTS — 20 marks

MARKS

Part A — The Creation of the Medieval Kingdoms, 1066–1406

Attempt the following questions using recalled knowledge and information from the sources where appropriate.

1. To what extent was William I's leadership the main reason why the Normans won the Battle of Hastings?

    (You must use recalled knowledge to present a **balanced account** of the influence of different factors and come to a **reasoned conclusion**.)

    8

Source A is from a chronicle written by a royal clerk in 1174.

Source A

> Whilst Henry was dealing with problems elsewhere in his kingdom, the king of Scotland, William the Lion, rebelled and attacked Northumberland. William's army committed terrible crimes wherever they went. Women and children were slaughtered and priests murdered inside their own churches. Next William travelled to Carlisle. His army besieged the castle and, by cutting off their supplies, forced the English to make a treaty with the Scots.

2. Evaluate the usefulness of **Source A** as evidence of the rebellions faced by Henry II during his reign.

    (You may want to comment on who wrote it, when they wrote it, why they wrote it, what they say or what has been missed out.)

    6

3. Explain the reasons why there was a Peasants Revolt in 1381.

    6

[Now go to SECTION 3 starting on *Page thirteen*]

SECTION 2 — BRITISH CONTEXTS — 20 marks

MARKS

Part B — War of the Three Kingdoms, 1603–1651

Attempt the following questions using recalled knowledge and information from the sources where appropriate.

1. To what extent were arguments between King James VI and I and Parliament the result of religious differences?

   (You must use recalled knowledge to present a **balanced account** of the influence of different factors and come to a **reasoned conclusion**.)

   8

2. Explain the reasons why Charles I was an unpopular monarch by 1640.

   6

Source A is from a letter dated 17 September 1649, written by Oliver Cromwell to the House of Commons.

Source A

> Our army came to Drogheda on 3rd September. On Monday 9th the battering guns began. I sent Sir Arthur Aston a request to surrender the town but received no satisfactory answer. Our guns then beat down the corner tower, and made gaps in the east and south walls. On the following day, after some fierce fighting, we entered the town. Several of the enemy, including Sir Arthur Aston, retreated into Mill Mount, a place very difficult to attack.

3. Evaluate the usefulness of **Source A** as evidence of what happened at Drogheda in Ireland during the Civil War.

   (You may want to comment on who wrote it, when they wrote it, why they wrote it, what they say or what has been missed out.)

   6

[Now go to SECTION 3 starting on *Page thirteen*]

SECTION 2 — BRITISH CONTEXTS — 20 marks

MARKS

Part C — The Atlantic Slave Trade, 1770–1807

Attempt the following questions using recalled knowledge and information from the sources where appropriate.

1. To what extent was the success of the abolitionist campaigns due to the work of campaigners such as Thomas Clarkson?

   (You must use recalled knowledge to present a **balanced account** of the influence of different factors and come to a **reasoned conclusion**.)

   8

2. Explain the reasons why many people in Britain continued to support the slave trade.

   6

Source A is from *Black Peoples of the Americas*, a book written by an historian in 1995.

Source A

> The planters in the Caribbean were afraid of a rebellion and they followed a policy of control through fear. Slaves had no rights. They were seen as possessions rather than human beings. Owners could deal with slaves exactly as they pleased and there was no punishment for owners who worked their slaves to death. Until the nineteenth century, no-one questioned owners burning or torturing their slaves.

3. Evaluate the usefulness of **Source A** as evidence of the treatment of slaves on the plantations.

   6

   (You may want to comment on who wrote it, when they wrote it, why they wrote it, what they say or what has been missed out.)

[Now go to SECTION 3 starting on *Page thirteen*]

SECTION 2 — BRITISH CONTEXTS — 20 marks

MARKS

Part D — Changing Britain, 1760–1900

Attempt the following questions using recalled knowledge and information from the sources where appropriate.

Source A is from a report on housing in Manchester, written by a doctor in 1832.

Source A

> The houses that the mill workers live in are poorly ventilated and do not have toilets. The streets are narrow, unpaved and worn into deep ruts. These ruts become the common resting place of mud, refuse and disgusting rubbish. In Parliament Street there is only one toilet for 380 inhabitants. The flow of muck from this toilet infests close-by houses and must be a source of disease.

1. Evaluate the usefulness of **Source A** as evidence of housing conditions in British cities in the nineteenth century.

    (You may want to comment on who wrote it, when they wrote it, why they wrote it, what they say or what has been missed out.)

    6

2. To what extent was new technology the main reason for improvements in coal mining by 1900?

    (You must use recalled knowledge to present a **balanced account** of the influence of different factors and come to a **reasoned conclusion**.)

    8

3. Explain the reasons why there was a decline in the use of canals after the 1840s.

    6

[Now go to SECTION 3 starting on *Page thirteen*]

SECTION 2 — BRITISH CONTEXTS — 20 marks

Part E — The Making of Modern Britain, 1880–1951

Attempt the following questions using recalled knowledge and information from the sources where appropriate.

1. To what extent was poor health the main cause of poverty by 1900?

    (You must use recalled knowledge to present a **balanced account** of the influence of different factors and come to a **reasoned conclusion**.)

    8

Source A is from the book *From the Cradle to the Grave: Social Welfare in Britain 1890s–1951* by historians and published in 2002.

Source A

> One of the groups of "deserving poor" that the Liberals aimed to help in Britain was the young. The Boer War and the condition of many recruits led politicians to act. The Liberal government knew that poorer children would be the soldiers of the future. Healthy children would grow up to be healthy soldiers and workers, and the British Empire would be stronger as a result.

2. Evaluate the usefulness of **Source A** as evidence of the reasons why the Liberals introduced reforms to help the young.

    (You may want to comment on who wrote it, when they wrote it, why they wrote it, what they say or what has been missed out.)

    6

3. Explain the reasons why the Second World War changed attitudes to welfare reform in Britain.

    6

[Now go to SECTION 3 starting on *Page thirteen*]

SECTION 3 — EUROPEAN AND WORLD CONTEXTS — 20 marks

MARKS

Part A — The Cross and the Crescent: the Crusades, 1071–1192

Attempt the following questions using recalled knowledge and information from the sources where appropriate.

1. Describe the use of castles in medieval times.   5

2. Explain the reasons why people joined the First Crusade.   5

Source A describes the relationship between Emperor Alexius and the Crusaders.

Source A

> Emperor Alexius was horrified when the Crusader knights arrived at Constantinople. Fearing they would attack his city, Alexius made the Crusaders camp outside and only allowed them to enter in small groups. In a desperate attempt to take charge of the army, Alexius offered treasure and supplies to the Crusaders who agreed to fight for him. Any Crusader who refused was attacked and forced to surrender. Although Alexius had asked the Pope for knights he did not trust them and made plans to remove them from Constantinople.

3. How fully does **Source A** describe the relationship between Emperor Alexius and the Crusaders? (Use **Source A** and recall.)   6

Sources B and C are about the character of Richard I.

Source B

> When the king of France left the Crusade, Richard vowed to fulfil his Christian duty and continue to Jerusalem. An excellent military commander, Richard used clever tactics to win key battles and drive the Muslims back. Richard had such a fearsome reputation that the Muslims dreaded facing him on the battlefield. Despite the danger involved Richard always fought alongside his men, courageously attacking the enemy.

Source C

> The Crusaders had been besieging Acre for two years before Richard arrived with his army. Richard immediately took charge of the attack and using his experience and leadership forced the city to surrender. Throughout the fighting Richard showed great bravery by defending his men and killing the enemy. When some Crusaders returned home, Richard refused to leave promising he would keep his oath to God and recapture Jerusalem.

4. Compare the views of **Sources B** and **C** as evidence of the character of Richard I. (Compare the sources overall and/or in detail.)   4

SECTION 3 — EUROPEAN AND WORLD CONTEXTS — 20 marks   MARKS

Part B — "Tea and Freedom": the American Revolution, 1774–83

Attempt the following questions using recalled knowledge and information from the sources where appropriate.

Source A explains why there was growing tension between Britain and the colonists.

Source A

> The war with France had ended in 1763. Although victory was widely celebrated, there were already voices being raised against British rule in the thirteen colonies. The decision to increase taxes on the colonists was very unpopular. Britain had gone to great expense to protect the colonies and wanted the colonies to pay some of this money back. The decision to maintain a standing army in the colonies also alarmed the colonists. The Stamp Act of 1765 provoked a furious reaction. Colonists responded by organising a boycott of British goods.

1. How fully does Source A explain why there was growing tension between Britain and the colonists by 1774? (Use Source A and recall.)   6

2. Describe the events of the Boston Tea Party and the British government's reaction to it.   5

3. Explain the reasons why Britain lost the war against the colonists.   5

Sources B and C are about the events that led to the British defeat at Saratoga.

Source B

> In June 1777 General Burgoyne set out from Canada with nearly 8,000 men but his progress was then slowed by mountains and dense forest. The British fought off American forces in September. However, unlike the Americans, Burgoyne had no reinforcements. In October, Burgoyne tangled with the Americans once again. He was forced to retreat and his army was trapped against the Hudson River. On 17 October, Burgoyne was forced to surrender almost 6,000 men and 30 cannons.

Source C

> General Burgoyne was eager to win fame for himself. He planned to march south to Albany. Another British army was due to join up with Burgoyne's forces. However, they were stopped by heavy resistance and Burgoyne's army was left on its own. Burgoyne decided to carry on but his progress was slowed by the difficult terrain and lack of supplies. The British were trapped at the little community of Saratoga and had no option but to surrender.

4. Compare the views of Sources B and C about the British defeat at Saratoga. (Compare the sources overall and/or in detail.)   4

SECTION 3 — EUROPEAN AND WORLD CONTEXTS — 20 marks

MARKS

Part C — The USA, 1850–1880

Attempt the following questions using recalled knowledge and information from the sources where appropriate.

1. Describe slave life on Southern plantations before the outbreak of the civil war.   **5**

2. Explain why there was a growth in tension between the Northern and Southern States by 1860.   **5**

Source A describes the reasons why some settlers and prospectors headed west after 1850.

Source A

> After 1850 large numbers of settlers and prospectors were heading west. They were attracted by the promise of a better life. Some were fed up with the cold winters in the east and were attracted by the warmer weather in California. Many farmers went west because they thought the land would be more fertile. Ranch owners, such as Charles Goodnight, quickly realised that the plains could be used to feed their huge herds of cattle. However, it was hard going. One person in ten died before they reached their destination.

3. How fully does **Source A** describe the reasons why large numbers of settlers and prospectors were attracted west after 1850? (Use **Source A** and recall.)   **6**

Sources B and **C** are about the Sand Creek Massacre in 1864.

Source B

> Black Kettle and other chiefs of the Cheyennes were opposed to hostilities with the whites. Yet their village was still attacked by Colonel Chivington, who commanded 900 to 1,000 men. There were 500 people in the village, two-thirds of whom were women and children. I rode over the field after the slaughter was over, and counted from 60 to 70 dead bodies. A large majority of the dead were women and children.

Source C

> In the Cheyenne camp there were about 1,200 people in the village and about 700 were warriors. My reason for making the attack was that I believed they were hostile to the whites. I estimate that there were 500 or 600 people killed. I saw only one woman who had been killed and I saw no dead children. We found the scalps of 19 white people in the camp.

4. Compare the views of **Sources B** and **C** about the events which took place during the Sand Creek Massacre of 1864. (Compare the sources overall and/or in detail.)   **4**

SECTION 3 — EUROPEAN AND WORLD CONTEXTS — 20 marks

MARKS

Part D — Hitler and Nazi Germany, 1919–1939

Attempt the following questions using recalled knowledge and information from the sources where appropriate.

1. Describe the rights all Germans had in the Weimar Republic.

5

Sources **A** and **B** are about hyperinflation in Germany.

Source A

> Workers were paid twice a day and when they were given their wages, they threw bundles of banknotes out of factory windows to waiting members of their families who would then rush to the shops to buy food or coal or clothes before the prices went up. Millions of people faced starvation due to hyperinflation. People such as pensioners who were living on fixed incomes found that prices rose much faster than their earnings.

Source B

> Almost overnight the life savings of many Germans became worthless. Some workers were paid twice a day and could spend their wages instantly. People who were paid monthly or depended on savings suffered because these could not keep up with price rises. Pensioners lived on fixed incomes. They always received the same amount of money each week. These incomes were now worth nothing. They faced homelessness and starvation.

2. Compare the views of **Sources A** and **B** on the effects of hyperinflation on the people of Germany. (Compare the sources overall and/or in detail.)

4

3. Explain the reasons why Hitler and the Nazi Party attracted so much support by January 1933.

5

Source C is about Nazi control of people's lives.

Source C

> Hitler and the Nazi Party aimed to control every part of people's lives, and that included their free time. The KDF (Strength through Joy Organisation) controlled most forms of entertainment. Each year around seven million people took part in KDF sports matches. Mass outings to the theatre and the opera were arranged. The KDF had its own symphony orchestra which toured the country. Workers were also provided with affordable holidays including cruises and walking or skiing holidays.

4. How fully does **Source C** describe how the Nazis controlled people's lives? (Use **Source C** and recall.)

6

SECTION 3 — EUROPEAN AND WORLD CONTEXTS — 20 marks   MARKS

Part E — Red Flag: Lenin and the Russian Revolution, 1894–1921

Attempt the following questions using recalled knowledge and information from the sources where appropriate.

1. Describe the methods used by the Tsar to control Russia before 1905.   5

2. Explain the reasons why the Tsar's control of Russia was threatened in 1905.   5

Source A describes some of the effects of the First World War on Russia.

Source A

> The outbreak of the First World War in August 1914 was to have a terrible impact on Russians. Russia went to war to support its friends and allies. Russian armies were in action against Germany and Austria-Hungary within only six days. Heart-breaking losses were suffered by the Tsar's armies during the early years of the war. Thousands of wounded soldiers were left lying untreated on the ground for days. Nurses and doctors lacked enough bandages to treat even a quarter of the wounds.

3. How fully does Source A describe the effects of the First World War on Russia? (Use Source A and recall.)   6

Sources B and C describe the events in Petrograd during February 1917.

Source B

> The disturbances which have begun in Petrograd are becoming more serious. Shortages of bread and flour cause panic. The workers are without jobs, the unemployed take the path to riot and revolt. The capital is in a state of anarchy. The Government is paralysed. The transport system has broken down. The suppliers of fuel and food are completely disorganised. There is wild shooting on the streets and troops are firing at each other.

Source C

> The situation was already very serious. Some of the factories had to close down and there were several thousand workmen unemployed. They wanted bread, but after waiting for hours in the queues outside the bakers' shops, many had been unable to get any. On Thursday, March 8, there had been a stormy sitting in the Duma and it was the bread shortage that was the cause of the unrest.

4. Compare the views of Sources B and C on the events in Petrograd during February 1917. (Compare the sources overall and/or in detail.)   4

SECTION 3 — EUROPEAN AND WORLD CONTEXTS — 20 marks   MARKS

Part F — Mussolini and Fascist Italy, 1919–1939

Attempt the following questions using recalled knowledge and information from the sources where appropriate.

1. Describe Mussolini's foreign policy up to 1939.   5

2. Explain the reasons why many Italians were unhappy with Mussolini's economic policies.   5

Source A describes the use of propaganda in Fascist Italy.

Source A

> Mussolini had long experience in the newspaper business and so he knew a thing or two about how to make effective propaganda. Mussolini's press office issued official versions of events which all the newspapers were expected to publish without question. The radio and cinema were also used to broadcast Fascist propaganda. News bulletins broadcast a daily diet of Mussolini's speeches and praised him as the saviour of Italy. The media played a very crucial role in the cult of "Il Duce."

3. How fully does **Source A** describe the use of propaganda in Fascist Italy?   (Use **Source A** and recall.)   6

Sources **B** and **C** are about opposition to Mussolini.

Source B

> The Fascists used terror and violence, but for the most part this was not necessary. Unpopular groups like the Communists and Socialists were treated brutally. Fascist policies benefited the rich to ensure their support. The signing of the Lateran agreement in 1929 was important in winning the support of Catholics. There was some opposition in the army but this was never carried out in a coordinated way.

Source C

> While there was opposition to the Fascists, this never really posed a threat to the government. While some army generals opposed Mussolini, others liked his aggressive attitude. Mussolini changed his policy towards the Roman Catholic Church. This new close relationship with the church reduced the threat of opposition from Catholics. Big businessmen and landowners supported a regime which always seemed to be on their side.

4. Compare the views of **Sources B** and **C** on opposition to Mussolini.   (Compare the sources overall and/or in detail.)   4

SECTION 3 — EUROPEAN AND WORLD CONTEXTS — 20 marks   MARKS

Part G — Free at Last? Civil Rights in the USA, 1918–1968

Attempt the following questions using recalled knowledge and information from the sources where appropriate.

Sources A and **B** are about immigrants in American cities in the 1920s.

Source A

> The early twentieth century saw a massive growth in immigration from Southern and Eastern Europe. Immigrants from the same country usually lived in the same areas of the city. These areas contained tenement slums which were damp, dark and filthy with no water supply, toilets or drains. Immigrants had to take any work they could get, usually low paid jobs such as labourers or servants.

Source B

> Finding a well-paid, skilled job was a common problem for poorly educated immigrants. Immigrants tended to live in their own communities: in New York there was a Polish district, a Jewish district and an Italian district. Tenement buildings in these areas were often five or six storeys high with rooms which lacked light or sanitation. Many of the new immigrants found that life in America was not what they expected.

1. Compare the views of **Sources A** and **B** about the living and working conditions of immigrants in American cities.   **4**

2. Describe the non-violent protests of the Civil Rights Movement in the 1950s and 1960s.   **5**

Source C is about the actions taken by federal authorities to help black Americans.

Source C

> Federal authorities did take action. President Truman issued orders to desegregate the US military in 1948. He also set up a President's Committee on civil rights in 1946 to report to him on how progress towards black civil rights could be made. However no legislation followed. In 1960 Congress passed a Civil Rights Act which established penalties for obstructing black voting. The assassination of President Kennedy in November 1963 came at the time he was preparing a Civil Rights Bill.

3. How fully does **Source C** describe the actions taken by federal authorities to improve civil rights for black Americans between 1945 and 1964? (Use **Source C** and recall.)   **6**

4. Explain the reasons why the Black Panthers gained the support of many black Americans.   **5**

SECTION 3 — EUROPEAN AND WORLD CONTEXTS — 20 marks

MARKS

Part H — Appeasement and the Road to War, 1918–1939

Attempt the following questions using recalled knowledge and information from the sources where appropriate.

1. Describe the military terms of the Treaty of Versailles.

5

Source A is about the weaknesses of the League of Nations.

Source A

> The USA refused to join as they were not interested in getting involved in the problems of other countries. Initially Russia was not invited to join, so another great country of the world was absent. Therefore, right from the start the League of Nations was actually rather weak. Taking decisions was difficult as the Assembly had to be unanimous and member states often could not agree. A further problem was that the League did not have its own army to back up its decisions.

2. How fully does **Source A** explain the reasons why the League of Nations was weak? (Use **Source A** and recall.)

6

3. Explain the reasons why Britain did not take military action against Germany's reoccupation of the Rhineland.

5

Sources B and **C** are about the Anschluss.

Source B

> Germany and Austria are now one. It was a mistake of the peacemakers at Versailles to forbid the union of Austria and Germany. The population of Austria comprised ethnic Germans, the majority of whom are enthusiastic about the Anschluss. The Austrians will not only feel at home as part of Germany, they will benefit financially too from an increase in trade with their German brothers.

Source C

> That there has been no fighting is proof of the desire of the Austrian people to belong to Germany. Austrians will also benefit from greater markets for their raw materials and manufactured goods. The union of these two countries should never have been forbidden at Versailles. Winston Churchill has argued that Austria is a small country "brutally struck down". I do not see what there is to complain about.

4. Compare the views of **Sources B** and **C** about the Anschluss. (Compare the sources overall and/or in detail.)

4

SECTION 3 — EUROPEAN AND WORLD CONTEXTS — 20 marks

MARKS

Part I — World War II, 1939–1945

Attempt the following questions using recalled knowledge and information from the sources where appropriate.

Sources **A** and **B** are about the German strategy of Blitzkrieg.

Source A

> Blitzkrieg was a tactic based on speed and surprise. It required the effective use of light tank units supported by planes and infantry. The tactic was developed by army officer Hans Guderian. He had written a military pamphlet called "Achtung Panzer" which got into the hands of Hitler. It was used effectively in the first years of the Second World War and resulted in the British and French armies being pushed back in just a few weeks to the beaches of Dunkirk.

Source B

> Hitler had spent four years in World War One fighting a static war with neither side moving far for months on end. He was enthralled by Guderian's plan that was based purely on speed and movement. When Guderian told Hitler that he could reach the French coast in weeks if an attack on France was ordered, fellow officers openly laughed at him. Once a strategic target had been selected, Stuka dive bombers were sent in to "soften" up the enemy, then the tanks approached, supported by infantry.

1. Compare the views of **Sources A** and **B** on the German strategy of Blitzkrieg. (Compare the sources overall and/or in detail.)   **4**

2. Describe what life was like for the ordinary citizens of Nazi occupied Europe.   **5**

Source C is about the activities of the French Resistance.

Source C

> The French Resistance movement developed in 1940. It helped Jews, and Allied airmen who had crash landed in France, to escape. Many resistance workers paid for their courage with their lives. Even school children were recruited to help smuggle people across the borders of northern and southern France. As well as this, the Resistance movement was crucial to undermining Nazi rule by producing publications of news and information. Nazi rule was further challenged by the Resistance who worked together to discover French collaboration.

3. How fully does **Source C** describe the activities of the French Resistance?   (Use **Source C** and recall.)   **6**

4. Explain the reasons why the Russian army was able to take over Berlin in 1945.   **5**

SECTION 3 — EUROPEAN AND WORLD CONTEXTS — 20 marks

MARKS

Part J — The Cold War, 1945–1989

Attempt the following questions using recalled knowledge and information from the sources where appropriate.

1. Explain the reasons why a Cold War developed after 1945.   5

Source A is about American intervention in Vietnam.

Source A

> The Americans intervened in Vietnam for several reasons. In a speech in March 1947 President Truman explained that America would resist the spread of Communism. This became known as the Truman Doctrine. In the 1950s the Americans had responded to French requests for assistance in Vietnam by giving money to try to halt the Vietminh. By the early 1960s it was clear that South Vietnam could not resist Communism without the support of American troops. Many in America believed war was necessary to stop the spread of Soviet influence.

2. How fully does **Source A** explain the reasons why Americans intervened in Vietnam? (Use **Source A** and recall.)   6

Sources B and **C** are about the crisis in Berlin in 1961.

> There is peace in Berlin today. The source of world trouble and tension is Moscow, not Berlin. And if war begins, it will have begun in Moscow and not Berlin. For the choice of war or peace is largely theirs, not ours. It is the Soviets who have stirred up this crisis. It is they who are trying to force a change. They have rejected an all-German peace treaty and the rule of international law.

Source C

> We can now look back on the Berlin crisis and say with confidence that this crisis was caused by Moscow. It was the brutal Soviet-backed regime in East Germany which caused so many people to leave. The Soviet domination of East Germany was a clear breach of international law. The Soviets rejected an American proposal for a peace treaty which would have dealt with all of the issues in Germany.

3. Compare the views of **Sources B** and **C** on the crisis in Berlin in 1961. (Compare the sources overall and/or in detail.)   4

4. Describe the impact of the Cuban Missile Crisis on international relations.   5

[END OF QUESTION PAPER]

SQA AND HODDER GIBSON NATIONAL 5 HISTORY 2014

General Marking Principles for National 5 History

There are six types of question used in this question paper. Each assesses a particular skill, namely:

A. Describe . . .
B. Explain the reasons why . . .
C. To what extent . . .
D. Evaluate the usefulness of Source . . .
E. Compare the views of Sources . . .
F. How fully does Source . . .

A. Questions that ask candidates to *Describe* . . . (5 or 6 marks)

Candidates must make a number of relevant, factual points. These should be key points. The points do not need to be in any particular order. Candidates may provide a number of straightforward points or a smaller number of developed points, or a combination of these.

Up to the total mark allocation for this question of 5 or 6 marks:

- **1 mark** should be given for each accurate relevant point
- **a second mark** should be given for any reason that is developed, as in the following example

Question: Describe the Liberal Welfare Reforms introduced between 1906 and 1914.

The Liberals brought in a number of welfare reforms that were aimed at helping the poorest people in society **(1 mark for knowledge)**. *They were particularly trying to help children and the elderly* **(a second mark for development)**.

B. Questions that ask candidates to *Explain the reasons why* . . . (5 or 6 marks)

Candidates must make a number of points that make the issue plain or clear, for example by showing connections between factors or causal relationships between events or ideas. These should be key reasons and may include theoretical ideas. There is no need for any evaluation or prioritising of these reasons. Candidates may provide a number of straightforward reasons or a smaller number of developed reasons, or a combination of these.

Up to the total mark allocation for this question of 5 or 6 marks:

- **1 mark** should be given for each accurate relevant point
- **a second mark** should be given for any reason that is developed, as in the following example

Question: Explain the reasons why the Liberals introduced their social welfare reforms between 1906 and 1914.

The Liberals introduced a variety of reforms in order to help the poorest in society as it had been shown that this group was suffering particular hardships. **(1 mark for a reason)** *Booth had identified that over 35% of Londoners were living in poverty* **(a second mark for development)**.

C. Questions that ask *To what extent* . . . (8 marks)

Candidates must make a judgement about the extent to which different factors contributed to an event or development, or to its impact. They are required to provide a balanced account of the influence of different factors and come to a reasoned conclusion based on the evidence presented.

Up to **5 marks** should be given for relevant, factual, key points of knowledge used to support factors: with **1 mark** given for each point. **If only one factor is presented, a maximum of 3 marks should be given for relevant points of knowledge.**

Up to **3 further marks** should be given for presenting the answer in a structured way and coming to a reasoned conclusion, as follows:

- **1 mark** for the answer being presented in a structured way, with knowledge being organised in support of different factors
- **1 mark** for a valid judgement or overall conclusion
- **1 mark** for a reason being provided in support of the conclusion

Example:

Some historians think the Liberals passed their welfare reforms to help the poorest people. The National Insurance Acts helped keep workers out of poverty. **(1 mark for knowledge)** *The introduction of old age pensions meant that families didn't have the burden of supporting the elderly.* **(1 mark for knowledge)**

However, other historians think they were more concerned with fighting off the Labour Party. **(1 mark for structure)** *Cutting the working day for miners was simply a way of buying their support.* **(1 mark for knowledge)** *The National Insurance Acts were targeted at working men who might be likely to support the Labour Party if they felt the Liberals didn't listen.* **(1 mark for knowledge)**

Others believe it was about national efficiency. Churchill and Lloyd George argued that Britain needed its people to be fitter to be able to compete. **(1 mark for knowledge)** *They were shocked by the state of the men who volunteered during the Boer War and wanted to solve this problem.* **(1 mark for knowledge)**

Overall, the Liberals were more concerned about helping the poor. **(1 mark for a conclusion)** *Most of their reforms were directed at helping the poor and it is clear from their speeches that this was what motivated them most.* **(1 mark for supporting a conclusion)**

D. Questions that ask candidates to *Evaluate the usefulness of a given source as evidence of* . . . (5 or 6 marks)

Candidates must evaluate the extent to which a source is useful by commenting on evidence such as the author, type of source, purpose, timing, content and omission.

Up to the total mark allocation for this question of 5 or 6 marks:

- a maximum of **4 marks** can be given for evaluative comments relating to author, type of source, purpose and timing

- a maximum of **2 marks** may be given for evaluative comments relating to the content of the source
- a maximum of **2 marks** may be given for evaluative comments relating to points of significant omission

Example:

Source A is useful as it was written in 1910 which was at the time when the Liberals were introducing their main reforms. **(1 mark)** *It was written by the Prime Minister so it may be less useful as he has a personal interest in making the reforms sound successful.* **(1 mark)** *It says "these reforms will make the lives of the poor infinitely better" which shows evidence of bias and makes it less useful.* **(1 mark)** *On the other hand it also says that the National Insurance Act would benefit working men by giving them unemployment benefits which is accurate so makes the source more useful.* **(1 mark)** *But it is less useful as it fails to mention that women would not really be covered by this Act.* **(1 mark)**

E. **Questions that ask candidates to *Compare the views of two given sources about* . . . (4 marks)**

Candidates must interpret evidence and make direct comparisons between sources. Candidates are expected to compare content directly on a point-by-point basis.

Up to the total mark allocation for this question of 4 marks:

A simple comparison will indicate what points they agree or disagree about and should be given **1 mark**. A developed comparison will be supported by specific references to each source and should be given **2 marks**.

Example:

Sources A and B agree that King Charles I was an ineffective ruler. **(1 mark for a simple comparison)**

The sources disagree about how far Charles I created his own problems. **(1 mark for a simple comparison)**

Source A agrees with Source B where it says "the king failed to maintain control of parliament" and Source B says "King Charles provoked his own people to rebel". **(a second mark for a developed comparison)**

The sources disagree about how much Charles I's problems were his own making, where Source A thinks Charles was a disaster as king, while Source B feels he was generally not bad but made some important mistakes. **(2 marks for a developed comparison)**

F. **Questions that ask *How fully does a given source explain/describe* . . . (5 or 6 marks)**

Candidates must make a judgement about the extent to which the source provides a full description/explanation of a given event or development.

Up to the total mark allocation for this question of 5 or 6 marks:

- candidates should be given up to **3 marks** for their identification of points from the source that support their judgement; each point from the source needs to be interpreted rather than simply copied from the source
- candidates should be given up to **4 marks** for their identification of points of significant omission, based on their own knowledge, that support their judgement
- a maximum of **2 marks** may be given for answers in which no judgement has been made

Example:

Source B explains the reasons why the Liberals introduced their reforms fairly well as it mentions their growing fear of the Labour party. **(1 mark)** *It mentions specifically the Welsh MPs such as Lloyd George who might lose their seats.* **(1 mark)** *It also deals with the raising of working class expectations which the new Labour Party might bring.* **(1 mark)** *However, it fails to mention their genuine concern for the masses which motivated many MPs.* **(1 mark)** *The poor state of health among volunteers for the Boer War had shocked many of them into demanding changes.* **(1 mark)** *Others, such as Churchill, felt that poverty was holding back Britain's competitiveness as a nation and must be changed.* **(1 mark)**

Section 1, Part A

1. *Candidates can be credited in a number of ways **up to a maximum of 5 marks**.*

Candidates must make a judgement about the usefulness of the source and support this by making evaluative comments on identified aspects of the source.

1 mark should be given for each relevant comment made, up to a **maximum of 5 marks in total**:

- a maximum of **4 marks** can be given for evaluative comments relating to the author, type of source, purpose and timing
- a maximum of **2 marks** may be given for comments relating to the content of the source
- a maximum of **2 marks** may be given for comments relating to points of significant omission

Examples of aspects of the source and relevant comments:

Aspect of the source	Possible comment
Author: Bishop Fraser of St Andrews	Author was the leading churchman and one of the Guardians who was well informed, so source may be more useful
Type of source: A letter	A personal communication so may be less guarded, so source may be more useful
Purpose: To seek Edward's help in keeping the peace	Purpose may have caused the writer to exaggerate the problem, so source may be less useful
Timing: October 1290	Written at the time there was fear that the Guardianship might fall apart so content may reflect these worries, so source may be less useful

Content	Possible comment
• Rumour that the Maid of Norway has died	Less useful as it is only passing on rumours
• But that she is very weak	Less useful as it contradicts itself
• Agreed to stay at Perth until we hear definite news	More useful as it indicates calmness in the crisis

Possible points of significant omission may include:

- Guardians in charge
- Factionalism among nobility
- Fears of civil war
- They looked to Edward as a respected older male relative of the royal family
- Edward had sufficient power to enforce any decision on the succession

2. *Candidates can be credited in a number of ways up to a maximum of 5 marks. They may take different perspectives on the events and may describe a variety of different aspects of the events.*

1 mark should be given for each accurate relevant key point of knowledge. A **second mark** should be given for each point that is developed, up to a maximum of **5 marks**. Candidates may achieve full marks by providing five straightforward points, by making three developed points, or a combination of these.

Possible points of knowledge may include:

- Murdered Sheriff of Lanark which made him an outlaw and forced him into open rebellion
- Attack on Ormsby showed early intentions to undermine the English administration
- His use of guerilla tactics was very successful
- He gathered a small force as his fame began to spread
- Worked with Andrew Moray to win the Battle of Stirling Bridge
- He served as Guardian and tried to establish trade with the Low Countries
- When he was defeated at the Battle of Falkirk he resigned the Guardianship
- His mission to Europe had little success
- His role ended when he was betrayed by his own people

3. *Candidates can be credited in a number of ways up to a maximum of 5 marks.*

Candidates must show a causal relationship between events.

Possible reasons may include:

- The Bruces were an important noble family and could use their status
- They had a lot of allies in Scotland and so could gather plenty of support
- Murder of Comyn removed opposition leadership and weakened any Scottish opposition
- Death of Edward I removed threat of English opposition
- Support of the Church from Wishart and Lamberton provided Bruce with legitimacy
- Bruce was able to use his base in Carrick as a starting point to defeat his Scottish enemies one by one
- Bruce was able to split Ross from Comyn, enabling him to tackle one at a time
- Bruce destroyed castles rather than allow a base for his enemies
- Edward II gave little help to his nobles in Scotland

4. *Candidates can be credited in a number of ways up to a maximum of 5 marks.*

Candidates must make an overall judgement about how fully the source explains the events. **1 mark** may be given for each valid point interpreted from the source or each valid point of significant omission provided. The candidate can achieve **up to 3 marks** for their interpretation of the parts of the source they consider are relevant in terms of the proposed question where there is also at least one point of significant omission identified to imply a judgement has been made about the limitations of the source. For full marks to be given each point needs to be discretely mentioned in terms of the question.

A maximum of 2 marks may be given for answers which refer only to the source.

Possible points which may be identified in the source include:

- English army had no room to move because they were surrounded by marshes and streams
- Bruce decided to take advantage of this mistake and to attack them
- The English were so jammed together and so tangled up that their leaders struggled to organise any defence
- They lost all confidence in Edward II

Possible points of significant omission may include:

- Bruce organised Scots into schiltrons which was an effective defensive formation
- Bruce chose the higher ground which gave a physical advantage
- Bruce prepared the ground behind him to protect from a rear attack
- Bruce trained his schiltrons to move which allowed them to respond to attacks
- Death of de Bohun demoralised the English
- The English had been arguing among themselves
- The English were camped on boggy ground which restricted their movement
- The English cavalry could not charge due to the congestion
- The English bowmen were defeated by the Scots
- Many English were trapped by the ditches by the Pelstream and Bannock burns

Section 1, Part B

1. *Candidates can be credited in a number of ways up to a maximum of 5 marks.*

Candidates must make an overall judgement about how fully the source explains the events. **1 mark** may be given for each valid point interpreted from the source or each valid point of significant omission provided. The candidate can achieve **up to 3 marks** for their interpretation of the parts of the source they consider are relevant in terms of the proposed question where there is also at least one point of significant omission identified to imply a judgement has been made about the limitations of the source. For full marks to be given, each point needs to be discretely mentioned in terms of the question.

A maximum of 2 marks may be given for answers which refer only to the source.

Possible points which may be identified in the source include:

- Guise took strong action against Protestants in Scotland
- Made more use of French officials
- Used more French soldiers to control key strongholds in Scotland
- She demanded a new tax

Possible points of significant omission may include:

- Mary Queen of Scots being Queen of France worried the Protestant Scottish nobles
- The marriage treaty said that Scotland was to become part of France
- The Protestants wanted to defend their religion against Mary of Guise
- The Protestants were encouraged by Queen Elizabeth
- The Protestants were encouraged by John Knox

2. *Candidates can be credited in a number of ways up to a maximum of 5 marks.*

Candidates must make a judgement about the usefulness of the source and support this by making evaluative comments on identified aspects of the source.

1 mark should be given for each relevant comment made, up to a **maximum of 5 marks in total:**

- a maximum of **4 marks** can be given for evaluative comments relating to the author, type of source, purpose and timing
- a maximum of **2 marks** may be given for comments relating to the content of the source
- a maximum of **2 marks** may be given for comments relating to points of significant omission

Examples of aspects of the source and relevant comments:

Aspect of the source	Possible comment
Author: Bishop Fraser of St Andrews	A young queen newly returned to Scotland
Type of source: A letter	Official government document
Purpose:	To calm the churchmen by ensuring payment to ministers of the Church of Scotland
Timing: 1566	At a time when the Reformation was very recent and suspicions persisted over her Catholicism

Content	Possible comment
• I determined that they should be paid in the future	Useful as it shows Mary's positive support of the church
• With the advice of my government officials	Less useful as it may imply pressure has been brought on Mary from her officials
• Decided to allocate the sum of £10,000 for their payment	More useful as it indicates the extent of her support of the church

Possible points of significant omission may include:

- Mary remained a Roman Catholic
- Mary wanted support from the church at a difficult time

3. *Candidates can be credited in a number of ways up to a maximum of 5 marks. They may take different perspectives on the events and may describe a variety of different aspects of the events.*

1 mark should be given for each accurate relevant key point of knowledge. **A second mark** should be given for each point that is developed, up to a maximum of **5 marks**. Candidates may achieve full marks by providing five straightforward points, by making three developed points, or a combination of these.

Possible points of knowledge may include:

- Estrangement of Mary and Darnley
- Distrust of Mary for the Scottish lords
- Mary turned to Bothwell
- Conspirators begged Mary for forgiveness
- Darnley not trusted by either Mary or the conspirators
- Darnley moved to Glasgow

4. *Candidates can be credited in a number of ways up to a maximum of 5 marks.*

Candidates must show a causal relationship between events.

Up to a **maximum of 5 marks in total**, 1 mark should be given for each accurate, relevant reason, and a **second mark** should be given for reasons that are developed. Candidates may achieve full marks by providing five straightforward reasons, three developed reasons, or a combination of these.

Possible reasons may include:

- 1580: the Pope's policy of encouraging plots against Elizabeth made English Protestants think Mary was a menace, especially since her son and heir was a Protestant
- 1585: after several plots, the English government passed a law stating that Mary would be executed if she was actively involved in any plot against Elizabeth
- 1585: Mary was moved to Chartley where English spies discovered how letters were smuggled
- 1586: Babington contacted Mary to inform her of his plans to kill Elizabeth and help Mary to escape
- Elizabeth hesitated to execute her cousin, the death warrant was concealed amongst a pile of letters and Elizabeth signed them all

Section 1, Part C

1. *Candidates can be credited in a number of ways up to a maximum of 5 marks.*

Candidates must show a causal relationship between events.

Up to a **maximum of 5 marks in total**, **1 mark** should be given for each accurate, relevant reason, and a **second mark** should be given for reasons that are developed. Candidates may achieve full marks by providing five straightforward reasons, three developed reasons, or a combination of these.

Possible reasons may include:

- Scots were excluded from trading with England's colonies
- The wars between England and France had reduced Scottish trade with France
- Scotland never gained from peace treaties at the end of these wars
- Failure of the Darien Scheme left Scotland near to bankruptcy; many blamed England for the failure of the scheme
- Queen Anne found it difficult to govern Scotland from Westminster; Scots accused Queen Anne of policies which were damaging to Scotland
- The Worcester Affair turned ordinary Scots against what they regarded as English pirates
- England feared a French threat in the future if the discontented Scots ever wanted to revive the Auld Alliance

2. *Candidates can be credited in a number of ways up to a maximum of 5 marks.*

Candidates must make a judgement about the usefulness of the source and support this by making evaluative comments on identified aspects of the source.

1 mark should be given for each relevant comment made, up to a **maximum of 5 marks in total**:

- a maximum of **4 marks** can be given for evaluative comments relating to the author, type of source, purpose and timing
- a maximum of **2 marks** may be given for comments relating to the content of the source
- a maximum of **2 marks** may be given for comments relating to points of significant omission

Examples of aspects of the source and relevant comments:

Aspect of the source	Possible comment
Author: A member of the Scottish government	Involved in the negotiations
Type of source: A letter	A personal communication so may be less guarded, so source may be more useful
Purpose: To encourage secrecy and avoid embarrassment	Purpose may have caused the writer to exaggerate the problem, so source may be less useful
Timing: 1707	At the time when there was a firm treaty negotiated

Content	Possible comment
• Impossible to state exactly how much was given	Less useful as it is vague on the details
• This has been kept a secret	More useful as it is honest about its refusal to divulge information
• Revealing this information at present would cause embarrassment	More useful as it explains the reasons for not divulging information

Possible points of significant omission may include:

- Other forms of bribery were used eg titles, jobs
- People kept changing sides
- Scottish Parliament was not well organised (eg Squadrone Volante)
- Opinion was sharply divided
- Many people recognised opportunities which the Treaty might provide

3. *Candidates can be credited in a number of ways up to a maximum of 5 marks.*

Candidates must make an overall judgement about how fully the source explains the events. **1 mark** may be given for each valid point interpreted from the source, or each valid point of significant omission provided. The candidate can achieve **up to 3 marks** for their interpretation of the parts of the source they consider are relevant in terms of the proposed question where there is also at least one point of significant omission identified to imply a judgement has been made about the limitations of the source. For full marks to be given, each point needs to be discretely mentioned in terms of the question.

A maximum of 2 marks may be given for answers which refer only to the source.

Possible points which may be identified in the source include:

- There was clear opposition among the towns in Scotland
- Fear that Scotland would lose business
- They would lose the ability to make their own decisions
- They would be throwing away all that their ancestors had fought to protect

Possible points of significant omission may include:

- The government threatened Scottish trade if the Union was not passed
- The government offered titles to people who supported the Union
- The government offered jobs to people who supported the Union
- They made their officials support the Union or they would not be paid
- They had soldiers in northern England and Ulster ready to go to Scotland
- The Equivalent made money available to Scotland.

4. *Candidates can be credited in a number of ways **up to a maximum of 5 marks**. They may take different perspectives on the events and may describe a variety of different aspects of the events.*

1 mark should be given for each accurate relevant key point of knowledge. A **second mark** should be given for each point that is developed, up to a maximum of **5 marks**. Candidates may achieve full marks by providing five straightforward points, by making three developed points, or a combination of these.

Possible points of knowledge may include:

- The Pound Sterling replaced the Pound Scots and coins changed
- English weights and measures replaced Scottish ones
- A Union flag replaced the Scottish flag
- New taxes applied in Scotland (Malt Tax)
- Customs and Excise men appeared in Scotland
- Scottish Parliament and Scottish nobles moved to London
- Scots Law was affected by appeals to the House of Lords
- The Patronage Act (1712) affected the Kirk
- Scots were beginning to trade freely with English colonies
- Money and jobs were going to England/Scottish manufacturers were ruined

Section 1, Part D

1. *Candidates can be credited in a number of ways **up to a maximum of 5 marks**.*

Candidates must make an overall judgement about how fully the source explains the events. **1 mark** may be given for each valid point interpreted from the source or each valid point of significant omission provided. The candidate can achieve **up to 3 marks** for their interpretation of the parts of the source they consider are relevant in terms of the proposed question where there is also at least one point of significant omission identified to imply a judgement has been made about the limitations of the source. For full marks to be given, each point needs to be discretely mentioned in terms of the question.

A maximum of 2 marks may be given for answers which refer only to the source.

Possible points which may be identified in the source include:

- The Irish potato famine of the mid-1840s led to a sharp increase in this immigration
- Some landlords evicted those who could not pay their rent
- Transport costs were cheap
- Wages in the west of Scotland continued to be higher than those in Ireland

Possible points of significant omission may include:

- They already had family in Scotland
- Scotland was close to Ireland so a short voyage
- Cotton mills
- Building railways
- Seasonal labour

- Better housing conditions than Ireland
- Jews and Italians escaping poverty or persecution

2. *Candidates can be credited in a number of ways **up to a maximum of 5 marks**. They may take different perspectives on the events and may describe a variety of different aspects of the events.*

1 mark should be given for each accurate relevant key point of knowledge. A **second mark** should be given for each point that is developed, up to a maximum of **5 marks**. Candidates may achieve full marks by providing five straightforward points, by making three developed points or a combination of these.

Possible points of knowledge may include:

- It brought new ideas and religions
- It was reflected in architecture
- Large numbers of poorer Jews arrived between 1880 and 1914. By 1919 over 9,000 lived in Glasgow alone. Most lived in the Gorbals and maintained separate identity, eg spoke Yiddish, the Jewish language
- Jewish immigrants tended to work in particular jobs such as peddling and hawking (selling door to door)
- Sweated labour was associated with immigrants and Jews in particular: tailoring and cigarette-making
- It encouraged immigration from other communities such as Italians and Lithuanians
- It provided raw materials for factories, such as cotton
- It provided jobs for Scots abroad and encouraged innovation
- Role of Empire as a market for Scottish goods and emigrants
- Empire helped the export-orientated Scottish economy to develop, at least up until 1914, especially in production of shipping, locomotives, etc
- Empire as a source of competition to Scottish economy: farm produce from Australia, Jute mill development in India, etc

3. *Candidates can be credited in a number of ways **up to a maximum of 5 marks**.*

Candidates must make a judgement about the usefulness of the source and support this by making evaluative comments on identified aspects of the source.

One mark should be given for each relevant comment made, up to a maximum of **5 marks in total**:

- a maximum of **4 marks** can be given for evaluative comments relating to the author, type of source, purpose and timing
- a maximum of **2 marks** may be given for comments relating to the content of the source
- a maximum of **2 marks** may be given for comments relating to points of significant omission

Examples of aspects of the source and relevant comments:

Aspect of the source	Possible comment
Author: Newspaper reporter	Eyewitness to these events who was well informed, so source may be more useful
Type of source: Newspaper	To inform the public but are often biased
Purpose: To explain the attraction of Australia to many farmers	Purpose may have caused the writer to exaggerate the problem, so source may be less useful
Timing: 30 May 1838	When people were just beginning to move away from the Highlands

Content	Possible comment
• Agents promised riches in Australia • They can't make farming pay in Scotland	Useful as it provides a balanced view of why some Scots left for Australia
• Highlanders crowded to see them	Less useful as it may be exaggerated
• They were desperate to possess the limitless quantity of land in Australia	More useful as it is accurate about the many Scots who moved to Australia from the Highlands

Possible points of significant omission may include:

- Money and letters sent home encouraged people to go
- Canada had great opportunities for farming
- Agents persuaded people by enthusiasm and pictures
- Poverty in Scotland encouraged emigration
- Some countries paid fares
- Advertisements persuaded people of benefits
- Landowners encouraged tenants to emigrate to gain greater profit from sheep
- The failure of the potato crop
- Kelp-making was no longer profitable

4. *Candidates can be credited in a number of ways up to a maximum of 5 marks.*

Candidates must show a causal relationship between events.

Up to a **maximum of 5 marks in total**, **1 mark** should be given for each accurate, relevant reason, and a **second mark** should be given for reasons that are developed. Candidates may achieve full marks by providing five straightforward reasons, three developed reasons, or a combination of these.

Possible reasons may include:

- Scots brought farming skills to Canada
- Scots developed sheep farming in Australia
- Tradesmen such as stonemasons helped the building industry in the USA
- They developed businesses, banks and trading companies
- Examples of contributions to economy and other aspects such as Andrew Carnegie (steel); Donald Mackay (Boston shipyards); Alan Pinkerton (detective agency); John Muir (national parks); examples such as paper-making in New Zealand; Hudson Bay Company

- Scots established education system, eg Canada
- Scots brought a tradition of hard work
- Scots were successful in the government of India
- They formed tight-knit communities to support each other

Section 1, Part E

1. *Candidates can be credited in a number of ways up to a maximum of 5 marks. They may take different perspectives on the events and may describe a variety of different aspects of the events.*

1 mark should be given for each accurate relevant key point of knowledge. A **second mark** should be given for each point that is developed, up to a maximum of **5 marks**. Candidates may achieve full marks by providing five straightforward points, by making three developed points or a combination of these.

Possible points of knowledge may include:

- Chlorine gas temporarily incapacitated the enemy
- Mustard gas and phosgene gas were more potent
- However, gas masks made it less effective
- Tanks spread fear among the enemy and provided cover for advancing soldiers
- However, they broke down and had limited strategic value
- Machine guns could kill large numbers
- But they often jammed
- Aircraft could spot enemy troop positions

2. *Candidates can be credited in a number of ways up to a maximum of 5 marks.*

Candidates must make a judgement about the usefulness of the source and support this by making evaluative comments on identified aspects of the source.

1 mark should be given for each relevant comment made, **up to a maximum of 5 marks in total**:

- a maximum of **4 marks** can be given for evaluative comments relating to the author, type of source, purpose and timing
- a maximum of **2 marks** may be given for comments relating to the content of the source
- a maximum of **2 marks** may be given for comments relating to points of significant omission

Examples of aspects of the source and relevant comments:

Aspect of the source	Possible comment
Author: Lieutenant George Craik	Eyewitness to the events but was an officer so has a particular perspective
Type of source: Memoirs	Personal recollections, but well after the events
Purpose: To explain the extent of the problems faced by officers at Loos	Purpose may have caused the writer to exaggerate the problem, so source may be less useful
Timing: 1915	At a point when the war had reached stalemate

Content	Possible comment
• The trenches were in not too bad a state	Useful as it is not exaggerated
• One problem for commanders was organising supplies and suitable living conditions	Useful as it describes a typical situation for officers
• To venture out into no man's land in daylight was instant death	Less useful as it shows a degree of exaggeration

Possible points of significant omission may include:

- Wet and muddy
- Trench foot and other diseases
- Use of tinned food
- Chlorine tablets to purify their water
- Snipers
- Shell shock

3. *Candidates can be credited in a number of ways up to a maximum of 5 marks.*

Candidates must make an overall judgement about how fully the source explains the events. **1 mark** may be given for each valid point interpreted from the source or each valid point of significant omission provided. The candidate can achieve **up to 3 marks** for their interpretation of the parts of the source they consider are relevant in terms of the proposed question where there is also at least one point of significant omission identified to imply a judgement has been made about the limitations of the source. For full marks to be given, each point needs to be discretely mentioned in terms of the question.

A maximum of 2 marks may be given for answers which refer only to the source.

Possible points which may be identified in the source include:

- Government needed to control the factories
- Clyde Workers' Committee was formed to campaign against the Munitions Act
- Engineers were forbidden from leaving the works where they were employed
- The editors were sent to prison for criticising the war

Possible points of significant omission may include:

- Unrest on Red Clydeside between 1915 and 1919 by skilled engineers who went on strike for more pay: "tuppence an hour"
- Anger over importation of English and American workers, paid more than Scots workers
- Clyde Workers Committee set up to protect munitions workers from compulsory long hours at low rates of pay under Munitions Act
- Strike at Beardmore's Steel Works over "dilution" by unskilled labour
- Clyde Workers' Committee organised strike demanding 40-hour week
- Industries changed over to war production

- Women used to replace men in semi-skilled work
- It provided a temporary reprieve for some industries which were in decline
- It interrupted supplies of raw materials

4. *Candidates can be credited in a number of ways up to a maximum of 5 marks.*

Candidates must show a causal relationship between events.

Up to a **maximum of 5 marks in total**, **1 mark** should be given for each accurate, relevant reason, and a **second mark** should be given for reasons that are developed. Candidates may achieve full marks by providing five straightforward reasons, three developed reasons, or a combination of these.

Possible reasons may include:

- Suffragist campaigns had gradually gained momentum before the War
- They gained support from across the social spectrum and included men as well as women
- They had gained voting rights in local elections
- There was a gradual widening of the franchise and a sense that it was only a matter of time
- Suffragette campaigns kept the issue in the public eye
- However, they alienated as many people as they attracted
- Their cessation during the war was welcomed
- Women's work during the war was recognised as significant
- Changes in work led to economic and social changes for women

Section 2, Part A

1. *Candidates can be credited in a number of ways up to a maximum of 6 marks.*

Candidates must make a judgement about the usefulness of the source and support this by making evaluative comments on identified aspects of the source.

1 mark should be given for each relevant comment made, up to a **maximum of 6 marks in total**:

- a maximum of **4 marks** can be given for evaluative comments relating to the author, type of source, purpose and timing
- a maximum of **2 marks** may be given for comments relating to the content of the source
- a maximum of **2 marks** may be given for comments relating to points of significant omission

Examples of aspects of the source and relevant comments:

Aspect of the source	Possible comment
Author: French	Useful as it comes from the home of chivalry
Type of source: Poetry	Less useful as it represents a romantic view rather than factual
Purpose: To encourage knights to remain true to the ideals of chivalry	Purpose may have caused the writer to exaggerate the problem in order to shock them into behaving, so source may be less useful
Timing: 12th century	Useful as it was written at the height of the age of chivalry

Content	Possible comment
• Many knights are failing to live by the Code of Chivalry	Less useful as it is vague on the extent of the problem
• They steal money from churches and rob pilgrims of their possessions	Less useful as it exaggerates the problem
• Spent years training to be the perfect soldier	More useful as it is accurate about what it took to become a knight

Possible points of significant omission may include:

- Showed mercy to their enemies
- Treated women with respect
- Fulfilled Christian duty
- Went on Crusade to the Holy Lands
- Protected the vulnerable
- Served their feudal overlords
- Served as mercenaries
- Made their way in the world through tournaments
- Served as sheriffs and crown officials

2. *Candidates can be credited in a number of ways up to a maximum of 8 marks.*

Candidates must use knowledge to present a balanced assessment of the influence of different possible factors and come to a reasoned conclusion. **Up to 5 marks** are allocated for relevant points of knowledge used to address the question. **1 mark** should be given for each relevant, factual key point of knowledge used to support a factor. **If only one factor is presented, a maximum of 3 marks should be given for relevant points of knowledge.**

Possible factors may include:	Relevant, factual, key points of knowledge to support this factor may include:
Barons had become too powerful during the civil war	• Castles had been built without permission • Barons had increased their power/king's authority had been reduced • Barons had private armies/hired mercenaries • Barons were stealing land from their weaker neighbours and increasing their power
Corruption in the legal system	• Sheriffs decided the laws in their own areas • Sheriffs were corrupt/could not be trusted • Barons were keeping the fines collected from criminals, instead of giving them to the king
Henry ruled too much to be able to control it all effectively	• Henry ruled from the Pyrenees to the Scottish border
Any other valid factor	

Up to 3 marks should be given for presenting the answer in a structured way, leading to a conclusion which addresses the question, as follows:

1 mark for the answer being presented in a structured way, with knowledge being organised in support of different factors

1 mark given for a valid judgement or overall conclusion

1 mark given for a reason being provided in support of the conclusion

3. *Candidates can be credited in a number of ways up to a maximum of 6 marks.*

Candidates must show a causal relationship between events.

Up to a **maximum of 6 marks in total**, **1 mark** should be given for each accurate, relevant reason, and a **second mark** should be given for reasons that are developed. Candidates may achieve full marks by providing five straightforward reasons, three developed reasons, or a combination of these.

Possible reasons may include:

- Sponsorship of kings such as David I encouraged new orders to set up in Scotland
- New orders were highly regarded and so found a steady flow of novices
- The Church became the most important landholder and could use its wealth to expand
- The Church was economically important and could use its economic position to expand
- It had cultural and trading links with Europe and attracted people from all over Europe
- It helped the poor and this encouraged new novices
- It provided religious services which raised its status in society

Section 2, Part B

1. *Candidates can be credited in a number of ways **up to a maximum of 6 marks**.*

Candidates must make a judgement about the usefulness of the source and support this by making evaluative comments on identified aspects of the source.

1 mark should be given for each relevant comment made, up to a **maximum of 6 marks in total**:

- a maximum of **4 marks** can be given for evaluative comments relating to the author, type of source, purpose and timing
- a maximum of **2 marks** may be given for comments relating to the content of the source
- a maximum of **2 marks** may be given for comments relating to points of significant omission.

Examples of aspects of the source and relevant comments:

Aspect of the source	Possible comment
Author: Parliamentarians	Less useful as it shows only one side of the argument
Type of source: Petition	Useful as it is carefully written to explain their complaints but less useful as it states an extreme case
Purpose: To force the king to accept their rights	Less useful as it will clearly be biased towards their views
Timing: 1628	At a time when Charles I was looking to raise taxes for wars in France

Content	Possible comment
• No man should be forced to make any gift, loan, donation, tax or similar charge to the Crown without consent of Parliament	Less useful as it is really only trying to claim Parliament's rights rather than protect people
• No free man should be detained in prison without due cause shown	Less useful as this is not something which affected many people
• Soldiers and sailors should not be housed upon private citizens without their agreement	More useful as it indicates a specific complaint which we know to have been the case

Possible points of significant omission may include:

- Charles I had tried to remove opposition from Parliament by appointing opponents as sheriffs instead
- Charles I used the Church of England to support his position
- Duke of Buckingham was becoming increasingly unpopular
- Charles I wanted to raise taxes for foreign wars
- Religious grounds of dispute between Crown and Parliament

2. *Candidates can be credited in a number of ways **up to a maximum of 8 marks**.*

Candidates must use knowledge to present a balanced assessment of the influence of different possible factors and come to a reasoned conclusion.

Up to 5 marks are allocated for relevant points of knowledge used to address the question. **1 mark** should be given for each relevant, factual key point of knowledge used to support a factor. **If only one factor is presented, a maximum of 3 marks should be given for relevant points of knowledge.**

Possible factors may include:	Relevant, factual, key points of knowledge to support this factor may include:
Religious differences	• Coronation service employed Anglican forms • Clergy in Scotland were told to wear Anglican surplices • Presbyteries were threatened with dissolution • Charles attempted to force a revised version of the Prayer Book on Scotland • Bishops were to be introduced into the Scottish Church • Anger over the Prayer Book led to St Giles Riot • The National Covenant 1638 rejected the canons
Resentment against Charles	• Scots resented Charles because he was an absentee king/visited Scotland only once • King sent an army to the borders of Scotland/Bishops Wars began
Resentment over economic situation	• Scotland was a poor country/many thought Charles did not care • He tried to raise taxes from the Scots
Any other valid factor	

Up to 3 marks should be given for presenting the answer in a structured way, leading to a conclusion which addresses the question, as follows:

1 mark for the answer being presented in a structured way, with knowledge being organised in support of different factors.

1 mark given for a valid judgement or overall conclusion.

1 mark given for a reason being provided in support of the conclusion.

3. *Candidates can be credited in a number of ways **up to a maximum of 6 marks**.*

Candidates must show a causal relationship between events.

Up to a maximum of 6 marks in total, **1 mark** should be given for each accurate, relevant reason, and a **second mark** should be given for reasons that are developed. Candidates may achieve full marks by providing five straightforward reasons, three developed reasons, or a combination of these.

Possible reasons may include:

- The Marquess of Newcastle was forced to fall back on the fortified city of York where he was besieged by Parliamentary armies under Sir Thomas Fairfax. However, Fairfax broke off the siege and marched his men south to prevent Rupert from reaching the approaches to York but Rupert surprised the Parliamentary generals by marching around their position and reaching the city anyway
- Rupert now ordered his tired men out from York to surprise the enemy but by the time the armies were in position it was late in the day, and Rupert, convinced that his foe would not attack until the morning, left the field in search of his supper
- Lord Newcastle retired to his coach for a quiet smoke and was unprepared
- The Parliamentary army surprised the Royalists by an attack which must have begun just as dusk was falling at 7pm
- The Royalist cavalry under Rupert was unable to resist the Parliamentary forces
- The Parliamentary infantry were the key to the victory

Section 2, Part C

1. *Candidates can be credited in a number of ways **up to a maximum of 6 marks.***

Candidates must make a judgement about the usefulness of the source and support this by making evaluative comments on identified aspects of the source.

One mark should be given for each relevant comment made, up to a **maximum of 6 marks in total**:

- a maximum of **4 marks** can be given for evaluative comments relating to the author, type of source, purpose and timing
- a maximum of **2 marks** may be given for comments relating to the content of the source
- a maximum of **2 marks** may be given for comments relating to points of significant omission

Examples of aspects of the source and relevant comments:

Aspect of the source	Possible comment
Author: Mungo Park	Useful as he was a British explorer in Africa and was well informed
Type of source: A travel memoir	Useful as he was an eyewitness but less useful as it was written after the events
Purpose: To describe the treatment of slaves in Africa	Purpose may have caused the writer to exaggerate the problem, so source may be less useful
Timing: 1799	At the height of British involvement in the slave trade

Content	Possible comment
• The African captives are usually secured by putting the right leg of one and the left leg of another into the same pair of fetters	Useful as it gives good details on how the slaves were treated
• By supporting the fetters with a string, they can just walk, though very slowly	Useful as it is accurate in its description
• Every four slaves are likewise fastened together by their necks with a strong rope or twisted thongs	Useful as it gives only factual details without bias or exaggeration

Possible points of significant omission may include:

- Some were beaten with whips to make them walk
- They sorted out the ones who would be strong enough to be useful

2. *Candidates can be credited in a number of ways **up to a maximum of 6 marks.***

Candidates must show a causal relationship between events.

Up to a **maximum of 6 marks in total**, **1 mark** should be given for each accurate, relevant reason, and a **second mark** should be given for reasons that are developed. Candidates may achieve full marks by providing five straightforward reasons, three developed reasons, or a combination of these.

Possible reasons may include:

- Slaves were controlled by strict laws or codes
- Slave risings lacked effective leadership
- Slave resistance was crushed by the better armed and organised whites
- Plantation owners often used black overseers to help them maintain control
- Punishments for escaping were very severe and acted as a deterrent
- Slaves lived in fear of being sold off/separated from their families if they broke the rules
- Slaves had little or no education and could be brainwashed into accepting plantation life
- Many islands were small and it was difficult for slaves to evade capture

3. *Candidates can be credited in a number of ways **up to a maximum of 8 marks.***

Candidates must use knowledge to present a balanced assessment of the influence of different possible factors and come to a reasoned conclusion. **Up to 5 marks** are allocated for relevant points of knowledge used to address the question. **1 mark** should be given for each relevant, factual key point of knowledge used to support a factor. **If only one factor is presented, a maximum of 3 marks should be given for relevant points of knowledge.**

Possible factors may include:	Relevant, factual, key points of knowledge to support this factor may include:
Role of Wilberforce	• Wilberforce motivated by his Christian principles • He was reluctant at first to pursue the matter in Parliament • Used his influence over Pitt to support the campaign • However, once he became convinced, he led the Parliamentary campaign for abolition
Other campaigners contributed too	• Quakers' anti-slavery committees had begun the campaigns • Contribution of anti-slavery campaigners, eg Thomas Clarkson • First-hand accounts from former slaves such as Equiano influenced people • Influence of religious groups/the churches • National anti-slavery campaigns involving meetings, petitions, leaflets
Changing attitudes	• People had begun to think of Africans as fellow human beings/regarded trade as unacceptable • Growing support in Parliament for abolition/trade with the West Indies was becoming less important to Britain • Many merchants supported free trade • Slavery began to be regarded as an inefficient way to produce goods
Any other valid factor	

Up to 3 marks should be given for presenting the answer in a structured way, leading to a conclusion which addresses the question, as follows:

1 mark for the answer being presented in a structured way, with knowledge being organised in support of different factors.

1 mark given for a valid judgement or overall conclusion.

1 mark given for a reason being provided in support of the conclusion.

Section 2, Part D

1. *Candidates can be credited in a number of ways **up to a maximum of 8 marks**.*

Candidates must use knowledge to present a balanced assessment of the influence of different possible factors and come to a reasoned conclusion. **Up to 5 marks** are allocated for relevant points of knowledge used to address the question. **1 mark** should be given for each relevant, factual key point of knowledge used to support a factor. **If only one factor is presented, a maximum of 3 marks should be given for relevant points of knowledge.**

Possible factors may include:	Relevant, factual, key points of knowledge to support this factor may include:
Improved medical knowledge	• Able to cure more diseases • Vaccinations prevented disease • Surgery improved and saved lives • Anaesthetics • Antiseptics • Better care for mothers and babies
Better living conditions	• Improvements in housing • Sanitation • Better diet • Improved working conditions
Clean water supply	• Removed the cause of diseases such as cholera and typhoid
Any other valid factor	

Up to 3 marks should be given for presenting the answer in a structured way, leading to a conclusion which addresses the question, as follows:

1 mark for the answer being presented in a structured way, with knowledge being organised in support of different factors.

1 mark given for a valid judgement or overall conclusion.

1 mark given for a reason being provided in support of the conclusion.

2. *Candidates can be credited in a number of ways **up to a maximum of 6 marks**.*

Candidates must make a judgement about the usefulness of the source and support this by making evaluative comments on identified aspects of the source.

One mark should be given for each relevant comment made, up to a **maximum of 6 marks in total**:

- a maximum of **4 marks** can be given for evaluative comments relating to the author, type of source, purpose and timing
- a maximum of **2 marks** may be given for comments relating to the content of the source
- a maximum of **2 marks** may be given for comments relating to points of significant omission

Examples of aspects of the source and relevant comments:

Aspect of the source	Possible comment
Author: Railway engineer	Useful as it was written by an eyewitness to the events
Type of source: Written recollections	Useful as it was based on personal experience but written later so less useful as they may have forgotten things
Purpose: To explain why some landowners resisted the railways	Purpose may have caused the writer to exaggerate the problem, so source may be less useful
Timing: 1840s	Useful as it was produced at the beginning of the railway expansion

Content	Possible comment
• Lady Seafield very decidedly told us that she hated railways	Less useful as it is only the views of the very wealthy
• "Cheap travel brought together such an objectionable variety of people"	Less useful as it exaggerates these views
• The railway would frighten away the grouse from his moors • What would become of the men who float timber down the Spey?	More useful as it provides details of their specific concerns

Possible points of significant omission may include:

- Benefits of travel
- Live further from work
- Spend time in the countryside
- Holidays
- Fear of accidents
- Spread of crime
- Fear of impact on farming

3. *Candidates can be credited in a number of ways up to a maximum of 6 marks.*

Candidates must show a causal relationship between events.

Up to a **maximum of 6 marks in total**, **1 mark** should be given for each accurate, relevant reason, and a **second mark** should be given for reasons that are developed. Candidates may achieve full marks by providing five straightforward reasons, three developed reasons, or a combination of these.

Possible reasons may include:

- Political protests created pressure for change
- Fear of revolution forced Parliament to listen
- Need to include middle classes in government because they were key to generating wealth
- Better education in towns made it more reasonable to extend the franchise
- Spread of radical ideas and moral arguments; equality became more of an issue
- Political benefits at Westminster for parties; they saw potential voters
- Population growth in the towns made them more politically sensitive
- Hyde Park riots put more pressure on the government
- Chartist movement provided organised political pressure for change

Section 2, Part E

1. *Candidates can be credited in a number of ways up to a maximum of 6 marks.*

Candidates must make a judgement about the usefulness of the source and support this by making evaluative comments on identified aspects of the source.

1 mark should be given for each relevant comment made, up to a **maximum of 6 marks in total**:

- a maximum of **4 marks** can be given for evaluative comments relating to the author, type of source, purpose and timing
- a maximum of **2 marks** may be given for comments relating to the content of the source
- a maximum of **2 marks** may be given for comments relating to points of significant omission

Examples of aspects of the source and relevant comments:

Aspect of the source	Possible comment
Author: Campaigner for change	Useful as it was an eyewitness but less useful as it has a clear bias
Type of source: A letter	A personal communication so may be less guarded, so source may be more useful
Purpose: To describe the extent of the poverty in London	Purpose may have caused the writer to exaggerate the problem, so source may be less useful
Timing: 1890	When poverty in London was at its worst

Content	Possible comment
• In one cellar a sanitary inspector reports finding a father, mother, three children and four pigs	Useful as it is very detailed
• In another room a missionary found a man ill with smallpox	Useful as it reflects what we know to have been fairly typical conditions in poorer areas
• Children running about half-naked and covered with dirt	Less useful as it exaggerates for effect

Possible points of significant omission may include:

- Lack of clean water in some towns
- Poor sewerage provision
- Overcrowding due to large families
- Poor quality of housing
- Social impact included alcohol issues and rise of temperance movements
- Lack of social mobility

2. *Candidates can be credited in a number of ways* **up to a maximum of 8 marks.**

Candidates must use knowledge to present a balanced assessment of the influence of different possible factors and come to a reasoned conclusion. **Up to 5 marks** are allocated for relevant points of knowledge used to address the question. **1 mark** should be given for each relevant, factual key point of knowledge used to support a factor. **If only one factor is presented, a maximum of 3 marks should be given for relevant points of knowledge.**

Possible factors may include:	Relevant, factual, key points of knowledge to support this factor may include:
Increasing popularity of the Labour party	• Trade Unions did not feel Liberals and Conservatives did enough for the poor • The new Labour Party stood for practical reforms to tackle poverty • Liberals thought of ways to help the poor because they thought they would lose votes to Labour
Concern for the poor	• Socialists felt a high level of poverty was wrong • Reports of Booth and Rowntree showed the scale of poverty • Many Liberal MPs represented poorer constituencies
National efficiency	• Worries about effect of poverty on the defence of the country • Concern that industrial output was being held back because of poverty • Countries such as Germany showed poverty could be tackled, eg pensions • Recruitment during the Boer War led to fears over defence due to fitness of many men
Any other valid factor	

Up to 3 marks should be given for presenting the answer in a structured way, leading to a conclusion which addresses the question, as follows:

1 mark for the answer being presented in a structured way, with knowledge being organised in support of different factors.

1 mark given for a valid judgement or overall conclusion.

1 mark given for a reason being provided in support of the conclusion.

3. *Candidates can be credited in a number of ways* **up to a maximum of 6 marks.**

Candidates must show a causal relationship between events.

Up to a **maximum of 6 marks in total**, **1 mark** should be given for each accurate, relevant reason, and a **second mark** should be given for reasons that are developed. Candidates may achieve full marks by providing five straightforward reasons, three developed reasons, or a combination of these.

Possible reasons may include:

- Beveridge Report showed the true nature of poverty and had widespread support
- Government ensured everyone had a fair share during the war and people wanted this to continue
- Ministry of Food ensured nation's health and safe food supply
- The public expected the Government to do more for them since this had worked well during the war
- Recognition of scale of poverty because of evacuation brought more support for change
- Bombing destroyed large amounts of housing and created an obvious need for intervention
- Labour Party's socialist ideology said there should be redistribution of wealth

Section 3, Part A

1. *Candidates can be credited in a number of ways* **up to a maximum of 4 marks.**

Candidates must make direct comparisons of the two sources, either overall or in detail. A simple comparison will indicate what points of detail or overall viewpoint they agree or disagree about and should be given **1 mark**. A developed comparison of the points of detail or overall viewpoint should be given **2 marks**. Candidates may achieve full marks by making four simple comparisons, two developed comparisons or by a combination of these.

Possible points of comparison may include:

Source A	Source B
Overall: Sources agree about the treatment of Jews Crusaders' brutal treatment of the Jews	Crusaders were ruthless killers
Many of the Crusaders were poor and hungry so they began stealing food and possessions from the Jews	Houses were robbed and valuables stolen
Some forced the Jews to change religion and become Christian	Those Jews who survived the massacre were forced to give up their faith and become Christians
Others, against the orders of Peter the Hermit, slaughtered the Jews	Immediately Peter the Hermit's army began attacking and killing Jewish men, women and children

2. *Candidates can be credited in a number of ways* **up to a maximum of 5 marks. They may take different perspectives on the events and may describe a variety of different aspects of the events.**

1 mark should be given for each accurate relevant key point of knowledge. A **second mark** should be given for each point that is developed, up to a **maximum of 5 marks.** Candidates may achieve full marks by providing five straightforward points, by making three developed points or a combination of these.

Possible points of knowledge may include:

- The Crusaders failed to starve the Muslims inside Nicaea into surrendering
- The governor of Nicaea, Kilij Arslan, was away fighting his Muslim neighbours; he did not return to protect the city
- The Crusaders asked Emperor Alexius for boats to blockade the city
- The city was surrounded and the Muslims inside had their supplies cut off
- Emperor Alexius agreed to let the Muslims go free in return for the city
- Without the knowledge of the Crusaders, the city was returned to Emperor Alexius in the middle of the night
- The Crusaders were denied their plunder of the city
- The relationship between Emperor Alexius and the Crusaders was damaged

3. *Candidates can be credited in a number of ways **up to a maximum of 5 marks**.*

Candidates must show a causal relationship between events.

Up to a **maximum of 5 marks in total**, **1 mark** should be given for each accurate, relevant reason, and a **second mark** should be given for reasons that are developed. Candidates may achieve full marks by providing five straightforward reasons, three developed reasons, or a combination of these.

Possible reasons may include:

- Crusaders used battering rams to weaken the city's defences
- Crusaders used siege towers to climb the city's walls
- Godfrey provided strong leadership in battle
- A Crusader killed the guards and let the other Crusaders in
- The Crusaders killed everyone inside the city: men, women and children

4. *Candidates can be credited in a number of ways **up to a maximum of 6 marks**.*

Candidates must make an overall judgement about how fully the source explains the events. **1 mark** may be given for each valid point interpreted from the source or each valid point of significant omission provided. The candidate can achieve **up to 3 marks** for their interpretation of the parts of the source they consider are relevant in terms of the proposed question where there is also at least one point of significant omission identified to imply a judgement has been made about the limitations of the source. For full marks to be given, each point needs to be discretely mentioned in terms of the question.

A maximum of 2 marks may be given for answers which refer only to the source.

Possible points which may be identified in the source include:

- Saladin was renowned for his knightly virtues
- Saladin, knowing that he was poorly supplied with delicacies, sent him a gift of the choicest fruits of the land
- Saladin sent a fine Arabian steed as a present for his rival
- Involved in almost daily combat

Possible points of significant omission may include:

- He united and led the Muslim world
- In 1187, he recaptured Jerusalem for the Muslims after defeating the King of Jerusalem at the Battle of Hattin
- When his soldiers entered the city of Jerusalem, they were not allowed to kill civilians, rob people or damage the city
- At Acre, Saladin agreed to pay a ransom for the people but somehow there was a breakdown in the process of payment and Richard ordered their execution
- Saladin lost at the Battle of Arsur in September 1191
- Saladin agreed a truce for pilgrims from the west to be allowed to visit Jerusalem without being troubled by the Muslims
- Saladin was a good negotiator – he refused the Crusaders' request to keep Ascalon
- He was respected by other Muslim leaders
- He never went back on a promise

Section 3, Part B

1. *Candidates can be credited in a number of ways **up to a maximum of 5 marks**.*

Candidates must show a causal relationship between events.

Up to a maximum of **5 marks in total**, **1 mark** should be given for each accurate, relevant reason, and a **second mark** should be given for reasons that are developed. Candidates may achieve full marks by providing five straightforward reasons, three developed reasons, or a combination of these.

Possible reasons may include:

- Britain had insisted on keeping troops in America after the French war
- The British had wanted the Americans to pay for their own defence/the Quartering Act meant they had to billet British soldiers
- Grenville had introduced measures after the war to raise revenue, eg the Sugar Act and the Stamp Duty Act which were resented
- Britain was taxing the colonists without giving them representation
- The British had attempted to prevent the Americans moving west
- George III was a tyrant, ruling from 3,000 miles away, who did not understand the colonists

2. *Candidates can be credited in a number of ways **up to a maximum of 6 marks**.*

Candidates must make an overall judgement about how fully the source explains the events. **1 mark** may be given for each valid point interpreted from the source or each valid point of significant omission provided. The candidate can achieve **up to 3 marks** for their interpretation of the parts of the source they consider are relevant in terms of the proposed question where there is also at least one point of significant omission identified to imply a judgement has been made about the limitations of the source. For full marks to be given, each point needs to be discretely mentioned in terms of the question.

A maximum of 2 marks may be given for answers which refer only to the source.

Possible points which may be identified in the source include:

- The Revolutionary War was waged by small armies
- Led by inefficient, even incompetent, commanders who fought muddled campaigns
- The men gathering in Boston were enthusiastic but badly armed and lacking supplies
- Most men were part-time and served for only a few months

Possible points of significant omission may include:

- They were badly armed and lacked supplies.
- Many American officers lacked training in the different types of warfare
- Were short of artillery and cavalry; many did not have a uniform

3. *Candidates can be credited in a number of ways **up to a maximum of 4 marks**.*

Candidates must make direct comparisons of the two sources, either overall or in detail. A simple comparison will indicate what points of detail or overall viewpoint they agree or disagree about and should be given **1 mark**. A developed comparison of the points of detail or overall viewpoint should be given **2 marks**. Candidates may achieve full marks by making four simple comparisons, two developed comparisons, or by a combination of these.

Possible points of comparison may include:

Source B	Source C
Overall: Agree that the British defeat was their own fault	
Cornwallis was defeated by a combination of difficult circumstances	Cornwallis made some basic errors
Cornwallis moved into Virginia and began to build a base at Yorktown	Cornwallis set up camp at Yorktown
In 1781, by late summer, Cornwallis's position at Yorktown was deteriorating fast	In August 1781, but this turned out to be a poor position
American forces prevented him from moving inland	American troops moved quickly to surround him and keep him there

4. *Candidates can be credited in a number of ways **up to a maximum of 5 marks**. They may take different perspectives on the events and may describe a variety of different aspects of the events.*

One mark should be given for each accurate relevant key point of knowledge. A **second mark** should be given for each point that is developed, up to a maximum of **5 marks**. Candidates may achieve full marks by providing five straightforward points, by making three developed points or a combination of these.

Possible points of knowledge may include:

- Capture of 1,000 British on 26 December 1776 at Trenton
- General Howe sends Cornwallis with 5,000 men to take revenge
- Cornwallis postpones attack and allows Washington's army to escape
- Poor leadership/tactics of British forces during 1777
- Lack of communication between the British armies
- Overconfidence of General Burgoyne
- Native Americans desert the British
- Defeat of Burgoyne's forces at Saratoga
- Surrender of 6,000 men and 30 cannon

Section 3, Part C

1. *Candidates can be credited in a number of ways **up to a maximum of 5 marks**. They may take different perspectives on the events and may describe a variety of different aspects of the events.*

1 mark should be given for each accurate relevant key point of knowledge. A **second mark** should be given for each point that is developed, up to a maximum of **5 marks**. Candidates may achieve full marks by providing five straightforward points, by making three developed points, or a combination of these.

Possible points of knowledge may include:

- Native Americans wanted freedom to roam/hunt; white Americans wanted to farm
- Treaty with the Native Americans broken: felt betrayed due to broken promises
- Grants to encourage gold prospecting alarmed Native Americans (Colorado & Montana in 1858/the Black Hills in 1874)
- Sacred land had to be protected by the Native Americans
- Many white Americans favoured setting up reservations but Native Americans objected to reservation life
- Hunting grounds disturbed by settlers and miners crossing Native American territory on the way to California and Oregon
- Issue of buffalo brought further conflict
- Development of the railways
- Clash of cultures: many white Americans saw Native Americans as savages/inferior
- Decline in Native American population: some Native American tribes were wiped out
- White/Native American tension led to atrocities/massacres/wars, eg Battle of Little Big Horn

2. *Candidates can be credited in a number of ways up to a maximum of 6 marks.*

Candidates must make an overall judgement about how fully the source explains the events. **1 mark** may be given for each valid point interpreted from the source or each valid point of significant omission provided. The candidate can achieve **up to 3 marks** for their interpretation of the parts of the source they consider are relevant in terms of the proposed question where there is also at least one point of significant omission identified to imply a judgement has been made about the limitations of the source. For full marks to be given, each point needs to be discretely mentioned in terms of the question.

A maximum of 2 marks may be given for answers which refer only to the source.

Possible points which may be identified in the source include:

- The Compromise of 1850 was created by Henry Clay and others to deal with the balance between slave and free states
- The Kansas-Nebraska Act of 1854
- The real issue occurred in Kansas where pro-slavery people of Missouri began to pour into the state to help force it to be slave
- The fight even erupted on the floor of the Senate when anti-slavery campaigner Charles Sumner was beat over the head by South Carolina's Senator, Preston Brooks

Possible points of significant omission may include:

- North-South Divide: Northern states opposed to slavery/Southern states in favour of slavery
- South saw slavery as central to its way of life/justified use of slaves
- Slavery perceived as a moral good/necessary evil by Southerners
- Horror of slave life (Uncle Tom's Cabin) intensified sectional feeling
- Northern anti-slavery propaganda inflamed South
- South was alarmed by election of Lincoln who wanted to halt spread of slavery
- Background to slavery issues played a part in dividing the nation (Fugitive State Laws, Dred Scott case, [1857], John Brown's Raid [1859])
- Fanatical leaders on either side who were unwilling to compromise
- South fearful of modernisation and movement of people to the North
- The Confederate attack on Fort Sumter forced Lincoln's hand

3. *Candidates can be credited in a number of ways up to a maximum of 5 marks.*

Candidates must show a causal relationship between events.

Up to a **maximum of 5 marks in total**, **1 mark** should be given for each accurate, relevant reason, and a **second mark** should be given for reasons that are developed. Candidates may achieve full marks by providing five straightforward reasons, three developed reasons, or a combination of these.

Possible reasons may include:

- The North had a larger and superior number of forces and soldiers
- They were better equipped
- They had more economic leverage to maintain their forces
- Moral cause spurred them on
- Role of General Grant was significant in providing better strategy
- Political leadership of Lincoln kept a focus on winning the war
- South was disorganised: infighting among Southern states

4. *Candidates can be credited in a number of ways up to a maximum of 4 marks.*

Candidates must make direct comparisons of the two sources, either overall or in detail. A simple comparison will indicate what points of detail or overall viewpoint they agree or disagree about and should be given **1 mark**. A developed comparison of the points of detail or overall viewpoint should be given **2 marks**. Candidates may achieve full marks by making four simple comparisons, two developed comparisons, or by a combination of these.

Possible points of comparison may include:

Source B	Source C
Overall: Agree about the brutality by whites and lack of resistance by blacks Failure to resist due to not understanding why this was happening	Reluctant to resist as they wanted to be seen as law-abiding
Hostility was shown to the school teachers like me who taught in schools for blacks	Teachers became key figures so they were frequently intimidated
They went at night and gave these warnings	These attacks usually took place at night
They were whipping me	Mutilated and murdered

Section 3, Part D

1. *Candidates can be credited in a number of ways up to a maximum of 5 marks. They may take different perspectives on the events and may describe a variety of different aspects of the events.*

1 mark should be given for each accurate relevant key point of knowledge. A **second mark** should be given for each point that is developed, up to a maximum of **5 marks**. Candidates may achieve full marks by providing five straightforward points, by making three developed points, or a combination of these.

Possible points of knowledge may include:

- Spartacist Revolt
- Political assassinations
- Kapp Putsch
- Constitutional disagreements
- Stab in the Back myth
- Reactions to Versailles

2. *Candidates can be credited in a number of ways up to a maximum of 6 marks.*

Candidates must make an overall judgement about how fully the source explains the events. **1 mark** may be given for each valid point interpreted from the source or each valid point of significant omission provided. The candidate can achieve **up to 3 marks** for their interpretation of the parts of the source they consider are relevant in terms of the proposed question where there is also at least one point of significant omission identified to imply a judgement has been made about the limitations of the source. For full marks to be given, each point needs to be discretely mentioned in terms of the question.

A maximum of 2 marks may be given for answers which refer only to the source.

Possible points which may be identified in the source include:

- On Friday afternoons, workers desperately rushed to the nearest store, where a queue had already formed
- When you arrived a pound of sugar cost two million marks but, by the time your turn came, you could only afford a half pound
- In the chaos, people pushed prams loaded with money
- We were devastated as life savings became worthless

Possible points of significant omission may include:

- It wiped out pensions
- It caused a degree of psychological trauma in the nation
- Bartering became common
- People preferred dollars as a more stable currency
- Debts were wiped out
- Some businessmen such as Stinnes benefited
- Businesses went bust due to lack of investment
- Increased political extremism
- Munich Putsch

3. *Candidates can be credited in a number of ways up to a maximum of 5 marks.*

Candidates must show a causal relationship between events.

Up to a **maximum of 5 marks in total**, **1 mark** should be given for each accurate, relevant reason, and a **second mark** should be given for reasons that are developed. Candidates may achieve full marks by providing five straightforward reasons, three developed reasons, or a combination of these.

Possible reasons may include:

- Weimar blamed for losing World War One/Stab in the Back
- Proportional representation produced weak governments

- The governments showed inability to curb extremism in politics
- Coalition governments lacked authority/seemed unable to solve problems facing Germany
- Weimar was blamed for economic hardships: Hyper-inflation/Depression
- Squabbling among politicians led to people losing respect for/faith in them
- Hitler promised strong, decisive leadership
- Nazi use of propaganda, eg held large public meetings/parades which excited many
- Use of intimidation/violence which attracted many/intimidated others
- Nazi programme: anti-Versailles, anti-Communist, anti-Jews had a great deal of support among ordinary Germans
- Hitler's promises: eg provision of jobs, reunite all Germans, re-militarisation
- The use of political tactics, eg refusal to join coalition governments allowed Hitler to outflank his opponents
- Success in elections brought greater publicity/legitimacy/financial backing
- Nazis gained widespread support as they seemed to offer something to most groups/classes in Germany

4. *Candidates can be credited in a number of ways up to a maximum of 4 marks.*

Candidates must make direct comparisons of the two sources, either overall or in detail. A simple comparison will indicate what points of detail or overall viewpoint they agree or disagree about and should be given **1 mark**. A developed comparison of the points of detail or overall viewpoint should be given **2 marks**. Candidates may achieve full marks by making four simple comparisons, two developed comparisons or by a combination of these.

Possible points of comparison may include:

Source B	Source C
Overall: Sources agree that Hitler had protected Germany from a serious threat Hitler saved Germany from the paramilitary threat	Hitler saved Germany
Hitler's courage in taking firm action has made him a hero	Hitler's personal popularity soared
Satisfaction that Hitler has acted	Welcomed the strong action against it
Serious threat posed by Rohm and the SA to Germany and her people	You have saved the German nation from serious danger

Section 3, Part E

1. *Candidates can be credited in a number of ways **up to a maximum of 5 marks**. They may take different perspectives on the events and may describe a variety of different aspects of the events.*

1 mark should be given for each accurate relevant key point of knowledge. A **second mark** should be given for each point that is developed, up to a maximum of **5 marks**. Candidates may achieve full marks by providing five straightforward points, by making three developed points or a combination of these.

Possible points of knowledge may include:

- Wages were low and working conditions were poor
- Working hours were very long/12-hour shifts
- High number of deaths from accidents and work-related health problems/poor diet
- Poor living conditions/shared rooms in tenement blocks/ barrack-style buildings next to factories
- No privacy or private space/shared beds occupied in shifts/curtains in place of walls
- Under surveillance by Okhrana/police spies infiltrated the unions
- The people did not have full voting rights
- Strikes/protests often put down by police or government troops, eg Bloody Sunday, Lena Goldfields
- Food shortages

2. *Candidates can be credited in a number of ways **up to a maximum of 6 marks**.*

Candidates must make an overall judgement about how fully the source explains the events. **1 mark** may be given for each valid point interpreted from the source or each valid point of significant omission provided. The candidate can achieve **up to 3 marks** for their interpretation of the parts of the source they consider are relevant in terms of the proposed question where there is also at least one point of significant omission identified to imply a judgement has been made about the limitations of the source. For full marks to be given, each point needs to be discretely mentioned in terms of the question.

A maximum of 2 marks may be given for answers which refer only to the source.

Possible points which may be identified in the source include:

- By 1905 there was a growing desire to overthrow the repressive government of Nicholas II
- There was a great deal of poverty in the cities and the countryside
- The revolutionary movement gained strength following Russia's humiliating defeat by Japan
- Revolutionary groups became much more organised

Possible points of significant omission may include:

- Impact of Bloody Sunday which angered people
- Shortages of food and fuel made people desperate
- High unemployment caused distress
- Discontent in the armed forces was increasing.

3. *Candidates can be credited in a number of ways **up to a maximum of 5 marks**.*

Candidates must show a causal relationship between events.

Up to a **maximum of 5 marks in total**, **1 mark** should be given for each accurate, relevant reason, and a **second mark** should be given for reasons that are developed. Candidates may achieve full marks by providing five straightforward reasons, three developed reasons, or a combination of these.

Possible reasons may include:

- The Provisional Government lacked legitimate authority to rule Russia
- It had taken too long to organise democratic elections
- It had needed others' help to defeat the Kornilov Coup
- It failed to solve key problems: food shortages/rising prices/unemployment
- The Provisional Government lost popularity as it continued the war and failure to deliver reforms in land ownership and working conditions
- Kerensky and the Provisional Government were seen as weak/were taken by surprise at Bolshevik growth **BUT** the failure of the July Days strengthened the Provisional Government
- Bolshevik propaganda was successful in putting over its policies
- They promised an end to war, give land to the peasants, food to the workers and an end to rule by the rich
- Lenin and the Bolsheviks appealed by being strong and organised
- The Bolsheviks had weapons (not handed back) after the Kornilov revolt
- The Bolsheviks had great support from the industrial workers in Petrograd/Moscow and gained control of the local Soviets
- The Bolsheviks had some military support to be able to seize key points in Petrograd
- Return of Bolshevik exiles/prisoners increased revolutionary fervour

4. *Candidates can be credited in a number of ways **up to a maximum of 4 marks**.*

Candidates must make direct comparisons of the two sources, either overall or in detail. A simple comparison will indicate what points of detail or overall viewpoint they agree or disagree about and should be given **1 mark**. A developed comparison of the points of detail or overall viewpoint should be given **2 marks**. Candidates may achieve full marks by making four simple comparisons, two developed comparisons, or by a combination of these.

Possible points of comparison may include:

Source B	Source C
Overall: Sources disagree about the nature of Trotsky's leadership. Trotsky was a great leader	Trotsky was ruthless
He was an inspirational leader	A ruthless leader who used strict discipline
He made rousing speeches to the troops and raised morale	When 200 soldiers deserted at Svyazhsk, Trotsky arrived and ordered the execution of one in every ten men in the regiment, as a warning to the rest
Over five million men joined the Red Army of their own free will	He forced people to join the Red Army to raise the number of troops

Section 3, Part F

1. *Candidates can be credited in a number of ways up to a maximum of 4 marks.*

Candidates must make direct comparisons of the two sources, either overall or in detail. A simple comparison will indicate what points of detail or overall viewpoint they agree or disagree about and should be given **1 mark**. A developed comparison of the points of detail or overall viewpoint should be given **2 marks**. Candidates may achieve full marks by making four simple comparisons, two developed comparisons, or by a combination of these.

Possible points of comparison may include:

Source A	Source B
Overall: Agree about the lack of resolve in the face of the Fascist threat Mussolini's threats of force were decisive in his victory	Lack of a resolute opposition allowed Mussolini to succeed
Put Mussolini in the position to threaten the government	Mussolini and his followers marched for Rome
The government decided to send in the army to stop Mussolini	The prime minister called out the army when the Fascists surrounded Rome
Victor Emmanuel III decided instead to give in to Mussolini's demands and appointed him head of a new government	The Italian king refused to use the military to squash Mussolini's "march".

2. *Candidates can be credited in a number of ways up to a maximum of 6 marks.*

Candidates must make an overall judgement about how fully the source explains the events. **1 mark** may be given for each valid point interpreted from the source or each valid point of significant omission provided. The candidate can achieve **up to 3 marks** for their interpretation of the parts of the source they consider are relevant in terms of the proposed question where there is also at least one point of significant omission identified to imply a judgement has been made about the limitations of the source. For full marks to be given, each point needs to be discretely mentioned in terms of the question.

A maximum of 2 marks may be given for answers which refer only to the source.

Possible points which may be identified in the source include:

- The leadership cult started almost as soon as Mussolini came to power
- His role as Duce of Fascism and Head of the Government had been secured by changes to the law
- Mussolini had undoubted charisma and political intelligence
- His main talents lay chiefly in the areas of acting and propaganda

Possible points of significant omission may include:

- Mussolini instituted a new calendar with Year 1 beginning with 1922
- He established "holy days" such as 23 March, to remind Italians of the advent of Fascism
- He included 21 April, the birth of the city of Rome, to emphasise his intention to recreate the greatness of the Roman Empire
- Shrines to Fascist martyrs with eternal flames were constructed and each Fascist party headquarters had to have a memorial chapel
- In Milan, a School of Mystical Fascism was founded in 1930. Mussolini used slogans such as "Believe, Obey, Fight" and "Mussolini is Always Right"
- Newspapers were forbidden to mention any signs of illness and even his birthdays were to be ignored as this would reveal his age
- His imperialist war in Ethiopia and his intervention in the Spanish Civil War were hailed as glorious crusades on behalf of civilisation and religion

3. *Candidates can be credited in a number of ways up to a maximum of 5 marks. They may take different perspectives on the events and may describe a variety of different aspects of the events.*

1 mark should be given for each accurate relevant key point of knowledge. A **second mark** should be given for each point that is developed, up to a maximum of **5 marks**. Candidates may achieve full marks by providing five straightforward points, by making three developed points or a combination of these.

Possible points of knowledge may include:

- He set Italy targets as he had with his Battle for Births
- The Battle for Land: this "battle" was to clear marshland and make it usable for farming and other purposes, eg roads built on them to improve Italy's infrastructure
- These schemes were labour intensive and employed a lot of people so they served a purpose in this area
- The Battle of the Lira: Mussolini inflated the value of the lira making exports more expensive
- This created unemployment at home as many industries could not sell their goods
- But, Italy got through the Depression in the 1930s better than Europe's industrial powerhouses simply because she was an agricultural nation
- The Battle for Grain: Mussolini wanted to make Italy economically stronger and near enough self-sufficient by growing more grain
- However, this was at the expense of fruit and vegetables
- Italian grain became expensive at home and the price of bread rose, which hit the poor the worst

4. *Candidates can be credited in a number of ways **up to a maximum of 5 marks.***

Candidates must show a causal relationship between events.

Up to a **maximum of 5 marks in total**, **1 mark** should be given for each accurate, relevant reason, and a **second mark** should be given for reasons that are developed. Candidates may achieve full marks by providing five straightforward reasons, three developed reasons, or a combination of these.

Possible reasons may include:

- He bought off key groups: the workers were promised an eight-hour day while an enquiry into the profits made by the industrialists during World War One was dropped
- The rich benefited from a reduction in death duties: now, under Mussolini, more of what someone had earned during their lifetime went to their family and not the government
- To get support from the Roman Catholic Church, religious education was made compulsory in all elementary schools
- He also sought the support of the Church by entering into the Lateran Treaty
- He introduced a Fascist Grand Council which would decide policy for Italy without consulting the non-Fascists in the government first
- Accusations that people were intimidated into voting for the Fascists or that Fascists took ballot papers from those who may have voted against Mussolini
- In November 1926, all rival political parties and opposition newspapers were banned in Italy
- In 1927, a secret police force was set up called the OVRA
- The death penalty was reintroduced for "serious political offences"

Section 3, Part G

1. *Candidates can be credited in a number of ways **up to a maximum of 5 marks**. They may take different perspectives on the events and may describe a variety of different aspects of the events.*

1 mark should be given for each accurate relevant key point of knowledge. A **second mark** should be given for each point that is developed, up to a maximum of **5 marks**. Candidates may achieve full marks by providing five straightforward points, by making three developed points, or a combination of these.

Possible points of knowledge may include:

- Skin colour identified them as "different" and marked them out for discrimination
- Whites felt they were superior to black migrants
- Blacks were seen as uneducated and unskilled and so were able to get only poorly-paid jobs
- White unskilled workers saw them as a threat to their jobs
- There was competition for jobs with immigrants to USA
- There were riots between blacks and whites in the North
- They were separated into ghetto communities in Northern cities
- Housing conditions were very poor

2. *Candidates can be credited in a number of ways **up to a maximum of 4 marks.***

Candidates must make direct comparisons of the two sources, either overall or in detail. A simple comparison will indicate what points of detail or overall viewpoint they agree or disagree about and should be given **1 mark**. A developed comparison of the points of detail or overall viewpoint should be given **2 marks**. Candidates may achieve full marks by making four simple comparisons, two developed comparisons, or by a combination of these.

Possible points of comparison may include:

Source A	Source B
Overall: Sources agree about the limited nature of the success of the boycott	Bus boycott had limited success but longer-term success was less
Bus boycott had limited success on its own	
His name was Martin Luther King and this was to be his first step towards becoming the leading figure in the Civil Rights Movement	Martin Luther King became involved in the Civil Rights Movement. He went on to become an African American leader who was famous throughout the world
The courts decided that segregation on Montgomery's buses was illegal	The US Supreme Court announced that Alabama's bus segregation laws were illegal
There were still white-only theatres, pool rooms and restaurants	Most other facilities and services in Montgomery remained segregated for many years to come

3. *Candidates can be credited in a number of ways **up to a maximum of 5 marks**.*

Candidates must show a causal relationship between events.

Up to a **maximum of 5 marks in total**, **1 mark** should be given for each accurate, relevant reason, and a **second mark** should be given for reasons that are developed. Candidates may achieve full marks by providing five straightforward reasons, three developed reasons, or a combination of these.

Possible reasons may include:

- NAACP was the moving force behind Supreme Court decisions
- The Supreme Court declared segregated schools unconstitutional
- Black pressure forced Eisenhower to propose a Civil Rights Act
- Civil Rights Movement was gaining heroes such as Rosa Parks
- Mass action such as Montgomery Bus Boycott was successful
- Protest at Little Rock saw black students admitted to a white school
- Details of Brown v Topeka Board of Education decision
- Rise of new civil rights' leaders such as Martin Luther King and SCLC
- Civil Rights Act

4. *Candidates can be credited in a number of ways **up to a maximum of 6 marks**.*

Candidates must make an overall judgement about how fully the source explains the events. One mark may be given for each valid point interpreted from the source or each valid point of significant omission provided. The candidate can achieve **up to 3 marks** for their interpretation of the parts of the source they consider are relevant in terms of the proposed question where there is also at least one point of significant omission identified to imply a judgement has been made about the limitations of the source.

For full marks to be given, each point needs to be discretely mentioned in terms of the question.

A maximum of 2 marks may be given for answers which refer only to the source.

Possible points which may be identified in the source include:

- Malcolm X was mistreated in his youth and this gave him a different set of attitudes to Martin Luther King
- While in jail, he was influenced by the ideas of Elijah Muhammad who preached hatred of the white race
- He believed that the support of non-violence was a sign that black people were still living in mental slavery
- He often used violent language and threats to frighten the government into action

Possible points of significant omission may include:

- Malcolm X claimed that even whites who appeared friendly were "wolves in sheep's clothing"
- He believed that non-violence deprived black people of their right to self-defence
- He claimed that peaceful protest gained little for most black people
- He didn't think non-violent campaigns tackled the problems for blacks in Northern cities

Section 3, Part H

1. *Candidates can be credited in a number of ways **up to a maximum of 5 marks**.*

Candidates must show a causal relationship between events.

Up to a **maximum of 5 marks in total**, **1 mark** should be given for each accurate, relevant reason, and a **second mark** should be given for reasons that are developed. Candidates may achieve full marks by providing five straightforward reasons, three developed reasons, or a combination of these.

Possible reasons may include:

- A strong Germany would restore balance of power
- To defend Europe from the threat from the east
- France had built the Maginot Line which was seen as an aggressive act
- Communism/Russia was a threat to Germany/Europe: Germany was the first line of resistance and had to be strong
- An army would be to unite all Germans/create Greater Germany/gain Lebensraum
- An army would be necessary to regain territory lost at Versailles
- Restoring Germany's military strength would gain popularity and economic growth for Germany

2. *Candidates can be credited in a number of ways **up to a maximum of 6 marks**.*

Candidates must make an overall judgement about how fully the source explains the events. **1 mark** may be given for each valid point interpreted from the source or each valid point of significant omission provided. The candidate can achieve **up to 3 marks** for their interpretation of the parts of the source they consider are relevant in terms of the proposed question where there is also at least one point of significant omission identified to imply a judgement has been made about the limitations of the source. For full marks to be given, each point needs to be discretely mentioned in terms of the question.

A maximum of 2 marks may be given for answers which refer only to the source.

Possible points which may be identified in the source include:

- The Great Depression meant that money could not be found for re-armament
- The government knew that the British people were totally opposed to war
- Chamberlain believed he could negotiate directly with Hitler
- Communist Russia was the real threat to peace in the world

Possible points of significant omission may include:

- British opinion felt that the Treaty of Versailles had been too harsh
- There was the fear of bombing from the air
- Chiefs of Staff warned the government that British forces were unprepared
- Britain had no reliable allies: Empire unwilling, France was not trusted and USA was isolationist

3. *Candidates can be credited in a number of ways* **up to a maximum of 4 marks.**

Candidates must make direct comparisons of the two sources, either overall or in detail. A simple comparison will indicate what points of detail or overall viewpoint they agree or disagree about and should be given **1 mark**. A developed comparison of the points of detail or overall viewpoint should be given **2 marks**. Candidates may achieve full marks by making four simple comparisons, two developed comparisons, or by a combination of these.

Possible points of comparison may include:

Source B	Source C
Overall: Sources disagree about the way the Anschluss was viewed. Anschluss was welcomed by the Austrians and would benefit Europe as a whole	Anschluss was a war-like act which threatened the rest of Europe
It is clear that Anschluss is popular among the Austrian people who are, after all, German in language and culture	We have permitted Hitler to brutally invade an independent country
Keeping Germany and Austria apart had been one of the more spiteful terms of Versailles and this wrong is now made right	The decision in 1919 to forbid Anschluss had been a very sensible one for limiting the war-like ambitions of Germany
Europe is likely to benefit from a period of peace and prosperity as Germany moves into a brighter future	Any intelligent person can see that an even more powerful Germany is a threat to the peace and stability of Europe

4. *Candidates can be credited in a number of ways* **up to a maximum of 5 marks.** *They may take different perspectives on the events and may describe a variety of different aspects of the events.*

1 mark should be given for each accurate relevant key point of knowledge. A **second mark** should be given for each point that is developed, up to a maximum of **5 marks**. Candidates may achieve full marks by providing five straightforward points, by making three developed points, or a combination of these.

Possible points of knowledge may include:

- Britain and France warned Germany off: the "May Crisis"
- Runciman mission failed to persuade Czechoslovakia to surrender Sudetenland to Germany
- Hitler and Chamberlain met after a further threat to attack Czechoslovakia
- Agreement was reached, but war became likely after demands at second meeting: "Black Wednesday"
- Third meeting: UK, France, Germany and Italy at Munich
- Czechoslovakia was pressurised into ceding Sudetenland to Germany

Section 3, Part I

1. *Candidates can be credited in a number of ways* **up to a maximum of 5 marks.**

Candidates must show a causal relationship between events.

Up to a **maximum of 5 marks in total**, **1 mark** should be given for each accurate, relevant reason, and a **second mark** should be given for reasons that are developed. Candidates may achieve full marks by providing five straightforward reasons, three developed reasons, or a combination of these.

Possible reasons may include:

- Hitler had given his full backing to Guderian's tactics
- In Britain and France, the cavalry regiments ruled supreme and they were adamant that tanks would not get any influence in their armies
- The High Commands of both countries were dominated by these old traditional cavalry regiments and their political pull was great
- In 1940, Britain and France still had a World War One mentality and didn't recognise the potential of the new weapons
- What tanks they had were poor compared to the German Panzers
- British and French tactics were outdated
- France hid behind the Maginot Line
- Effective use of Blitzkrieg tactics in the early stages
- Stalin refused to engage with the Germans until Stalingrad

2. *Candidates can be credited in a number of ways* **up to a maximum of 4 marks.**

Candidates must make direct comparisons of the two sources, either overall or in detail. A simple comparison will indicate what points of detail or overall viewpoint they agree or disagree about and should be given **1 mark**. A developed comparison of the points of detail or overall viewpoint should be given **2 marks**. Candidates may achieve full marks by making four simple comparisons, two developed comparisons, or by a combination of these.

Possible points of comparison may include:

Source B	Source C
Overall: Sources disagree about the effectiveness of the Resistance movements Resistance movements were too weak to make much of an impact	Resistance movements were well organised and made a big impact
The resistance movements of Europe had found it hard to make much of an impression on the might of the German military	The French Resistance scored key victories against the German occupation forces
German army commanders indicated that the resistance movements were an irritant but no more than this	Resistance members discovered French collaborators, killed many ranking Nazi officials, and destroyed trains, convoys, and ships used by the German army
The devastating attacks of 1939 to 1941 had given little time for each country to prepare a secret army to undermine the invaders	Resistance members organised themselves in secret

3. *Candidates can be credited in a number of ways **up to a maximum of 6 marks.***

Candidates must make an overall judgement about how fully the source explains the events. **1 mark** may be given for each valid point interpreted from the source, or each valid point of significant omission provided. The candidate can achieve **up to 3 marks** for their interpretation of the parts of the source they consider are relevant in terms of the proposed question where there is also at least one point of significant omission identified to imply a judgement has been made about the limitations of the source. For full marks to be given, each point needs to be discretely mentioned in terms of the question.

A maximum of 2 marks may be given for answers which refer only to the source.

Possible points which may be identified in the source include:

- The Soviets sent him a birthday present in the form of an artillery barrage right into the heart of the city
- The Western Allies joined in with a massive air raid
- 14-16 year-old boys who had "volunteered" for the "honour" to be accepted into the SS and to die for their Führer in the defence of Berlin
- Boys who were found hiding were hanged as traitors by the SS

Possible points of significant omission may include:

- Russians advanced westward as much as 40 kilometres a day through East Prussia, Lower Silesia, East Pomerania, and Upper Silesia
- The first defensive preparations at the outskirts of Berlin were made on 20 March, when the newly appointed commander of Army Group Vistula, General Gotthard Heinrici, correctly anticipated that the main Soviet thrust would be made over the Oder River
- Before the main battle in Berlin commenced, the Soviets managed to encircle the city as a result of their success in the battles of the Seelow Heights and Halbe
- Marshal Ivan Konev's 1st Ukrainian Front had pushed in the north through the last formations of Army Group Centre
- The German defences consisted of several depleted, badly equipped, and disorganised *Wehrmacht* and Waffen-SS divisions, which included many SS foreign volunteers, as well as many *Volkssturm* and Hitler Youth members
- Within the next few days, the Soviets rapidly advanced through the city and reached the city centre where close combat raged
- Before the battle was over, Hitler and a number of his followers committed suicide
- The city's defenders finally surrendered on 2 May
- However, fighting continued to the north-west, west and south-west of the city until the end of the war in Europe on 8 May
- German units fought westward so that they could surrender to the Western Allies rather than to the Soviets

4. *Candidates can be credited in a number of ways **up to a maximum of 5 marks.** They may take different perspectives on the events and may describe a variety of different aspects of the events.*

1 mark should be given for each accurate relevant key point of knowledge. A **second mark** should be given for each point that is developed, up to a **maximum of 5 marks**. Candidates may achieve full marks by providing five straightforward points, by making three developed points or a combination of these.

Possible points of knowledge may include:

- The Imperial Japanese Army was locked in war with China and could not be spared to defend the home islands
- Japan had so few fighter aircraft and trained pilots left, they decided not to risk such precious assets and did not try to intercept either atomic bombing raids because they were such small formations
- The US shipyards and factories were every bit as productive as Yamamoto had feared
- The Americans progressed methodically from island to island
- By August 1945, 67 Japanese cities had been destroyed by conventional TNT and incendiary bombs and some two million Japanese civilians had been killed by the terror bombing
- Curtis LeMay complained that he had no worthwhile targets against which to task his bombers. The Japanese fleet was gone, with what ships that remained decommissioned and rusting at anchor

- The embargo was starving the home islands to death
- Japanese industry collapsed for want of raw materials
- After the fall of Saipan (and the consequent fall of the Tojo Cabinet), the Japanese peace movement grew exponentially and more and more peace overtures were sent to Washington by way of Sweden, Switzerland, Moscow and elsewhere
- Two atomic bombs were dropped on Hiroshima and Nagasaki which shocked the Japanese
- However, Douglas MacArthur, Dwight Eisenhower, Chester Nimitz and Chief of Staff Leahy (to name but a few) recommended against using the bombs because they were unnecessary to end the war and would not save lives

Section 3, Part J

1. *Candidates can be credited in a number of ways **up to a maximum of 6 marks**.*

Candidates must make an overall judgement about how fully the source explains the events. **1 mark** may be given for each valid point interpreted from the source, or each valid point of significant omission provided. The candidate can achieve **up to 3 marks** for their interpretation of the parts of the source they consider are relevant in terms of the proposed question where there is also at least one point of significant omission identified to imply a judgement has been made about the limitations of the source. For full marks to be given, each point needs to be discretely mentioned in terms of the question.

A maximum of 2 marks may be given for answers which refer only to the source.

Possible points which may be identified in the source include:

- To the American government, placing missiles on Cuba was a war-like act by the Soviets
- They believed that the Soviet Union intended to supply a large number of powerful nuclear weapons
- Spy photographs proved the offensive purpose of the missiles which were pointed directly at major American cities
- It was estimated that within a few minutes of them being fired, 80 million Americans would be dead

Possible points of significant omission may include:

- America refused to trade with Cuba after Batista's fall
- The American government backed a rebellion against Castro: "Bay of Pigs"
- The Bay of Pigs worsened the situation and pushed Cuba closer to the USSR
- Khrushchev complained about American missile bases in Turkey
- Kennedy declared a naval blockade of Cuba
- Americans prepared for a head-on clash
- USSR tried to set up missile bases in Cuba
- Khrushchev backed down

2. *Candidates can be credited in a number of ways **up to a maximum of 5 marks**.*

Candidates must show a causal relationship between events.

Up to a **maximum of 5 marks in total**, **1 mark** should be given for each accurate, relevant reason, and a **second mark** should be given for reasons that are developed. Candidates may achieve full marks by providing five straightforward reasons, three developed reasons, or a combination of these.

Possible reasons may include:

- Record numbers of East Germans were escaping to the West
- Those who left East Berlin were young and well educated
- Agents were using West Berlin as a centre of operations against East Germany and the Soviet Union
- West Berlin was a shining example of capitalism in the middle of communist East Germany and had to be isolated
- Future of Berlin had been in dispute since the end of World War II
- Khrushchev needed a foreign policy success to divert attention from domestic problems

3. *Candidates can be credited in a number of ways **up to a maximum of 4 marks**.*

Candidates must make direct comparisons of the two sources, either overall or in detail. A simple comparison will indicate what points of detail or overall viewpoint they agree or disagree about and should be given **1 mark**. A developed comparison of the points of detail or overall viewpoint should be given **2 marks**. Candidates may achieve full marks by making four simple comparisons, two developed comparisons, or by a combination of these.

Possible points of comparison may include:

Source B	Source C
Overall: Sources disagree about the tactics used by the Vietcong The Vietcong used guerilla tactics	The Vietcong engaged the Americans in open warfare
The Vietcong generally avoided large-scale attacks on the enemy but continually harassed their troops and installations	Thousands of Vietcong launched wave after wave of attacks on our camp
This limited the scale of their casualties to only a handful at a time	The Vietcong body count was reported to have been 800, but I thought it was more
They travelled light, carrying basic weapons and few supplies	They had all kinds of Chinese and Russian weapons, such as flamethrowers and rocket launchers

4. *Candidates can be credited in a number of ways* **up to a maximum of 5 marks**. *They may take different perspectives on the events and may describe a variety of different aspects of the events.*

1 mark should be given for each accurate relevant key point of knowledge. A **second mark** should be given for each point that is developed, up to a maximum of **5 marks**. Candidates may achieve full marks by providing five straightforward points, by making three developed points, or a combination of these.

Possible points of knowledge may include:

- Non-proliferation treaty was signed in 1968
- SALT talks agreed to limit testing of nuclear weapons
- USA begins to sell the USSR wheat in 1970s
- The end of the Vietnam War eased tension
- USA and USSR signed Helsinki agreement in 1975
- Changing personalities among the leadership of the USA and USSR
- Joint space mission between USA and USSR in 1975
- Role of Gorbachev

NATIONAL 5 HISTORY MODEL PAPER 1

Section 1, Part A

1. *You should try to make 5 separate points from recall.*

You could mention:

- The death of Alexander III
- The death of the Maid of Norway
- The Guardians asked Edward to decide who would be king
- Edward demanded that the (thirteen) Competitors recognise him as overlord
- Edward chose Balliol
- John Balliol did homage to King Edward

You can always get extra marks if you bring in more information to back up a point you are making. E.g. the first event that contributed to Edward becoming overlord was the death of Alexander III (**1 mark**). This severely weakened Scotland as he had no son to succeed him (**1 mark**).

5

2. *Start off by saying that the source partly explains Edward's decision. This allows you to go on to show what is and what is not in the source.*

The source mentions:

- The Scots organised a rebellion against Edward
- The Scots rejected Edward's claim to be Scotland's overlord
- Scotland made an alliance with France against England

However the source does not mention:

- The Scots refused to obey Edward's order to help him fight against the French
- The Scots invaded the north of England
- The Scots attacked Carlisle
-

5

3. *You should try to make 5 separate points from recall.*

You could mention:

- Wallace organised the army of Scotland
- He defeated the English at Stirling Bridge
- He accepted the position of joint Guardian of Scotland
- He developed the idea of fighting in schiltrons
- He continued to resist Edward until he was executed

You can always get extra marks if you add more information to back up a point you are making. E.g. the leadership of Wallace was important because he managed to organise the army of Scotland (**1 mark**) using guerrilla tactics against the English occupation (**1 mark**).

5

4. *You need to make 5 clear points about the usefulness of the source.*

You would probably start by arguing that the source does provide useful evidence about Bruce's tactics. Comment on who wrote the source, when it was written and why it was written:

- The author is an English monk who was present at the time of the raid

- The source was written at the time of the raid
- The source was written to describe what happened when Bruce's army invaded England

However, you could say that the source is likely to be biased because it was written by an English monk.

You should then comment on the information contained in the source:

- The source tells us that Bruce's army attacked Durham and Richmond
- English people had to resort to paying the Scots not to attack their town

You would gain marks by pointing out that in some ways the source is less useful because of important information that has not been mentioned. E.g. Bruce sent his brother to attack Ireland, and asked the Pope to overturn his excommunication.

5

Section 1, Part B

1. *You should try to make 5 separate points from recall.*

You could mention:

- Henry wanted to break the Auld Alliance between Scotland and France
- The Scots announced that they considered the Treaty of Greenwich was void
- The government of Scotland was becoming more friendly towards France
- The French had bribed Arran to change his mind about the Treaty of Greenwich
- Henry intended to force the Scots into changing their mind

You can always get extra marks if you add more information to back up a point you are making. E.g. the Scots had angered Henry when they claimed that the Treaty of Greenwich was void (**1 mark**). This Treaty had arranged for Mary to marry Henry's son (**1 mark**).

5

2. *You need to make 5 clear points about the usefulness of the source.*

You would probably start by arguing that the source does provide useful evidence about the growth of Protestantism. Comment on who wrote the source, when it was written and why it was written:

- The source was written when Protestantism was growing in Scotland
- It was written by John Knox an important Protestant leader of the time
- It was written to provide an account of the growth of Protestantism

You should then comment on the information contained in the source:

- It tells us that John Knox felt able to return to Scotland and preach openly

However, you could say that the source is likely to be biased because it was written by John Knox who was biased in favour of Protestantism.

You would gain marks by pointing out that in some ways the source is less useful because of important information that has not been mentioned. E.g. Elizabeth I's accession to the throne in England also encouraged the growth of Protestantism in Scotland

5

3. *Start off by saying that the source partly describes how well Mary ruled Scotland. This allows you to go on to show what is and what is not in the source.*

The source mentions:

- She established a successful government
- She defeated nobles who challenged her authority
- Her religious policy was tolerant and ahead of its time

However the source does not mention:

- She was more concerned about furthering her claim to the English throne
- She left the running of Scotland to a small group of nobles
- She failed to deal with religious problems in Scotland

5

4. *You should try to make 5 separate points from recall.*

You could mention:

- Mary was Elizabeth's heir
- Her presence encouraged opposition to Queen Elizabeth in England
- Plots to remove Elizabeth and place Mary on the throne
- There would be dangers in allowing Mary to return to Scotland
- There would be dangers in allowing Mary to go to France

You can always get extra marks if you add more information to back up a point you are making. E.g. there were a number of plots to remove Elizabeth and place Mary on the throne (**1 mark**) for example the Ridolfi Plot (**1 mark**).

5

Section 1, Part C

1. *You should try to make 5 separate points from recall.*

You could mention:

- The English ship, Worcester was seized at Leith
- Captain Green and two of his crew were arrested and put on trial for piracy
- They were found guilty and sentenced to death
- Queen Anne's government in England wanted her to pardon them
- Queen Anne wanted her Scottish Government to pardon them
- Captain Green and the two crewmen were hanged

You can always get extra marks if you bring in more information to back up a point you are making. E.g. Captain Green and two of his crewmen were hanged (**1 mark**). An Edinburgh mob put pressure on the Scottish Government not to pardon them (**1 mark**).

5

2. *You need to make 5 clear points about the usefulness of the source.*

You would probably start by arguing that the source does provide useful evidence about the Treaty of Union. Comment on who wrote the source, when it was written and why it was written:

- Written shortly after the Treaty of Union therefore a primary source
- Written by someone who had traveled in Scotland during the time
- Written to describe reaction to the Treaty in Scotland

You should then comment on the information contained in the source:

- Scots called the people who had negotiated the Union traitors
- Scots wanted to remain Scotsmen

You would gain marks by pointing out that in some ways the source is less useful because of important information that has not been mentioned e.g:

- some Scots supported the Union
- some believed it would make Scotland wealthier

6

3. *Start off by saying that the source partly describes the arguments against the Union. This allows you to go on to show what is and what is not in the source.*

The source mentions:

- Scots feared that they would have little influence over government decisions
- Businesses in Scotland would suffer as a result of English imports
- The Treaty had been signed because of English bribes

However the source does not mention:

- Presbyterians feared a British parliament dominated by Anglican church
- Fears of reduction in status of Scottish nobility in British parliament
- Fear of new taxes
- Fear of taking on English debt

5

4. *You should try to make 5 separate points from recall.*

You could mention:

- Scotland had not become richer
- There was fear that English imports were ruining Scottish businesses
- There were new Customs and Excise taxes
- They disliked the changes in Scotland's weights, measures, money, etc
- Nobles and important politicians had left Edinburgh for London
- The House of Lords had allowed "patronage" in the Church of Scotland (Patronage Act)

You can always get extra marks if you add more information to back up a point you are making. E.g. there were new Customs and Excise taxes (**1 mark**) for example a Malt Tax was introduced (**1 mark**).

5

Section 1, Part D

1. *You should try to make 5 separate points from recall.*

You could mention:

- Scotland was close to Ireland
- Travel was cheap
- There was work to be found in cotton/textile factories
- Many found work as navigators of the canals and railways
- There was work to be found on farms at harvest time
- Many Irish had already settled in Scotland which encouraged more to come

You can always get extra marks if you add more information to back up a point you are making. E.g. there was work to be found in cotton/textile factories (**1 mark**) which often provided jobs for the whole family (**1 mark**).

5

2. *You need to make 5 clear points about the usefulness of the source.*

You would probably start by arguing that the source does provide useful evidence about the impact of the Irish on law and order. Comment on who wrote the source, when it was written and why it was written:

- Comes from a newspaper which reported on events in Scotland
- Published during a time of Irish immigration
- Written to describe the impact of Irish immigrants

You should then comment on the information contained in the source:

- Describes an attack by Irish navvies
- Describes how the police responded to the attack

However, you might point out that the source is taken from a Scottish newspaper and is less likely to give the Irish side of the story.

You would gain marks by pointing out that in some ways the source is less useful because of important information that has not been mentioned. E.g. most Irish immigrants were hardworking and law-abiding.

5

3. *Start off by saying that the source partly explains why Scots emigrated. This allows you to go on to show what is and what is not in the source.*

The source mentions:

- Landlords paid travelling costs
- Rent arrears written off so that emigrants had money
- Landlords often bought their cattle
- Edinburgh and Glasgow made a contribution towards their expenses in emigrating

However the source does not mention:

- Highlands and Islands Emigration Society (HIES) gave assistance
- Charities e.g. Barnardos, helped orphans/young women to emigrate
- Countries such as Australia and Canada sent agents to advise on emigration
- Family members living abroad gave encouragement and sent money for travel

5

4. *You should try to make 5 separate points from recall.*

You could mention:

- Scots brought farming skills to Canada
- Scots developed sheep farming in Australia
- Tradesmen such as stone masons helped the building industry in USA
- Developed businesses, banks and trading companies
- Scots established education system e.g. Canada
- Scots brought a tradition of hard work

You can always get extra marks if you bring in more information to back up a point you are making. E.g. Scots developed businesses in their new countries (**1 mark**) for example Andrew Carnegie's success in the American steel industry (**1 mark**).

5

Section 1, Part E

1. *You need to make 5 clear points about the usefulness of the source.*

You would probably start by arguing that the source does provide useful evidence about the use of new technology during the First World War. Comment on who wrote the source, when it was written and why it was written:

- The source was written by someone who was involved in developing new technology
- It was written in 1918 not long after the invention of the tank
- It was written to explain how the tank was used

You should then comment on the information contained in the source:

- The tank helped to deal with enemy machine guns

You would gain marks by pointing out that in some ways the source is less useful because of important information that has not been mentioned. E.g. early tanks were very unreliable and very slow moving.

5

2. *Start off by saying that the source partly describes the changing role of women during the war. This allows you to go on to show what is and what is not in the source.*

The source mentions:

- Women took over jobs vacated by men
- They carried out vital work in the munitions industry
- They kept transport going
- They had to take on greater responsibility in the home

However the source does not mention:

- Women worked on farms
- They coped with food shortages/ rationing
- They joined the armed services

5

3. *You should try to make 5 separate points from recall.*

You could mention:

- Lack of investment and foreign competition resulted in decline of the coal industry
- The demand for ships declined
- Shipyards were hit by labour disputes
- Other countries increased their steel making

- Jute prices collapsed after the war
- The collapse of foreign markets for herring greatly affected the industry
- Cheap foreign imports of food competed with agriculture when trade was resumed after the war

You can always get extra marks if you bring in more information to back up a point you are making. E.g. the demand for ships declined (**1 mark**) for example Clyde yards produced warships which were no longer needed after the war (**1 mark**).

5

4. *You should try to make 5 separate points from recall.*

You could mention:

- Militancy gained a lot of negative publicity
- Many campaigners felt that militant action undermined their efforts
- Government determined not to give into acts of vandalism/force
- Attacks on MPs alienated support/turned many people against the cause who had previously supported votes for women
- Violent actions e.g. window smashing annoyed the public
- Upset Suffragists/damaged Suffragist campaign
- Once imprisoned Suffragettes could no longer campaign effectively

You can always get extra marks if you add more information to back up a point you are making. E.g. militancy gained a lot of negative publicity (**1 mark**) newspapers such as the Daily Mail condemned the Suffragettes as mad and irresponsible (**1 mark**).

5

Section 2, Part C

1. *You need to make 6 clear points about the usefulness of the source.*

You would probably start by arguing that the source does provide useful evidence about the treatment of slaves on the Middle Passage. Comment on who wrote the source, when it was written and why it was written:

- The source was written by a slave who had experienced the Middle Passage
- Written in 1789 at the time of the slave trade
- Written to describe what the Middle Passage was like

You should then comment on the information contained in the source:

- The source mentions terrible conditions below decks
- It mentions the shrieks of the women

You would gain marks by pointing out that in some ways the source is less useful because of important information that has not been mentioned. E.g. the source does not mention slaves being forced to exercise on deck.

6

2. *You should try to make 5 separate points from recall.*

You could mention:

- Millions of enslaved people taken from Africa
- Mostly strong young males and females
- Some African kings became rich through selling slaves to Europeans
- Europeans sold cloth, alcohol and firearms to Africans
- Some tribes went to war against neighbouring tribes in order to capture people to enslave
- Some tribes carried out raids on other tribes to kidnap people to enslave

You can always get extra marks if you bring in more information to back up a point you are making. E.g. some African Kings grew rich through selling slaves to Europeans (**1 mark**). For example the Kings of Dahomey earned fortunes from enslaving neighbouring tribes (**1 mark**).

5

3. *You should try to make 5 separate points from recall.*

You could mention:

- Slaves were often branded by their owners
- Slaves were punished severely for minor crimes
- Slaves were paired off by their owner for breeding purposes
- Slave families could be split up by their owners
- Female slaves were subjected to sexual abuse by their owners
- Slaves were forced to work very long hours

You can always get extra marks if you add more information to back up a point you are making.
E.g. slaves were punished severely for minor crimes (**1 mark**). A runaway might be whipped and forced to wear a collar (**1 mark**).

5

4. *For this type of question you must say whether you think the sources agree or not and then support your decision by making two comparisons using evidence from the sources.*

For this question you would probably decide that the two sources agree. You could then back this up with two of the following comparisons:

- Source A says that plantation owners had political influence and Source B supports this by saying that the plantation owners allied themselves with important groups to promote the case for slavery
- Source A points out that there were British ports which relied on the slave trade and Source B backs this up by mentioning that dozens of British ports relied on the slave trade
- Source A says that people believed that the trade had helped them to make Britain wealthy and prosperous and Source B supports this by pointing out that slavery seemed vital to the continuing prosperity of Britain

4

Section 2, Part D

1. *You should try to make 5 separate points from recall.*

You could mention:

- Revolution in agriculture helped feed the urban population
- Fertility of mothers increased as a result of an improved diet
- Improved medical knowledge e.g. better understanding of the connection between dirt and disease/bacteria
- Vaccinations against killer diseases: 1853 smallpox; 1897 tetanus, etc
- Improvements in sanitation e.g. flushing toilet

You can always get extra marks if you add more information to back up a point you are making. E.g. revolution in agriculture helped feed the urban population (**1 mark**) and scientific farming methods increased the range of food crops (**1 mark**).

5

2. *You need to make 6 clear points about the usefulness of the source.*

You would probably start by arguing that the source does provide useful evidence about working conditions in cotton mills. Comment on who wrote the source, when it was written and why it was written:

- The source was written by a visitor to a cotton mill
- The source was written during a time when working conditions were being improved
- The source was written to describe what a cotton mill was like

You should then comment on the information contained in the source:

- The source mentions that the factory is well ventilated
- The source mentions that there were guards on dangerous machinery

You would gain marks by pointing out that in some ways the source is less useful because of important information that has not been mentioned. E.g. factory acts had been introduced to improve working conditions especially for children, and many mill owners did not obey the new regulations.

6

3. *You should try to make 5 separate points from recall.*

You could mention:

- More use of steam powered machinery for pumping water
- Improvements made to ventilation
- Wider use of mechanical cage lifts
- Davy Lamp which reduced pit explosions
- Metal props made roof falls less likely
- Coal cutting machinery available from the 1880s

You can always get extra marks if you bring in more information to back up a point you are making. E.g. more use of steam powered machinery for pumping water (**1 mark**). This allowed deeper mining to be safer (**1 mark**).

5

4. *For this type of question you must say whether you think the sources agree or not and then support your decision by making two comparisons using evidence from the sources.*

For this question you would probably decide that the two sources agree. You could then back this up with two of the following comparisons:

- Source A mentions working class anger at the Whig government over the 1832 act. Source B describes working class Fury at continuing restriction on voting which remained after the Act

- Source A mentions people's anger at the Poor Law and Source B tells us about the hatred of the poor law

- Source A mentions working class people being confident about forming their own organizations. Source B mentions a working class backlash

4

Section 2, Part E

1. *You need to make 6 clear points about the usefulness of the source.*

You would probably start by arguing that the source does provide useful evidence about the causes of poverty in the early 20th century. Comment on who wrote the source, when it was written and why it was written:

- The source was written by a Liberal MP who would be well informed about problems in Britain

- The source was written in the early 20th century when the causes of poverty were being debated

- The source was written to explain the causes of poverty

You could argue that the source is less useful because the author was a liberal reformer and could be biased.

You should then comment on the information contained in the source:

- The source mentions that some men's earnings are not enough to keep a family

- It mentions that some people find it difficult to find work

You would gain marks by pointing out that in some ways the source is less useful because of important information that has not been mentioned. E.g. the lack of free secondary education made it difficult for young people to escape poverty, and the lack of affordable housing.

6

2. *For this type of question you must say whether you think the sources agree or not and then support your decision by making two comparisons using evidence from the sources.*

For this question you would probably decide that the two sources agree. You could then back this up with two of the following comparisons:

- Source A says that the reforms were in no sense a welfare state and Source B says that reforms were not designed to free people from poverty

- Source A says that the reforms targeted small areas of poverty and Source B mentions that only certain types of worker were supported for sickness and unemployment

- Source A says that the poor law was still necessary and Source B says that only some people were freed from having to seek poor relief

4

3. *You should try to make 5 separate points from recall.*

You could mention:

- Middle class people became more aware of the problems of poverty through the experience of evacuation

- People from different classes also came together to do air-raid duties like firewatching

- People from different classes were brought together in the air-raid shelters

- Both rich and poor faced the same problems such as bomb damage to their homes

- People were more sympathetic towards people living in inadequate housing due to the blitz

You can always get extra marks if you bring in more information to back up a point you are making. E.g. people from different classes were brought together in the air-raid shelters (**1 mark**). Better off people learned about the problems of the poor for themselves (**1 mark**).

5

4. *You should try to make 5 separate points from recall.*

You could mention:

- Beveridge proposed a system which was open to everyone regardless of wealth

- There would be no return to the hated means test

- The National Health Service would be free to everyone meaning that poor people could receive good medical attention

- Proposed a fair insurance scheme where everyone would pay the same contribution to receive the same benefits

- Promised every family an allowance for every child

You can always get extra marks if you add more information to back up a point you are making. E.g. there would be no return to the hated means test (**1 mark**) and benefits would be universal and based on contributions (**1 mark**).

5

Section 3, Part B

1. *You should try to make 6 separate points from recall.*

You could mention:

- Colonists were angered by the passing of the Tea Act in 1773 which allowed the East India Company to undercut the colonial merchants and smugglers

- Bostonians disguised themselves as Mohawk Indians and boarded the three tea ships

- Tea was emptied into the water of Boston harbour

- Some of the tea was stolen

- King George III and Parliament were outraged when they heard of these events

- Lord North rejected the offer of compensation from some of the colonial merchants

- Led to the passing of the "Intolerable Acts"

You can always get extra marks if you bring in more information to back up a point you are making. E.g. led to the passing of the "Intolerable Acts" (**1 mark**) such as the Massachusetts Act (**1 mark**).

6

2. *You need to make 6 clear points about the usefulness of the source.*

You would probably start by arguing that the source does provide useful evidence about what happened at Lexington and Concord in April 1775. Comment on who wrote the source, when it was written and why it was written:

- The source was written only a month after events at Lexington and Concord/written at the start of the year
- The source was written by the leaders of the colonies, who would have detailed/first hand knowledge of what had taken place
- The source was written to condemn the actions of the British army

You might want to point out ways in which the source is less useful, for example the writers of the source were leaders of the colonies so might be biased against the British.

You should then comment on the information contained in the source:

- The attack is described as unprovoked
- The colonists were cruelly slaughtered

You would gain marks by pointing out that in some ways the source is less useful because of important information that has not been mentioned. E.g. militia in Massachusetts had been training for war and spies had warned of the British army's movements and counter-attack was launched at Concord.

6

3. *If the question starts with "To what extent" you must write a balanced answer.*

In this question you should show that you understand that the involvement of foreign countries caused difficulties for Britain in the War of Independence?

You could mention:

- The French attacked British colonies in the Caribbean and elsewhere which undermined Britain's control
- The French harassed British shipping in the Atlantic interfering with trade
- Britain lost control of the seas for the first time that century
- Britain found it more difficult to reinforce and supply its forces in America.
- France provided the colonies with finance
- France provided the colonies with military assistance – soldiers, gunpowder
- Spain distracted Britain by attacking Gibraltar
- A Franco-Spanish force threatened Britain with invasion in 1779

You should then balance your answer by giving other reasons for Britain's defeat such as:

- Leadership qualities of George Washington
- Public opinion with in Britain was split over the war
- Military leadership was poor
- Major defeats at Saratoga and Yorktown
- Supplying an army fighting so far away from Britain posed major problems
- Colonists knew the territory on which battles were fought

Finish with a conclusion giving an overall answer to the question supported with a reason for the judgement you have made. E.g. overall, Spain and France played an important part in the defeat but it was the weaknesses of the British forces as shown in their military disasters at Saratoga and Yorktown, which were the main reasons for the defeat of Britain in the Wars of Independence.

8

Section 3, Part C

1. *You should try to make 6 separate points from recall.*

You could mention:

- White Americans believed in Manifest Destiny
- Native Americans wanted a home where the buffalo roam while the white Americans wanted to farm
- Treaty made with the Native Americans was broken
- White settlers had a 'property attitude' towards land
- Native Americans believed that Great Spirit had created land for their care
- Grants to encourage gold prospecting alarmed Native Americans
- Sacred land had to be protected by the Native Americans
- Many white Americans favoured setting up reservations
- Native Americans objected to reservation life
- Loss of freedoms associated with the move back to reservations

You can always get extra marks if you add more information to back up a point you are making. E.g. white Americans believed in Manifest Destiny (**1 mark**), a belief in being able to occupy land from the Pacific to the Atlantic (**1 mark**).

6

2. *You need to make 6 clear points about the usefulness of the source.*

You would probably start by arguing that the source does provide useful evidence about the impact of Reconstruction on black people in the South. Comment on who wrote the source, when it was written and why it was written:

- The source was written by a visitor to the South
- The source is taken from a diary written at the time of reconstruction
- The source was written to describe the impact of Reconstruction on black people in the South

You should then comment on the information contained in the source:

- The source mentions that black people were living in shabby conditions
- The source mentions violence used against black people

You would gain marks by pointing out that in some ways the source is less useful because of important information that has not been mentioned. E.g. secret organizations were set up in the South to terrorise black people. Black people were too poor to move.

6

3. *If the question starts with "To what extent" you must write a balanced answer.*

In this question you should show that you understand that differing attitudes to the union brought about Civil War.

You could mention:

- North Eastern States were in favour of a strong Union with power exercised from the centre
- Southern States believed States Rights should not be infringed upon by federal government
- Southern States held that it was their right to secede from the union if it was no longer acting in their interests
- Northern states believed that the South had no right to secede

You should then balance your answer by giving other reasons such as:

- North believed in protection of trade through tariffs
- South relied on free trade
- Northerners were opposed to the expansion of slavery
- Southerners believed that the expansion of slavery was necessary

Finish with a conclusion giving an overall answer to the question supported with a reason for the judgement you have made. E.g. overall, attitudes to the union were an important cause of the Civil War but it was the conflicts over the expansion of slavery, which was the main cause of the war.

8

Section 3, Part D

1. *You should try to make 6 separate points from recall.*

You could mention:

- The Spartacists had no organised plan for an armed revolution
- The Government used the Freikorps to crush the revolt
- The well equipped Freikorps quickly crushed the revolt
- The Freikorps used artillery to recapture buildings in Berlin
- The Spartacist leaders Karl Liebknecht and Rosa Luxemburg were arrested
- Both Spartacist leaders were executed/murdered by the Freikorps

You can always get extra marks if you add more information to back up a point you are making. E.g. the Government used the Freikorps to crush the revolt (**1 mark**). The Freikorps received support for their actions from the German army (**1 mark**).

6

2. *You need to make 6 clear points about the usefulness of the source.*

You would probably start by arguing that the source does provide useful evidence about Germany at the end of the First World War. Comment on who wrote the source, when it was written and why it was written:

- The source was written by an eye witness
- The source was written to describe Germany at the end of the war

You might want to argue that in some ways the source is less useful for example:

- The writer of the source is looking back at events which may be less reliable

You should then comment on the information contained in the source:

- The source mentions gunfire on the streets
- The source mentions the authors shock at the announcement of the armistice

You would gain marks by pointing out that in some ways the source is less useful because of important information that has not been mentioned. E.g. Germany had signed the armistice unconditionally. A socialist government took power at the end of the war.

6

3. *If the question starts with "To what extent" you must write a balanced answer.*

In this question you should show that you understand that Hitler's success was due to violence and intimidation.

You could mention:

- Violent activities of the SA
- Destruction of opposition offices and printing presses
- Intimidation of opposition Reichstag deputies

You should then balance your answer by giving other reasons such as:

- Divisions in opposition
- Economic chaos led Germans to support extremism
- Hitler offered simple solutions to Germany's problems

Finish with a conclusion giving an overall answer to the question supported with a reason for the judgement you have made. E.g. overall, violence and intimidation played a major part in Hitler's success but Hitler was also able to convince enough Germans to vote for him to allow him to gain power "legally".

8

Section 3, Part E

1. *You should try to make 5 separate points from recall.*

You could mention:

- Most Russians were religious
- Close link between the Church and the Tsar
- The Church supported the Tsar's rule
- Orthodox Church was the largest in Russia
- Orthodox Church was very wealthy
- Orthodox Church controlled education
- Orthodox Church encouraged the people to regard the Tsar as their "little father"

You can always get extra marks if you add more information to back up a point you are making. E.g. most Russians were religious (**1 mark**) and priests were held in high regard (**1 mark**).

6

2. *If the question starts with "To what extent" you must write a balanced answer.*

In this question you should show that you understand how the Russo-Japanese war caused the 1905 Revolution.

You could mention:

- The Tsar had hoped that a short, successful war would unite the country and boost his popularity
- The war had gone very badly from the start and the Tsar was blamed
- There were stories of soldiers and sailors being killed due to the incompetence of their leaders

You should then balance your answer by giving other reasons such as:

- There was growing poverty among workers and peasants
- There was rising unemployment in the cities
- There were food shortages
- The cruelty of the Tsar's government/secret police

Finish with a conclusion giving an overall answer to the question supported with a reason for the judgement you have made. E.g. overall, the war was the most important cause of the 1905 Revolution because defeat provided the spark which led to the explosion of discontent against the Tsar.

8

3. *You need to make 6 clear points about the usefulness of the source.*

You would probably start by arguing that the source does provide useful evidence about the problems facing the Provisional Government. Comment on who wrote the source, when it was written and why it was written:

- The source was written by the leader of the Provisional Government who would be aware of events in Russia
- The source was written at the time when the Provisional Government was facing problems
- It was written to describe the problems facing the Provisional Government

You should then comment on the information contained in the source:

- The source mentions defeat at the front
- The source also mentions shortages of food and land

You would gain marks by pointing out that in some ways the source is less useful because of important information that has not been mentioned. E.g. opposition groups such as the Bolsheviks were plotting the downfall of the Provisional Government. The Soviets were interfering in the government of Russia.

6

Section 3, Part G

1. *You should try to make 6 separate points from recall.*

You could mention:

- European immigrants often arrived with little wealth or possessions
- They faced discrimination on the grounds of race or religion
- They faced discrimination in most areas of life and work simply because they were immigrants

- They did the poorest jobs with lowest pay
- They lived in poor housing often in unsanitary slums
- They became stereotyped by public and media as a threat
- They were blamed for political extremism e.g. Red Scare

You can always get extra marks if you bring in more information to back up a point you are making. E.g. faced discrimination on the grounds of race or religion (**1 mark**). Many were Catholics or Jews whilst most old immigrants were protestant (**1 mark**).

6

2. *You need to make 6 clear points about the usefulness of the source.*

You would probably start by arguing that the source does provide useful evidence about attitudes towards black Americans in the South at the time of the Civil Rights Movement. Comment on who wrote the source, when it was written and why it was written:

- The source was written by a person from Alabama which is in the deep South
- The source was written at the time of the growth of the Civil Rights Movement
- The source was written to describe the attitude of southerners to black people

You might want to comment on ways in which the source is less useful:

- The source was written by a leader of the KKK who would have extreme views

You should then comment on the information contained in the source:

- Black people should ignore what Northerners say
- Black people should work hard

You would gain marks by pointing out that in some ways the source is less useful because of important information that has not been mentioned. E.g. does not mention support for segregation in the South or that many southerners regarded black people as inferior.

6

3. *If the question starts with "To what extent" you must write a balanced answer.*

In this question you should show that you understand that their experiences in the Second World War encouraged the growth of the Civil Rights Movement.

You could mention:

- Black servicemen overseas had some experience of integration
- Some black people gained employment in war industries where they were treated as equals
- Government propaganda described the war as a fight for freedom which highlighted the lack of freedom for black people

You should then balance your answer by giving other reasons such as:

- Hardship and humiliation caused by the Jim Crow laws
- Segregation of schools, transport, etc
- Inequality faced by black Americans in employment and housing

Finish with a conclusion giving an overall answer to the question supported with a reason for the judgement you have made. E.g. overall, the experience of the Second World War encouraged the growth of the Civil Rights Movement but other reasons such as the injustices of segregation were important in keeping it going.

8

Section 3, Part H

1. *You should try to make 5 separate points from recall.*

You could mention:

- Britain allowed Germany to break the Treaty of Versailles
- British government and public opinion had revised their attitude to the Treaty of Versailles and agreed it was too harsh
- Britain did not protest about the reintroduction of conscription
- Britain took no action over the creation of a German air force
- the Anglo-German Naval Agreement allowed Germany to build a navy
- Britain accepted the reoccupation of the Rhineland

You can always get extra marks if you bring in more information to back up a point you are making. E.g. Britain accepted the reoccupation of the Rhineland (**1 mark**). Members of the government felt Germany was only going into its own backyard (**1 mark**).

6

2. *You need to make 6 clear points about the usefulness of the source.*

You would probably start by arguing that the source does provide useful evidence about Britain's attitude to Czechoslovakia in 1938. Comment on who wrote the source, when it was written and why it was written:

- The source was written by the British ambassador who would reflect British attitudes
- The source was written at the time of the Czech crisis
- The source was written to influence British attitudes towards Czechoslovakia

You might want to comment on ways in which the source is less useful:

- The source was written by a supporter of appeasement

You should then comment on the information contained in the source:

- Says that Czechoslovakia must take some blame
- Says that the Czechs cannot be trusted

You would gain marks by pointing out that in some ways the source is less useful because of important information that has not been mentioned. E.g. Czechs had grievances that were genuine.

6

3. *If the question starts with "To what extent" you must write a balanced answer.*

In this question you should show that you understand that fear of bombing was a reason why British people wanted to avoid war during the 1930s.

You could mention:

- British people felt that the bomber would always get through
- British people overestimated Germany's aerial threat
- British people were frightened by images of air raids from the Spanish Civil War

You should then balance your answer by giving other reasons such as:

- Many British people believed that Germany had genuine grievances which should be settled peacefully
- Many British people supported the League of Nations
- Most British people had memories of the death and destruction caused by the Great War

Finish with a conclusion giving an overall answer to the question supported with a reason for the judgement you have made. E.g. overall, fear of bombing was an important reason why British people wanted to avoid another war but there were also important reasons for them to believe that war was unnecessary.

8

Section 3, Part I

1. *If the question starts with "To what extent" you must write a balanced answer.*

In this question you should show that you understand that sea power played a part in American success in the war with Japan.

You could mention:

- Sea power based on aircraft carriers allowed for air power to support landings and sea battles e.g. Midway
- Sea power victory at the Battle of Midway destroyed major part of Japanese fleets and therefore their ambitions in the Pacific. Four out of five Japanese aircraft carriers sunk, along with cruisers and destroyers
- Sea power allowed for "island hopping" to push Japanese forces back in the Pacific
- Sea power, especially US submarine fleet, contributed to blockade of Japan and led to a lack of resources for Japanese war effort

You should then balance your answer by giving other reasons such as:

- US code breakers successfully intercepted and read most Japanese communication during the war and knew what the enemy plans were
- Codebreakers were vital to victory at Midway
- US used Navaho language in their codes that Japanese could not break
- Codebreakers knew about the journey of Japanese Navy Commander Yamamoto to the South Pacific. He was intercepted, shot down and killed
- US resources and men – better equipped
- US development of A bomb and attack on Hiroshima and Nagasaki

Finish with a conclusion giving an overall answer to the question supported with a reason for the judgement you have made. E.g. overall, sea power was an important reason for American success in the war against Japan but the overall military superiority of the United States and the devastation it was able to inflict on Japan itself was the most important reason for American victory.

2. *You need to make 6 clear points about the usefulness of the source.*

You would probably start by arguing that the source does provide useful evidence about attitudes towards the atomic bombing of Japan. Comment on who wrote the source, when it was written and why it was written:

- The source was written by a member of the US government who would be aware of the facts around the use of the bomb
- The source was written shortly after the bomb had been used against Japan
- The source was written to explain why the bomb should not have been dropped

You might want to comment on ways in which the source is less useful:

- The source was written by an opponent of the bomb showing possible bias

You should then comment on the information contained in the source:

- The bomb was unnecessary because Japan was already on the verge of defeat
- The bomb was unnecessary because the blockade was working

You would gain marks by pointing out that in some ways the source is less useful because of important information that has not been mentioned. E.g. the bomb ended the war more quickly than other methods would have done, and probably saved the lives of many US servicemen who would have had to continue with conventional tactics.

6

3. *You should try to make 5 separate points from recall.*

You could mention:

- British and American forces advancing from the west
- Russians were advancing from the east
- Soviets managed to encircle Berlin
- Allied airforces controlled the skies over Germany
- The German defences consisted of several depleted, badly equipped, and disorganised units
- Hitler and a number of his followers committed suicide

You can always get extra marks if you bring in more information to back up a point you are making. E.g. allied airforces controlled the skies over Germany (**1 mark**) and were bombing German cities day and night (**1 mark**).

6

Section 3, Part J

1. *If the question starts with "To what extent" you must write a balanced answer.*

In this question you should show that you understand that the developing arms race was the main cause of the Cold War.

You could mention:

- Stalin was angry with Truman for not informing them about the development of the bomb
- Use of atomic bombs on Hiroshima and Nagasaki started the nuclear arms race
- USSR developed it's own atomic bomb – first test 1949

8

- Both USA and USSR raced to develop the first hydrogen bomb

You should then balance your answer by giving other reasons such as:

- USA remembered that USSR had made an alliance with Hitler in 1939
- USSR remembered that the USA had supported the white forces during the Civil War
- USA opposed the conquest of Eastern Europe by the USSR at the end of WW2
- USSR felt that USA had deliberately delayed entry into the war against Hitler
- USA was capitalist and USSR was Communist
- USSR wanted control of West Berlin but USA was determined to keep it free
- Berlin blockade and airlift

Finish with a conclusion giving an overall answer to the question supported with a reason for the judgement you have made. E.g. overall, the developing arms race was an important cause of tension but it was the difference in ideologies between communist USSR and capitalist USA that was the main reason for the tension between the two superpowers before 1950. The USA was desperate to stop the spread of communism and the USSR wanted protection against another attack from capitalist countries.

8

2. *You should try to make 6 separate points from recall.*

You could mention:

- Many of those conscripted avoided enlisting by draft dodging
- Students protested against President Johnson
- Large demonstrations against the war often lead to violent clashes
- Students held protests in many universities across the USA e.g. Kent State
- Prominent figures such as Martin Luther King spoke out against the war
- Many musicians of the time wrote and performed anti-Vietnam songs
- Vietnam veterans spoke out against the war

You can always get extra marks if you bring in more information to back up a point you are making. E.g. many of those conscripted avoided enlisting by draft dodging (**1 mark**) many protestors burned their draft cards to demonstrate their opposition to the war (**1 mark**).

6

3. *You need to make 6 clear points about the usefulness of the source.*

You would probably start by arguing that the source does provide useful evidence about the Soviet attitude to détente. Comment on who wrote the source, when it was written and why it was written:

- The source was written by the leader of the Soviet Union
- The source was written at the time of détente
- The source was written to explain why the Soviets wanted détente

You should then comment on the information contained in the source:

- The source mentions the need to avoid another war
- The source mentions that progress has already been made with détente

You would gain marks by pointing out that in some ways the source is less useful because of important information that has not been mentioned. E.g. Soviets wanted détente because of the rising cost of defence (**1 mark**). Soviets were fearful that they were falling behind in the arms race (**1 mark**).

6

NATIONAL 5 HISTORY MODEL PAPER 2

Section 1, Part A

1. *You should try to make 5 separate points from recall.*

You could mention:

- Alexander III's sons had all died before him
- Alexander's heir was an infant
- King Edward was the Maid's great uncle
- There were other people who thought they should rule (Balliol, Bruce)
- There was danger of a Civil War in Scotland
- Many Scottish nobles had land in England and looked to Edward for help

You can always get extra marks if you add more information to back up a point you are making. E.g. Alexander's heir was an infant (**1 mark**). Many Scots thought that a girl would not be able to rule (**1 mark**).

2. *You should try to make 5 separate points from recall.*

You could mention:

- John Balliol and the Scots had made an alliance with France against Edward
- John Balliol's men had attacked the north of England
- King Edward had defeated King John's army at Dunbar
- King Edward had pursued King John to the north of Scotland
- King John had surrendered to King Edward
- King Edward had stripped King John of his title and crown

You can always get extra marks if you bring in more information to back up a point you are making. E.g. John Balliol and the Scots had made an alliance with France against Edward (**1 mark**). This was known as the Auld Alliance (**1 mark**).

3. *You need to make 5 clear points about the usefulness of the source.*

You would probably start by arguing that the source does provide useful evidence about what happened at Falkirk. Comment on who wrote the source, when it was written and why it was written:

- The Source was written by an English Chronicler whose job was to record events of the time
- The source was written in 1298 not long after the battle
- The source was written to describe what happened at the Battle of Falkirk

You should then comment on the information contained in the source:

- The source mentions the use of schiltrons
- The source mentions that the Scottish horsemen fled the scene

However, you might mention that the source was written by an English chronicler so may be biased against the Scots.

You would gain marks by pointing out that in some ways the source is less useful because of important information that has not been mentioned. E.g. It does not mention that Edward failed to capture Wallace. It does not mention that the English archers played a decisive part in Edward's victory.

4. *Start off by saying that the source partly explains why it took so long for Bruce to be accepted. This allows you to go on to show what is and what is not in the source.*

The source mentions:

- Bruce had to force many Scots to abandon King John Balliol
- He had to force Scots to reject Edward II as overlord
- Bruce's efforts to spread the war to other parts of Britain were not successful

However the source does not mention:

- It took a long time to drive the English out of their castles in Scotland
- Bruce had been excommunicated so some people could not accept him as King
- Bruce took several years to defeat the Comyns and their allies

Section 1, Part B

1. *You should try to make 5 separate points from recall.*

You could mention:

- Protestantism had been spreading across Scotland
- The Catholic Church had been executing leading Protestants
- Cardinal Beaton had been supporting the French interests in Scotland
- The assassins tricked their way into St Andrews Castle
- Cardinal Beaton barricaded himself in his room
- Protestants broke the door down and stabbed him to death

You can always get extra marks if you bring in more information to back up a point you are making. E.g. the Catholic Church had been executing leading Protestants (**1 mark**) for example George Wishart was burned at the stake (**1 mark**).

2. *You need to make 5 clear points about the usefulness of the source.*

You would probably start by arguing that the source does provide useful evidence about what happened at Falkirk. Comment on who wrote the source, when it was written and why it was written:

- The source was written by a historian who would have studied the details of the murder
- The source was written many years after the event with the advantage of hindsight
- The source was written to describe Mary's actions at the time of Darnley's death

You should then comment on the information contained in the source:

- The source mentions that Mary had the valuable furniture removed from the house
- She had persuaded Darnley to come to Edinburgh

You would gain marks by pointing out that in some ways the source is less useful because of important information that has not been mentioned. E.g. letters were later found which showed Mary's support for the murder of Darnley.

3. *You should try to make 5 separate points from recall.*

You could mention:

- Bothwell was suspected of being involved in the murder of Darnley
- The Scottish nobles persuaded Mary to marry Bothwell
- Bothwell kidnapped Mary
- many believed Mary really wanted to marry Bothwell
- people would not accept being ruled by a murderess
- Mary married Bothwell in a Protestant ceremony

You can always get extra marks if you add more information to back up a point you are making. E.g Bothwell kidnapped Mary (**1 mark**) although some believe that she went with him voluntarily (**1 mark**).

4. *Start off by saying that the source partly describes the plot. This allows you to go on to show what is and what is not in the source.*

The source mentions:

- Mary sent coded letters concealed in a beer keg
- Elizabeth's men knew about the plot from the start because they had a spy in Mary's household
- Mary sent a letter approving the assassination of Elizabeth

However the source does not mention:

- Mary's letter was decoded by a spy
- The letters were presented to Elizabeth

Section 1, Part C

1. *You should try to make 5 separate points from recall.*

You could mention:

- The Worcester was seized in Leith harbour
- The Scots said that Captain Green of the Worcester had sunk one of their ships
- Scots said Green was a pirate
- The Scots thought that Queen Anne was going to order Green to be freed
- Green and two of his crewmen were hanged at Leith

You can always get extra marks if you add more information to back up a point you are making. E.g. the Worcester was seized in Leith Harbour (**1 mark**) this was revenge for English involvement in the seizure of a ship belonging to the Company of Scotland (**1 mark**).

2. *You need to make 5 clear points about the usefulness of the source.*

You would probably start by arguing that the source does provide useful evidence about Scottish attitudes to the Union. Comment on who wrote the source, when it was written and why it was written:

- The source was written by a spy working in Scotland
- The source was written at a time of protests against the Union
- The source was written to describe protests against the Union

You should then comment on the information contained in the source:

- The source describes a large Edinburgh mob protesting against the Union
- The source mentions the Scots calling the English "dogs"

You would gain marks by pointing out that in some ways the source is less useful because of important information that has not been mentioned. E.g. there were protests in many towns across Scotland. Scots feared that the Union would affect trade.

3. *You should try to make 5 separate points from recall.*

You could mention:

- The Jacobites promised to cancel the Act of Union
- Its supporters (Queen Anne and Hanoverians) became unpopular so the Jacobites became popular
- The Scots objected to Excise Duty and other taxes which would go if the Union was ended
- Scottish traders felt threatened by goods coming in from England
- Jacobites were "native"
- Scots felt that their country had been "taken over" by the English

You can always get extra marks if you bring in more information to back up a point you are making. E.g. Jacobites were seen by many Scots as "native" (**1 mark**). The Hanoverians were from Germany (**1 mark**).

4. *Start off by saying that the source partly describes the effects of the Union. This allows you to go on to show what is and what is not in the source.*

The source mentions:

- Money and jobs are going to England
- Scottish manufacturers are ruined
- Scottish troops are in English service

However the source does not mention:

- The Malt Tax and Customs and Excise were unpopular
- The Equivalent was not paid as promised
- Scots were beginning to trade freely with English colonies

Section 1, Part D

1. *You should try to make 5 separate points from recall.*

You could mention:

- Work was available on farms
- There was work in textile factories
- There was building work on the canals and railways
- There was work in the coal mines
- Wages were higher in Scotland
- Housing was available
- Many Irish had already settled in Scotland
- Scotland was close by

You can always get extra marks if you bring in more information to back up a point you are making. E.g. housing was available (**1 mark**) because Scottish towns were growing in size at this time (**1 mark**).

2. *You should try to make 5 separate points from recall.*

You could mention:

- The Irish had a reputation for criminal activity
- Irish navvies were shown as especially violent and lawless
- Scots thought they were taking Scottish jobs
- Scots saw them as competition for housing
- Scots felt the Irish were responsible for lowering wage rates
- Religious tensions

You can always get extra marks if you add more information to back up a point you are making. E.g. there were religious tensions between Scots and Irish (**1 mark**) most Irish were Catholic whereas Scots were Protestant (**1 mark**).

3. *You need to make 5 clear points about the usefulness of the source.*

You would probably start by arguing that the source does provide useful evidence about the reasons for Scottish emigration. Comment on who wrote the source, when it was written and why it was written:

- The source was written by an immigration agent from Canada
- The source was written in 1875 at a time of emigration from Scotland
- The source was written to describe attempts to encourage Scots to emigrate

You should then comment on the information contained in the source:

- The source mentions agents from different countries competing to attract immigrants
- The source mentions posters offering free passages.

You would gain marks by pointing out that in some ways the source is less useful because of important information that has not been mentioned. E.g. push factors such as some landlords were willing to assist their tenants to emigrate and some landlords would buy their tenants cattle from them.

4. *Start off by saying that the source partly describes the impact of Scottish emigrants. This allows you to go on to show what is and what is not in the source.*

The source mentions:

- Scots dominated government in Canada and Australia
- Scots dominated the Canadian fur trade
- A Scot founded the Australian sheep industry

However the source does not mention:

- Scots involvement in banking
- Scots helped to develop the education systems

Section 1, Part E

1. *You should try to make 5 separate points from recall.*

You could mention:

- Government organised a poster campaign
- Appeal to patriotism
- Desire to escape boring or difficult jobs
- Peer pressure
- War was not expected to last long
- Proud tradition of soldiering in Scotland

You can always get extra marks if you add more information to back up a point you are making. E.g. the government poster campaign (**1 mark**) for example the poster showing Kitchener saying "your country needs you" (**1 mark**).

2. *You should try to make 5 separate points from recall.*

You could mention:

- Subjected to ridicule/verbal abuse/white feathers
- Newspaper campaigns against them (e.g. articles or cartoons attacking conscientious objectors)
- Many conscientious objectors were physically assaulted
- Objectors were forced to appear before military tribunals
- Many sent to front as stretcher bearers/faced same risks as regular soldiers
- Some accepted non combat duties (e.g. ambulance drivers)
- Imprisonment of absolutists/pacifists

You can always get extra marks if you bring in more information to back up a point you are making. E.g. pacifists were often imprisoned (**1 mark**) they were singled out for harsh treatment for example were not given clothes (**1 mark**).

3. *Start off by saying that the source partly describes the effect of war on employment in Scotland. This allows you to go on to show what is and what is not in the source.*

The source mentions:

- Unemployment was higher in Scotland than elsewhere in the UK
- Unemployment was often long term
- Skilled workers left without work

However the source does not mention:

- Heavy industries laid off many workers
- New opportunities for women e.g. secretarial work

4. *You need to make 5 clear points about the usefulness of the source.*

You would probably start by arguing that the source does provide useful evidence about the contribution of the Suffragettes. Comment on who wrote the source, when it was written and why it was written:

- The source was written by Millicent Fawcett who was involved in the campaign
- The source was written in 1912 at a time of Suffragette militancy
- The source was written to describe the part played by the Suffragettes in the campaign for female suffrage

You should then comment on the information contained in the source.

- The Suffragettes were successful in drawing attention to their cause
- Many campaigners for the vote viewed the Suffragette's methods with disgust

You would gain marks by pointing out that in some ways the source is less useful because of important information that has not been mentioned. E.g. suffragettes won respect by stopping their campaign to support the war effort in 1914.

Section 2, Part C

1. *You need to make 6 clear points about the usefulness of the source.*

You would probably start by arguing that the source does provide useful evidence about resistance on the plantations. Comment on who wrote the source, when it was written and why it was written:

- The source was written by a historian who would have studied the period
- The source was written many years after slavery making it a secondary source
- It was written to describe resistance on the plantations

You should then comment on the information contained in the source:

- The source mentions the strict laws and codes to which slaves were subjected
- It mentions that slaves who broke laws were hunted down

You would gain marks by pointing out that in some ways the source is less useful because of important information that has not been mentioned. E.g. some slaves were successful in escaping and formed communities of escaped slaves such as the Maroons in Jamaica.

2. *If the question starts with "To what extent" you must write a balanced answer.*

In this question you should show that you understand that the abolitionist movement was important in bringing an end to the slave trade for the following reasons:

- Abolitionists such as Clarkson travelled to Britain educating people about what the trade was like
- Freed slaves such as Equiano published stories about their experiences
- Abolitionists such as Wilberforce put the case for abolition in Parliament
- Abolitionists organized petitions to Parliament against the slave trade

You should then balance your answer by giving other reasons for the end to the slave trade:

- The Quakers had campaigned against slavery before the Abolitionist movement began
- The Evangelical Christian movement spoke out against slavery
- Indian sugar was produced more cheaply without the use of slaves

- The rise of new industries such as coal and iron provided more profitable investments than slave produced products

Finish with a conclusion giving an overall answer to the question supported with a reason for the judgment you have made. E.g. overall, the Abolitionist movement was influential in ending the slave trade but economic reasons such as the development of sugar production in India were probably more important.

3. *You should try to make 6 separate points from recall.*

You could mention:

- New, profitable industries were growing in Britain
- The "sugar island" colonies were becoming less important
- Britain began to trade more with India and East Asia
- Slavery was seen as an inefficient way to produce goods
- More and more people began to recognise Africans as fellow human beings

You can always get extra marks if you add more information to back up a point you are making. E.g. Britain began to trade more with India and East Asia (**1 mark**). Sugar could be produced more cheaply in India without the use of slaves (**1 mark**).

Section 2, Part D

1. *If the question starts with "To what extent" you must write a balanced answer.*

In this question you should show that you understand that better sanitation did lead to improvements in health. You could mention:

- Piped water from clean reservoirs
- Piped sewerage systems
- Introduction of water closets

You should then balance your answer by giving other reasons such as:

- Control of the lethal diseases of childhood
- Victorian hospital building programs in Scottish cities
- Local Government Act 1889 – appointment of Medical Officers

Finish with a conclusion giving an overall answer to the question supported with a reason for the judgment you have made. E.g. overall, improvements in sanitation played an important part in tackling killer diseases such as cholera. However, better medical care also played a part in improving health.

2. *You should try to make 6 separate points from recall.*

You could mention:

- The need for fuel boosted the coal industry
- The need for tracks and locomotives boosted iron industry
- Postal services/communication became quicker and more efficient
- Railways provided cheaper transport of raw materials and manufactured goods
- Boost to employment for railway building
- Decline of canals

You can always get extra marks if you bring in more information to back up a point you are making. E.g. the need for fuel boosted the coal industry (**1 mark**). A reliable supply of fuel was needed for the growing number of steam locomotives (**1 mark**).

3. *You need to make 6 clear points about the usefulness of the source.*

You would probably start by arguing that the source does provide useful evidence about the importance of the Radical Wars. Comment on who wrote the source, when it was written and why it was written:

- The source was written many years after the event with the benefit of hindsight
- Written by reputable historians who will have researched the relevant primary sources
- Written to describe the Radical War

You should then comment on the information contained in the source:

- The source mentions that only a few workers took up arms
- The source mentions that the armed radicals found no support in Glasgow

You would gain marks by pointing out that in some ways the source is less useful because of important information that has not been mentioned. E.g. the radicals were urging people to commit treason the government took the threat seriously and sent troops to Glasgow.

Section 2, Part E

1. *You need to make 6 clear points about the usefulness of the source.*

You would probably start by arguing that the source does provide useful evidence about poverty at the end of the 19th century. Comment on who wrote the source, when it was written and why it was written:

- The source was produced at a time of poverty
- Aberdeen organisation representative of an industrial city which would experience more poverty
- Produced to show their willingness to help the "deserving poor"/sober and industrious who may become ill

You should then comment on the information contained in the source:

- Source says drinking and laziness are causes of poverty
- Source says only those willing to work and stay sober are to be helped

You would gain marks by pointing out that in some ways the source is less useful because of important information that has not been mentioned. E.g. some believed poverty was not always the fault of the individual (low wages/size of family/irregularity of work). Other causes of poverty as the fault of the individual such as gambling.

2. *You should try to make 5 separate points from recall.*

You could mention:

- Rationing helped encourage the idea of universal sharing of the nation's food supply rich and poor classes were mixing in society who previously had little in common
- War highlighted problems that could be overcome by government action

- The poor health of some city children evacuated to the country highlighted the problems of poverty
- Suffering of war caused a determination to create a better society once the war was over
- Other reforms had been made by the government during the war such as free health care for war wounded and bomb victims, Emergency Milk and Meals scheme, etc

You can always get extra marks if you bring in more information to back up a point you are making. E.g. war highlighted problems that could be overcome by government action (**1 mark**). This was highlighted by the Beveridge Report (**1 mark**).

3. *If the question starts with "To what extent" you must write a balanced answer.*

In this question you should show that you understand that free health care was important in getting people to welcome the Labour reforms.

You could mention:

- Free prescriptions under the new NHS
- Free dental care
- Free optical care

You should then balance your answer by giving other reasons such as:

- Free secondary education for all
- A National Insurance scheme to cover everybody
- A major new house building programme

Finish with a conclusion giving an overall answer to the question supported with a reason for the judgment you have made. E.g. overall, free health care was one of the most important reasons why people welcomed the Labour Reforms because it was a reform which benefitted everyone.

Section 3, Part B

1. *You should try to make 5 separate points from recall.*

You could mention:

- The British had been patrolling the seas to prevent smuggling/impose customs
- The British vessel Gaspée ran aground off the coast of Rhode Island
- The vessel was attacked by a crowd of local men
- The commander of the Gaspée was wounded by a musket shot
- The British government launched an investigation into the incident

You can always get extra marks if you bring in more information to back up a point you are making. E.g. the British government launched an investigation into the incident (**1 mark**) the people of Rhode Island refused to cooperate with the investigation (**1 mark**).

2. *Start off by saying that the source partly describes what happened at Bunker Hill. This allows you to go on to show what is and what is not in the source.*

The source mentions:

- British navy opened fire on the colonists
- The British charged the hill three times
- Eventually the colonists were driven back

However the source does not mention:

- British soldiers were left exposed to American musket fire as they made their way up the hill
- Bright uniforms of British soldiers made them easy targets
- British suffered 1000 casualties
- Colonists only suffered 400 casualties

3. *For this type of question you must say whether you think the sources agree or not and then support your decision by making two comparisons using evidence from the sources.*

For this question you would probably decide that the two sources agree. You could then back this up with two of the following comparisons:

- Source A says Cornwallis' position at Yorktown was deteriorating fast. Source B supports this by saying that Cornwallis ended up being in a poor position
- Source A points out that American forces prevented Cornwallis' Forces from moving inland. Source B backs this up by mentioning American troops moved in quickly to contain Cornwallis
- Source A says that the French defeated the British fleet in Chesapeake Bay and Source B supports this by pointing out that the French defeated the British fleet in a naval battle near Yorktown

4. *You should try to make 5 separate points from recall.*

You could mention:

- Poor leadership of British forces e.g. Howe, Cornwallis
- Tactical errors made by Britain e.g. Yorktown, Saratoga
- British army was small in number
- British soldiers were not properly trained/equipped to cope with terrain and conditions
- Colonial army was effectively led by George Washington
- Colonists had greater forces/able to call on minutemen when required
- Colonists benefited from assistance from foreign powers

You can always get extra marks if you bring in more information to back up a point you are making. E.g. the British army was small in number (**1 mark**) and had to rely on mercenary forces (**1 mark**).

Section 3, Part C

1. *You should try to make 5 separate points from recall.*

You could mention:

- They were chased from territory to territory as their numbers grew
- Their property was attacked
- They were condemned for their polygamy
- They were persecuted because of their beliefs
- They eventually found a place of safety in Utah

You can always get extra marks if you bring in more information to back up a point you are making. E.g. their property was attacked (**1 mark**). For example Mormon banks were burned to the ground (**1 mark**).

2. *Start off by saying that the source partly explains the outbreak of the war. This allows you to go on to show what is and what is not in the source.*

The source mentions:

- Lincoln sent a naval expedition to supply Fort Sumter
- Confederates opened fire on the fort
- Major Anderson surrendered
- The firing on Fort Sumter set off an outburst of patriotic fever in the North

However the source does not mention:

- Lincoln chose to ignore advice not to supply Fort Sumter
- The flying of the Union flag in Charleston harbour was seen as a provocative act by the South
- Lincoln immediately called for volunteers to avenge Fort Sumter

3. *You should try to make 5 separate points from recall.*

You could mention:

- Gave black Americans very few civil rights
- Prevented many black Americans from voting
- Prevented them from serving on juries
- Prevented from owning guns
- Restricted their right to own property
- Restrictions could not be overturned by northern politicians

You can always get extra marks if you bring in more information to back up a point you are making. E.g. restricted their right to own property (**1 mark**) also restricted the rights of black Americans to rent property (**1 mark**).

4. *For this type of question you must say whether you think the sources agree or not and then support your decision by making two comparisons using evidence from the sources.*

For this question you would probably decide that the two sources agree. You could then back this up with two of the following comparisons:

- Source A says the author was dismayed their life had shown no improvement for black people. Source B supports this by saying that attempts to improve conditions for black people had little effect in the South
- Source A points out that many black Americans remained in the South. Source B backs this up by mentioning because they were too poor, many stayed in the South
- Source A says that some white Americans felt justified in lynching and using violence against black people and Source B supports this by pointing out that secret organisations were set up to terrorise black people

Section 3, Part D

1. *You should try to make 5 separate points from recall.*

You could mention:

- Germany lost land to France, Belgium and Poland
- Germany was blamed for starting the First World War and ordered to pay reparations
- Germany's armed forces were reduced in size
- Germany was forbidden from uniting with Austria
- Germany lost all her overseas colonies
- The Rhineland was demilitarised

You can always get extra marks if you bring in more information to back up a point you are making. E.g. Germany lost land to France, Belgium and Poland (**1 mark**). This contributed to the problem of millions of German speaking people living outside Germany (**1 mark**).

2. *You should try to make 5 separate points from recall.*

You could mention:

- Enabling Act meant Hitler could pass laws without agreement of the Reichstag
- All political parties declared illegal
- Nazis employed spies/Gestapo agents
- Fear of the concentration camps deterred dissent
- Opponents arrested which weakened opposition groups
- Nazis controlled the media which inhibited free speech
- Nazis kept tight control of the young/Nazi-controlled education
- Nazi propaganda indoctrinated the German people
- Widespread support for the Nazis

You can always get extra marks if you bring in more information to back up a point you are making. E.g. fear of the concentration camps deterred dissent (**1 mark**) these were used to imprison anyone suspected of opposition to the Nazis (**1 mark**).

3. *Start off by saying that the source partly explains why Germans supported the Nazis. This allows you to go on to show what is and what is not in the source.*

The source mentions:

- The Nazis were seen as preferable to the Communists
- The Nazis appeared to be well disciplined
- Nazi propaganda pamphlets

However the source does not mention:

- Hitler offered simple solutions to economic problems
- Hitler promised to end the shame of the Versailles settlement
- Hitler offered scapegoats for Germany's problems

4. *For this type of question you must say whether you think the sources agree or not and then support your decision by making two comparisons using evidence from the sources.*

For this question you would probably decide that the two sources agree. You could then back this up with two of the following comparisons:

- Source A says that their weekends were crammed full with sporting activities and Source B says there was an emphasis on activity and sport
- Source A says that these were fun and Source B points out that many young Germans enjoyed activity and sport
- Source A says that this had a bad effect on school work and Source B felt that education was being downgraded

Section 3, Part E

1. *Start off by saying that the source partly explains why national minorities disliked Russification. This allows you to go on to show what is and what is not in the source.*

The source mentions:

- Non-Russians had to use the Russian language
- Russian clothing and customs were to be used
- Russian officials were put in to run regional governments
- Poles were told to change and become Russian citizens

However the source does not mention:

- Russians were the minority – only 44% of population
- Catholic Poles and Asiatic Muslims were pressurised to convert to Russian Orthodoxy
- Jews were persecuted for being "anti-Russian"
- Russian was used in schools and law courts

2. *You should try to make 5 separate points from recall.*

You could mention:

- The Tsar announced his October Manifesto
- A limited vote was extended to the peasants and industrial workers
- Many Liberals accepted these terms and ceased opposing the Tsar
- Right wing supporters of the Tsar began a wave of attacks on Jews and liberal intellectuals who had continued their opposition
- Witte was appointed Chairman of the Council of Ministers and arrested the entire St Petersburg soviet
- The troops stayed loyal to the Tsar and crushed opposition in Moscow
- The general strike came to an end as the middle classes withdrew their support
- The government announced the end of redemption dues to placate the peasants

You can always get extra marks if you bring in more information to back up a point you are making. E.g. the Tsar announced the October Manifesto (**1 mark**) this accepted cabinet government, free speech and a constitution for Russia (**1 mark**).

3. *You should try to make 5 separate points from recall.*

You could mention:

- Germany helped him to return to Russia
- Lenin travelled to Finland in a sealed train
- Lenin arrived at the Finland Station in Petrograd
- He made a speech calling for a second revolution
- He called for non cooperation with the Provisional Government
- He called for an end to the war
- He demanded land for the peasants
- He said that the Soviets should take control of Russia

You can always get extra marks if you bring in more information to back up a point you are making. E.g. Germany helped him to return to Russia (**1 mark**) they arranged for him to travel from Switzerland to Finland (**1 mark**).

4. *For this type of question you must say whether you think the sources agree or not and then support your decision by making two comparisons using evidence from the sources.*

For this question you would probably decide that the two sources mainly disagree.

You could then back this up with two of the following comparisons:

- Source A says that the Bolsheviks did not have the support of the Russian people but Source B says they had massive support
- Source A says that the revolution was caused by the chaos of war but Source B says it was brought about by people who had enough of misery/wanted a better life
- Source A says the Bolsheviks led the revolution but Source B says they simply guided it

Section 3, Part G

1. *You should try to make 5 separate points from recall.*

You could mention:

- Campaigned against immigration in the 1920s especially Jews and Roman Catholics
- Acted anonymously e.g. wore robes and hoods/ activities took place at night
- Used violence against opponents
- Used intimidation of black Americans e.g. fiery crosses/house burnings
- Infiltrated government e.g. 16 senators gained election in 1920s with KKK help
- Infiltrated state officials and police
- Large peaceful demonstrations e.g. 1928 march down Pennsylvania Avenue, Washington DC
- KKK was less active after 1925 as membership fell following allegations of corruption amongst Klan leadership

You can always get extra marks if you bring in more information to back up a point you are making. E.g. KKK used violence against its opponents (**1 mark**). For example there were lynchings where black people accused of crimes against whites were whipped and sometimes killed (**1 mark**).

2. *You should try to make 5 separate points from recall.*

You could mention:

- Hardship and humiliation caused by the Jim Crow laws
- Segregation of schools, transport, etc
- Inequality faced by black Americans in employment and housing
- Impact of 2nd World War e.g. black servicemen overseas had some experience of integration
- Refusal of southern states to desegregate following "Brown v Topeka"
- Success of the Montgomery Bus Boycott
- Effective leadership of the movement e.g. Martin Luther King
- Success of protests e.g. Birmingham, Washington, Selma
- Growing support from whites e.g. student groups like CORE

You can always get extra marks if you bring in more information to back up a point you are making. E.g. the hardship and humiliation caused by Jim Crow encouraged the growth of the Civil Rights Movement (**1 mark**). Some of these laws dated back 90 years (**1 mark**).

3. *For this type of question you must say whether you think the sources agree or not and then support your decision by making two comparisons using evidence from the sources.*

For this question you would probably decide that the two sources agree. You could then back this up with two of the following comparisons:

- Source A says this was to be Martin Luther King's first step towards becoming the leading figure in the Civil Rights Movement. Source B supports this by saying that as a result of the boycott, Martin Luther King became involved in the Civil Rights Movement
- Source A points out that the boycott lasted over a year. Source B backs this up by mentioning that the bus company's services were boycotted by 99% of Montgomery's African Americans for over a year
- Source A says that the courts decided that segregation on Montgomery's buses was illegal. Source B supports this by pointing out that the US Supreme Court announced that Alabama's bus segregation laws were illegal

4. *Start off by saying that the source partly explains why Malcolm X opposed non-violent protest. This allows you to go on to show what is and what is not in the source.*

The source mentions:

- Malcolm's mistreatment in his youth gave him different attitudes towards whites from Martin Luther King
- He became influenced by the ideas of Elijah Mohammed who preached hatred of white people
- He believed that support of non violence was a sign that black people were still living in mental slavery
- He believed violent language and threats would frighten the authorities into action

However the source does not mention:

- Malcolm X claimed that even whites who appeared friendly were "wolves in sheep's clothing"
- He believed that non violence deprived black people of their right to self-defense
- He claimed that peaceful protest gained little for most black people
- He didn't think non violent campaigns tackled the problems for black people in the northern cities

Section 3, Part H

1. *Start off by saying that the source partly explains the situation. This allows you to go on to show what is and what is not in the source.*

The source mentions:

- Germany withdrew from the Disarmament Conference
- Germany withdrew from the League
- France lost Poland as an ally

However the source does not mention:

- Hitler announced conscription
- The German army would rise to 500,000
- Hitler tried to take over Austria in 1934
- Hitler reoccupied the Rhineland

2. *You should try to make 5 separate points from recall.*

You could mention:

- German population was growing
- German territory had been restricted
- Germany needed access to food and raw materials
- Hitler wanted to regain territory lost by Versailles Treaty
- Austria should be annexed to Germany
- Belief that the Germans needed Lebensraum
- German minorities had a right to belong to Germany, e.g. Sudeten Germans

You can always get extra marks if you bring in more information to back up a point you are making. E.g. belief that the Germans needed Lebensraum (**1 mark**). Land in Eastern Europe for settlement and raw materials (**1 mark**).

3. *For this type of question you must say whether you think the sources agree or not and then support your decision by making two comparisons using evidence from the sources.*

For this question you would probably decide that the two sources disagree. You could then back this up with two of the following comparisons:

- Source A says Sudeten Germans should return to Germany. Source B disagrees with this by saying that the Sudetenland had never been part of Germany
- Source A points out that Sudeten Germans resented being part of Czechoslovakia since 1919. Source B disagrees by mentioning that Sudeten German unrest originated in the early 1930s
- Source A says that Sudeten Germans had been persecuted as ethnic minority and Source B opposes this by pointing out that they had been treated with respect

4. *You should try to make 5 separate points from recall.*

You could mention:

- Germany invaded Czechoslovakia in March 1939 breaking the Munich Agreement
- Great Britain sped up her rearmaments programme/ led to conscription
- Hitler demanded the return of Danzig from Poland
- Germany demanded permission to build a road and railway line through Poland
- Britain promised to defend Poland if she were attacked
- August 1939 Germany and Russia signed the Nazi-Soviet Non Aggression Pact
- September Germany invaded Poland
- Britain declared war on Germany

You can always get extra marks if you bring in more information to back up a point you are making. E.g. August 1939 Germany and Russia signed the Nazi-Soviet Non Aggression Pact (**1 mark**). This left Hitler free to attack Poland without fear of Russian opposition (**1 mark**).

Section 3, Part I

1. *You should try to make 5 separate points from recall.*

You could mention:

- Hitler had given his full backing to Guderian's tactics
- In 1940, Britain and France still had a World War One mentality and didn't recognise the potential of the new weapons
- What tanks they had were poor compared to the German Panzers
- British and French tactics were outdated
- Britain still had the mentality that as an island we were safe as our navy would protect us
- France hid behind the Maginot Line

You can always get extra marks if you bring in more information to back up a point you are making. E.g. what tanks they had were poor compared to the German Panzers (**1 mark**) which had thicker armour plating and superior weaponry (**1 mark**).

2. *Start off by saying that the source partly explains the effectiveness of resistance groups. This allows you to go on to show what is and what is not in the source.*

The source mentions:

- They gathered intelligence for the Allies
- They organised discovered French collaborators
- They killed many ranking Nazi officials
- They destroyed trains used by the German army

However the source does not mention:

- They ran cafes
- They made radio contact with Britain
- They concealed art works stolen by the Nazis

3. *You should try to make 5 separate points from recall.*

You could mention:

- Need for total secrecy
- Preserve element of surprise by landing in Normandy rather than using shortest crossing point
- Lack of natural harbours on Normandy coast
- Need for suitable weather conditions
- Lack of cover for troops on the beaches
- Providing troops with accurate information about enemy positions

You can always get extra marks if you bring in more information to back up a point you are making. E.g. lack of natural harbours on Normandy coast (**1 mark**) need for artificial "mulberry" harbours to land equipment and supplies (**1 mark**).

4. *For this type of question you must say whether you think the sources agree or not and then support your decision by making two comparisons using evidence from the sources.*

For this question you would probably decide that the two sources disagree. You could then back this up with two of the following comparisons:

- Source A says using the atomic bomb was a mistake. Source B disagrees by saying that using the atomic bomb was justified

- Source A points out that Japanese were already defeated and ready to surrender. Source B disagrees with this by mentioning that the Japanese government had decided to fight on to the last man
- Source A says that Hiroshima and Nagasaki was of no real help in our war against Japan and Source B opposes this by pointing out that Hiroshima and Nagasaki made them surrender sooner

Section 3, Part J

1. *You should try to make 5 separate points from recall.*

You could mention:

- The Soviet take-over of Eastern European countries had increased tension between East and West
- Churchill's Iron Curtain speech
- Offer of Marshall aid to all European countries
- Berlin airlift had increased tension between East and West
- Allies merged their zones to form West Germany
- NATO was formed in 1949
- NATO expanded in 1951 to include Greece and Turkey
- West Germany joined NATO in 1955

You can always get extra marks if you bring in more information to back up a point you are making. E.g. allies merged their zones to form West Germany, (**1 mark**). This formalised the division of Germany, increasing tension (**1 mark**).

2. *For this type of question you must say whether you think the sources agree or not and then support your decision by making two comparisons using evidence from the sources.*

For this question you would probably decide that the two sources disagree. You could then back this up with two of the following comparisons:

- Source A says the Soviet Union had the idea of installing a small number of nuclear missiles on Cuba. Source B disagrees with this by saying that Americans believed that the Soviets planned to place a large number of their missiles in Cuba
- Source A points out that Khrushchev did not want to start a war. Source B opposes this view by mentioning Americans regarded Soviet action as a warlike act
- Source A says that purpose of missiles was just to defend Cuba from American attack but Source B disagrees with this pointing out that missiles had an offensive purpose pointed directly at major American cities

3. *Start off by saying that the source partly explains why America became involved in Vietnam. This allows you to go on to show what is and what is not in the source.*

The source mentions:

- France asked America for assistance in Vietnam
- America feared that Vietnam would become communist
- They believed that they could establish a friendly government in South Vietnam, under the leadership of President Diem
- America feared that a civil war was developing in South Vietnam

However the source does not mention:

- America was increasingly concerned about the influence of China in south-east Asia
- There was a widespread belief in the Domino Theory
- There was a fear that other countries e.g. Thailand, Laos, Burma, Cambodia even New Zealand and Australia could fall to communism
- There was a general concern that America was falling behind in the Cold War at this time and needed to make a stand against communism
- American "advisors" had been in Vietnam to support the government of Diem since the early 1960s
- Gulf of Tonkin incident led America to become involved in a full scale war in Vietnam

4. *You should try to make 5 separate points from recall.*

You could mention:

- There had been a massive increase of refugees fleeing to the West
- Many people living in East Berlin saw that West Berlin was wealthier and had a more democratic society
- Many East Germans were unhappy at being separated from friends and family in the West
- It was felt that Berlin was a centre for western spies
- The East German government took the decision to close the border between East and West Berlin and build a wall.

You can always get extra marks if you bring in more information to back up a point you are making. E.g. there had been a massive increase of refugees fleeing to the West (**1 mark**). In the six months up to June 1961, 103,000 East Germans had fled through Berlin (**1 mark**).

NATIONAL 5 HISTORY MODEL PAPER 3

Section 1, Part A

1. *For this type of question you must say whether you think the sources agree or not and then support your decision by making two comparisons using evidence from the sources.*

For this question you would probably decide that the two sources disagree. You could then back this up with two of the following comparisons:

- Source A says that Balliol claimed to be descended from the eldest line of the family of David, Earl of Huntingdon. Source B disagrees with this – it did not matter that he was descended from the eldest of David's daughters
- Source A points out that it did not matter that Balliol was a generation younger than Bruce. Source B disagrees saying that Bruce was one generation closer to royalty than Balliol
- Source A says that the feudal law of primogeniture always supported the eldest line of the family and Source B denies this by pointing out that the feudal law of primogeniture did not apply to kingdoms

4

2. *You should try to make 5 separate points from recall.*

You could mention:

- The Bruces never supported him
- Balliol had accepted Edward as his overlord
- he was unable to stop Edward interfering
- he was defeated at Dunbar
- he was stripped of his title by Edward

You can always get extra marks if you add more information to back up a point you are making. E.g. he was unable to stop Edward interfering (**1 mark**) Edward heard legal appeals from Scots (**1 mark**).

5

3. *Start off by saying that the source partly explains the situation. This allows you to go on to show what is and what is not in the source.*

The source mentions:

- The Scots allowed as many of the English to cross the bridge as they could hope to defeat
- They slaughtered all who had crossed over
- Cressingham was killed
- De Warenne escaped

However the source does not mention:

- Scots hid on the Abbey Craig
- The English chose to cross the forth using the narrow bridge
- The English knights were forced to fight on marshy ground
- The English were defeated

6

4. *You should try to make 5 separate points from recall.*

You could mention:

- He murdered Comyn
- He ruined the Comyns by destroying their lands
- He destroyed the power of the Comyns' friends
- He captured castles
- He defeated Edward at Bannockburn
- He forced Scottish nobles to accept him as king

You can always get extra marks if you bring in more information to back up a point you are making. E.g. he destroyed the power of the Comyns' friends (**1 mark**) for example he defeated the MacDougalls (**1 mark**).

5

Section 1, Part B

1. *Start off by saying that the source partly explains why Henry interfered in Scotland. This allows you to go on to show what is and what is not in the source.*

The source mentions:

- Henry wanted Mary to marry his son
- Henry wanted to reduce French influence in Scotland
- Scotland and England had been at war
- Henry wanted to spread Protestantism

However the source does not mention:

- Mary had become queen in 1542 but had no husband
- Scots had broken their agreement to the marriage
- Henry aimed to enforce the Treaty of Greenwich
- Scottish protestants wanted Henry's support

6

2. *You should try to make 5 separate points from recall.*

You could mention:

- She was a woman so many Scots felt she would be incapable of ruling Scotland
- She was young and lacked experience
- She was Catholic and Scotland had recently become Protestant
- She had strong ties with France and many Scots feared French influence
- Scottish nobles had become used to running the country themselves

You can always get extra marks if you bring in more information to back up a point you are making. E.g. she had strong ties with France and many Scots feared French influence (**1 mark**) as was seen in Huntley's Rebellion (**1 mark**).

5

3. *For this type of question you must say whether you think the sources agree or not and then support your decision by making two comparisons using evidence from the sources.*

For this question you would probably decide that the two sources agree. You could then back this up with two of the following comparisons:

- Source A says Mary's supporters fought on for several years. Source B supports this by saying that Mary's supporters did not give up until 1573

- Source A points out that Moray and Lennox were killed. Source B backs this up by mentioning the death of the two regents
- Source A says that Edinburgh castle was captured and Source B supports this by pointing out that the castle was forced to surrender in 1573

4

4. *You should try to make 5 separate points from recall.*

You could mention:

- Elizabeth was Protestant and Mary was Catholic
- Elizabeth feared that Mary would return to Scotland and make it a base for opposition to her rule
- Elizabeth was supporting the Protestants who were now ruling Scotland
- Elizabeth was aware of plots against her to make Mary Queen of Britain
- Elizabeth feared the consequences of executing Mary

You can always get extra marks if you add more information to back up a point you are making. E.g. Elizabeth feared the consequences of executing Mary (**1 mark**). She did not want to give the idea that it was alright for queens to be executed (**1 mark**).

5

Section 1, Part C

1. *Start off by saying that the source partly explains why Scots invested in Darien. This allows you to go on to show what is and what is not in the source.*

The source mentions:

- Scottish prosperity depended on farming which suffered from bad weather and poor soil
- Scottish overseas trade was limited
- Scots thought that England's prosperity came from its overseas trade based on colonies
- Paterson promised them a colony where "trade will increase and money will make money"

However the source does not mention:

- The Hanoverian years made Scotland poorer
- Scots had seen huge profits made by the East India Company
- Scotland did not have any colonies
- They were told Darien was in a key location on the Isthmus of Panama between two oceans

6

2. *For this type of question you must say whether you think the sources agree or not and then support your decision by making two comparisons using evidence from the sources.*

For this question you would probably decide that the two sources agree. You could then back this up with two of the following comparisons:

- Source A says some Scots believed trading with England's colonies would make Scotland a richer country. Source B supports this by saying that Scots were angry that they could not make money by trading with England's colonies

- Source A points out that Scotland's trade (with France) was badly affected by England's frequent wars. Source B backs this up by mentioning they wanted to reduce the bad effects of England's war on Scotland's trade (Wine Act)
- Source A says that The Act of Security offered a shared monarch in return for access to England's colonies and Source B supports this by pointing out that they demanded access to England's colonies in return for sharing a monarch

4

3. *You should try to make 5 separate points from recall.*

You could mention:

- It promised "the Equivalent"
- It paid arrears of wages to those who supported the Union
- It insisted that government officials in Scotland support the Union
- It sent Argyll and Queensberry to organize support for the Union
- It paid bribes
- It offered well paid jobs
- It threatened military action

You can always get extra marks if you bring in more information to back up a point you are making. E.g. it threatened military action (**1 mark**). It made it clear that it had military forces in northern England and Ireland, which were ready to take action (**1 mark**).

5

4. *You should try to make 5 separate points from recall.*

You could mention:

- Queen Anne was to be succeeded by Hanoverians
- Hanoverians were seen as "foreign" compared to the "Scottish" Stuarts
- Hanoverian succession alarmed Catholics
- James VIII was ready to lead a rebellion
- Scots regretted the loss of their parliament
- The Equivalent had neither been paid promptly nor in cash

You can always get extra marks if you add more information to back up a point you are making. E.g. Hanoverian succession alarmed Catholics (**1 mark**). The Hanoverians were Protestant whereas Queen Ann was tolerant of Catholicism (**1 mark**).

5

Section 1, Part D

1. *You should try to make 5 separate points from recall.*

You could mention:

- Most of the Irish population lived in poverty
- They subsisted on a diet based on milk and potatoes
- They had very poor housing conditions
- There was little industry in the south of Ireland so unemployment was common
- In 1845 the potato crop was ruined by blight
- Millions of Irish people faced starvation

You can always get extra marks if you bring in more information to back up a point you are making. E.g. they had very poor housing conditions (**1 mark**) and large families often shared small hovels with their livestock (**1 mark**).

5

2. *Start off by saying that the source partly explains the importance of the church. This allows you to go on to show what is and what is not in the source.*

The source mentions:

- Church gave them a place to worship
- They could be baptized, married and buried
- Priests would listen to their problems
- Church offered a centre for social life

However the source does not mention:

- Priests could write letters for them
- Priests helped to find housing and work
- Provided charity in time of need

6

3. *You should try to make 5 separate points from recall.*

You could mention:

- The Highland Clearances
- Potato famine in the 1840s
- Decline of highland industries
- Rising cost of farmland
- Assisted passages
- Letters from relatives
- Higher wages

You can always get extra marks if you add more information to back up a point you are making. E.g. decline of highland industries (**1 mark**), for example the kelp industry (**1 mark**).

5

4. *For this type of question you must say whether you think the sources agree or not and then support your decision by making two comparisons using evidence from the sources.*

For this question you would probably decide that the two sources disagree. You could then back this up with two of the following comparisons:

- Source B says land was of poor quality. Source C denies this by saying that he has prepared good land and is preparing more
- Source B points out that he is lonely. Source C disagrees with this by mentioning that the community is doing well
- Source B says that he wants to return to Scotland and Source C disagrees saying that "this is the best place in the whole world"

4

Section 1, Part E

1. *Start off by saying that the source partly explains why so many Scots volunteered. This allows you to go on to show what is and what is not in the source.*

The source mentions:

- Opportunity for adventure
- Dangers were ignored
- War hysteria
- Anti-German propaganda

However the source does not mention:

- Government organised a poster campaign
- Appeal to patriotism
- Desire to escape boring or difficult jobs
- War was not expected to last long

6

2. *You should try to make 5 separate points from recall.*

You could mention:

- Women took on new jobs previously thought to be "male occupations"
- Women had to cope with food shortages
- Women had to cope with rationing
- Women had to keep the family going without male support
- Women had to cope with bereavement

You can always get extra marks if you bring in more information to back up a point you are making. E.g. women took on new jobs previously thought to be "male occupations" (**1 mark**). They drove buses and trams (**1 mark**).

5

3. *You should try to make 5 separate points from recall.*

You could mention:

- Foreign customers had developed their own industries
- Foreign customers had gone elsewhere for heavy goods
- Lack of investment in modernization during the war
- Less demand for warships in peacetime
- New industries were more profitable for investors

You can always get extra marks if you add more information to back up a point you are making. E.g. foreign customers had developed their own industries (**1 mark**). For example, countries in Asia had developed their own textile industry (**1 mark**).

5

4. *For this type of question you must say whether you think the sources agree or not and then support your decision by making two comparisons using evidence from the sources.*

For this question you would probably decide that the two sources partly agree. You could then back this up with two of the following comparisons:

- Source A says that the government feared a socialist rising and Source B supports this by pointing out that the government was worried about the loyalty of the police and armed forces
- Source A says the workers were ready to carry out a socialist rising. Source B disagrees saying that socialist leaders had little support for their plans

- Source A points out that by Saturday, Clydeside could have been in the workers hands. Source B disagrees saying that the workers went to watch football on Saturday

4

Section 2, Part C

1. *You need to make 6 clear points about the usefulness of the source.*

You would probably start by arguing that the source does provide useful evidence about the treatment of slaves on the Middle Passage. Comment on who wrote the source, when it was written and why it was written:

- The source was written by a historian who would have studied the period
- The source was written many years after slavery ended, giving the benefit of hindsight
- It was written to describe what the Middle Passage was like

You should then comment on the information contained in the source:

- The source mentions that slaves were whipped to make them exercise
- It mentions that the slaves were given poor food

You would gain marks by pointing out that in some ways the source is less useful because of important information that has not been mentioned. E.g. female slaves were often subjected to sexual abuse.

6

2. *You should try to make 6 separate points from recall.*

You could mention:

- The main British ports were London, Bristol and Liverpool
- Glasgow did not share in British Empire trade until 1707 and did not trade in large numbers. However the port did profit from the sugar trade which was closely linked to the slave trade
- Until 1698 London was the only port permitted to trade in African slaves. Shipping and support services all profited from the monopoly. Entrepeneurs were prepared to take risks necessary on the triangular trade
- The City of London profited from financial services provided such as insurance and loans. Banks were established such as Barclays to provide loans to other merchants
- Bristol merchants spent profits on fine buildings in the city centre
- Industries around Bristol such as copper smelting, sugar refining and glass making grew as a result of the slave trade
- Liverpool docks were deep and large and could supply, service and unload large slave ships. Those facilities made Liverpool into richest of slave trading centre
- The Liverpool dockland was filled with sugar warehouses

You can always get extra marks if you add more information to back up a point you are making. E.g. the slave trade was very profitable (**1 mark**). Merchants could make a profit at every point of the triangle (**1 mark**).

6

3. *If the question starts with "To what extent" you must write a balanced answer.*

In this question you should show that you understand that the Zong was important to the growth of the abolitionist campaign:

- The Zong case showed the cruelty of the Middle Passage
- The case was widely reported in newspapers
- Abolitionists such as Sharp publicized the case

You should then balance your answer by giving other reasons for this success:

- Importance of the Quaker campaign against the slave trade
- Importance of other court cases which highlighted the cruelty of slavery e.g. Somerset case
- Importance of the contribution of freed slaves in Britain such as Equiano
- Importance of the campaign in Parliament

Finish with a conclusion giving an overall answer to the question supported with a reason for the judgement you have made. E.g. the case of the Zong was important to the growth of the Abolitionist movement because the shocking details of the case were widely publicized and turned people against the trade. However, other factors such as contribution of freed slaves were also important.

8

Section 2, Part D

1. *You should try to make 6 separate points from recall.*

You could mention:

- The increase in urban population had led to severe overcrowding
- Housing was often built to a poor standard e.g. lacked ventilation/sun light
- The lack of proper sanitation
- People in cities often had poor diet e.g. lack of access to fresh milk, fruit and vegetables
- Poor city dwellers had limited access to proper medical care
- Poor working conditions often led to ill-health

You can always get extra marks if you bring in more information to back up a point you are making. E.g. one reason for poor health was the increase in the urban population, which led to overcrowding (**1 mark**). Whole families would often have to share one or two rooms allowing disease to spread (**1 mark**).

6

2. *You need to make 6 clear points about the usefulness of the source.*

You would probably start by arguing that the source does provide useful evidence about improvements in technology in the textile industry. Comment on who wrote the source, when it was written and why it was written:

- The source was written at a time of improvement in the textile industry
- The source was written by an eyewitness
- The source was written to describe how changes in technology in textile manufacture affected people

You should then comment on the information contained in the source:

- The source mentions improvements in living standards
- The source mentions harmful effects of new technology on workers' health

You would gain marks by pointing out that in some ways the source is less useful because of important information that has not been mentioned. E.g. new technology made some skilled workers redundant and there were accidents caused by the new machinery.

6

3. *If the question starts with "To what extent" you must write a balanced answer.*

In this question you should show that you understand that the Radicals posed a threat to order in Scotland.

You could mention:

- Radical notices were posted in Glasgow calling on people to revolt
- Workers in Glasgow and surrounding towns attempted a rebellion
- One group of armed Radicals marched on Glasgow
- A group of armed Radicals marched towards the Carron Iron Works
- There was widespread fear of violent disorder

You should then balance your answer by giving other reasons such as:

- Only a few workers took up arms
- The Radicals were too disorganised to carry out their plan
- Forces involved are too weak to pose any serious threat
- At Bonnymuir the troops easily crushed the Radicals
- The Glasgow uprising of 1820 was small scale

Finish with a conclusion giving an overall answer to the question supported with a reason for the judgement you have made. E.g. overall, although the Radicals caused concern among the population they lacked support and were too disorganized to pose a serious threat to order in Scotland.

8

Section 2, Part E

1. *You should try to make 6 separate points from recall.*

You could mention:

- The information produced by surveys of poverty by Booth and Rowntree showed the extent of poverty among children and the elderly
- Investigators had drawn attention to the fact that many poor children got no benefit from their education due to hunger/ill-health
- Socialist groups campaigned for school meals and old age pensions
- Recruits for the army during the Boer war failed the basic army medical
- Poor state of workers made it more difficult for Britain to compete with other countries
- Countries like Germany appeared to have benefited from the introduction of pensions

- Some younger Liberal MPs became convinced that direct action to help children and the elderly was necessary

You can always get extra marks if you add more information to back up a point you are making. E.g. Socialist groups campaigned for school meals and old age pensions (**1 mark**). Liberals were concerned that they might lose votes to the new Labour Party (**1 mark**).

6

2. *You need to make 6 clear points about the usefulness of the source.*

You would probably start by arguing that the source does provide useful evidence about attitudes to the welfare state after the Second World War. Comment on who wrote the source, when it was written and why it was written:

- The author was Prime Minister at the beginning of 1945 and would know about welfare reform

- The source comes from a speech made at a time when welfare reform was being debated

- It was written to explain why Welfare Reform was not necessary

You should also comment on what the source says:

- The source tells us that Labour reformers were unrealistic dreamers

- It says that British people should be free to plan their own lives

You could decide however that in some ways the source is less useful because:

- Churchill was campaigning against Labour's plans for reform so he could be biased

- His party was heavily defeated in the election, which suggests that his views were not widely supported

You could also decide that in some ways the source is less useful because of important information that has not been mentioned:

- Many British people supported the idea of welfare reform

- Beveridge Report was very popular in Britain/ sold thousands of copies

6

3. *If the question starts with "To what extent" you must write a balanced answer.*

In this question you should show that you understand how rationing helped to change attitudes towards poverty.

You could mention:

- Rationing was introduced by the government to try to ensure that food was distributed equally to everyone

- The government was stepping in to make sure that poor people were not deprived of food because of rising prices

- Many people thought that this kind of intervention by the government was fair

You should then balance your answer by giving other reasons such as:

- Many people agreed with government support for victims of bombing

- Evacuation made more middle class people aware of the effects of poverty

- The war brought a desire for a fairer society after the war

- Many people supported/were influenced by the Beveridge Report of 1942

Finish with a conclusion giving an overall answer to the question supported with a reason for the judgement you have made. E.g. overall, the experience of rationing was very important in changing attitudes to poverty because everybody had to accept that there was need to ration food.

8

Section 3, Part B

1. *Start off by saying that the source partly explains why many colonists had turned against British rule. This allows you to go on to show what is and what is not in the source*

The source mentions:

- People were persuaded by Paine that the British government were abusing the rights of the American people

- Paine's ideas were very popular

- The King had rejected the Olive Branch Petition

- The British were using mercenary soldiers to help them run the colonies

However the source does not mention:

- Anger at unfair taxation

- Colonists felt that actions of the British government were damaging trade

- Anger among the colonists about the growing number of British soldiers in the colonies

- Acts of violence by the British e.g. Boston Massacre

- Lack of representation in the British parliament

5

2. *You need to make 5 clear points about the usefulness of the source.*

You would probably start by arguing that the source does provide useful evidence about why the Boston Massacre took place. Comment on who wrote the source, when it was written and why it was written:

- The source was written by a British officer who was involved in the massacre

- The source was written shortly after the massacre took place

- The source was written to explain why the massacre took place

You should then comment on the information contained in the source:

- A British soldier fired accidently

- The British were attacked by a great number

You might want to comment on ways in which the source is less useful:

- The source was written by a British soldier which makes it biased

You would gain marks by pointing out that in some ways the source is less useful because of important information that has not been mentioned. E.g. there had been a build up of tension between the colonists and the British people in Boston were furious about the new system of taxation that had been imposed.

5

3. *You should try to make 5 separate points from recall.*

You could mention:

- France provided the colonies with military assistance; soldiers, gunpowder, etc
- The French attacked British colonies in the Caribbean and elsewhere
- The French harassed British shipping in the Atlantic
- Foreign intervention caused Britain to lose its control of the seas
- Foreign intervention made it more difficult for Britain to reinforce and supply its forces in America
- Spain distracted Britain by attacking Gibraltar
- A Franco-Spanish force threatened Britain with invasion in 1779

You can always get extra marks if you bring in more information to back up a point you are making. E.g. France provided the colonies with military assistance soldiers, gunpowder etc. (**1 mark**) and loans to pay for military supplies (**1 mark**).

5

4. *You should try to make 5 separate points from recall.*

You could mention:

- Most colonists were of British descent
- Many colonists were becoming wealthy through trade with Britain
- Some loyalists believed that the conflict was the colonists's fault
- Some colonists had loyalty to the British king
- Some colonists feared the spread of revolutionary ideas

You can always get extra marks if you add more information to back up a point you are making. E.g. some colonists had loyalty to the British king (**1 mark**) and they hoped to win favour with the British government (**1 mark**).

5

Section 3, Part C

1. *Start off by saying that the source partly explains the situation. This allows you to go on to show what is and what is not in the source.*

The source mentions:

- Hunters shot buffalo to provide meat for settlers
- Settlers crossed into sacred land of Native Americans
- Settlers shot buffalo for sport

However the source does not mention:

- Settler's attitude to land ownership offended Natives
- Settlers broke treaties
- Building of railroads

5

2. *You should try to make 5 separate points from recall.*

You could mention:

- Many Northerners felt slavery was morally wrong
- It violated the principles of democracy
- Growth in abolitionist feeling
- Horror of slave life intensified sectional feeling
- Dred Scott decision intensified sectional feeling

- Republican party campaigned against the expansion of slavery

You can always get extra marks if you add more information to back up a point you are making. E.g. horror of slave life intensified sectional feeling (**1 mark**). The novel *Uncle Tom's Cabin* was widely read in the North (**1 mark**).

5

3. *You should try to make 5 separate points from recall.*

You could mention:

- Prevent slavery being extended beyond its current limits
- Free land for farmers
- Grant land to build railroads/subsidise the building of transcontinental railway
- Mining and timber companies would get cheap federal land
- High tariffs to protect northern industries
- Preserve the Union
- Encourage westward expansion

You can always get extra marks if you bring in more information to back up a point you are making. E.g. encourage westward expansion (**1 mark**). Republicans were committed to the idea of Manifest Destiny (**1 mark**).

5

4. *You need to make 5 clear points about the usefulness of the source.*

You would probably start by arguing that the source does provide useful evidence about the effects of the Ku Klux Klan's tactics on black Americans. Comment on who wrote the source, when it was written and why it was written:

- Source written by a historian who would have studied the period
- Source written many years after the event with the benefit of hindsight
- Source written to explain the effects of the KKK on black Americans

You should then comment on the information contained in the source:

- The source mentions the Klan wearing robes to conceal their identity
- The source also mentions KKK lynching its victims

You would gain marks by pointing out that in some ways the source is less useful because of important information that has not been mentioned. E.g. KKK had supporters in positions of importance in the South.

5

Section 3, Part D

1. *You should try to make 5 separate points from recall.*

You could mention:

- Hitler and some Nazis interrupted a meeting at a Munich Beer Hall
- Von Kahr and Bavarian leaders were threatened into offering support to the Nazis
- Von Kahr and other leaders later their withdrew support and ordered the putsch to be crushed
- Next day Hitler marched to the town centre in Munich with 3,000 Nazis

- Nazi supporters were forced back by troops and police
- Hitler was later arrested
- Hitler was tried and imprisoned

You can always get extra marks if you bring in more information to back up a point you are making. E.g. Hitler and some Nazis interrupted the meeting (**1 mark**). Goering and 25 Nazis burst in to the Beer Hall (**1 mark**).

5

2. *Start off by saying that the source partly explains the situation. This allows you to go on to show what is and what is not in the source.*

The source mentions:

- No one party was ever able to win a majority of the seats in the Reichstag
- Germany was ruled by a series of coalitions which many thought provided only weak government
- Many felt that politicians were too busy arguing among themselves to solve the country's problems

However the source does not mention:

- Weimar Republic was associated in people's minds with the capitulation in WWI
- It was also blamed for the signing of the Versailles settlement
- Many blamed the government for Germany's economic problems

5

3. *You should try to make 5 separate points from recall.*

You could mention:

- Little cooperation between opposition groups
- Opposition leaders were arrested put in concentration camps or killed
- Opposition groups were often infiltrated by the Gestapo/spies
- All opposition was declared illegal after 1933 (Enabling Act)
- Trade Unions were declared illegal
- Intimidation by the SS
- Nazis controlled the media
- Nazis kept a tight control over the young

You can always get extra marks if you add more information to back up a point you are making. E.g. Nazis controlled the media (**1 mark**), which issued a stream of constant Nazi propaganda (**1 mark**).

5

4. *You need to make 5 clear points about the usefulness of the source.*

You would probably start by arguing that the source does provide useful evidence about militarism in Nazi Germany. Comment on who wrote the source, when it was written and why it was written:

- Source written by historians who would have studied the period
- Source written some years after the events with the benefit of hindsight
- Source written to describe the Nazi regime

You should then comment on the information contained in the source:

- The source mentions military discipline on work-camps
- The source also mentions that workers were encouraged to see themselves as soldiers of work

You would gain marks by pointing out that in some ways the source is less useful because of important information that has not been mentioned. E.g. military style discipline in the Hitler Youth and similar discipline in schools.

5

Section 3, Part E

1. *You need to make 5 clear points about the usefulness of the source.*

You would probably start by arguing that the source does provide useful evidence about Nicholas II. Comment on who wrote the source, when it was written and why it was written:

- The source was written by someone who lived under the Tsar's rule
- The source was written some time after the Tsar's rule with hindsight
- The source was written to describe the Tsar's rule

You might want to comment on ways in which the source is less useful:

- The source was written by an enemy of the Tsar so likely to be biased

You should then comment on the information contained in the source:

- The source mentions the Tsar was unreliable
- The source also mentions his stupidity

You would gain marks by pointing out that in some ways the source is less useful because of important information that has not been mentioned. E.g. the Tsar had been brought up to be an autocrat. The Tsar was dedicated to his family.

5

2. *You should try to make 5 separate points from recall.*

You could mention:

- Striking factory workers in St Petersburg marched to the Winter Palace
- The march was led by Father Gapon, a police spy
- The workers wanted to petition the Tsar about their working conditions/long hours and low pay
- The crowd was large (200,000) but peaceful and included women and children
- Marchers wore their Sunday clothes, sang hymns and carried icons
- Mounted Cossacks at the front charged the marchers
- Soldiers panicked and opened fire, killing and injuring many

You can always get extra marks if you bring in more information to back up a point you are making. E.g. marchers wore their Sunday clothes, sang hymns and carried icons (**1 mark**). Some carried portraits of the Tsar (**1 mark**).

5

3. *You should try to make 5 separate points from recall.*

You could mention:

- The war was going badly
- Defeats and losses blamed on Tsar and Tsarina
- Influence of Rasputin
- Peasants opposed conscription
- Middle classes wanted democratic reforms
- Workers faced shortages, inflation and unemployment

You can always get extra marks if you add more information to back up a point you are making. E.g. workers faced shortages and inflation (**1 mark**), which had reached 300% by February 1917 (**1 mark**).

5

4. *Start off by saying that the source partly explains why the Bolsheviks were able to stay in power in Russia. This allows you to go on to show what is and what is not in the source.*

The source mentions:

- Landlord's right to property was abolished so land could be redistributed
- Sovnarkom could pass new laws
- Elections held to the Constitutional Assembly
- Cheka set up to wipe out counter-revolutionary activity

However the source does not mention:

- Signed armistice with Germany
- Constitutional Assembly was closed down after one meeting
- Censorship of media

5

Section 3, Part G

1. *You should try to make 5 separate points from recall.*

You could mention:

- The laws enforced separate schools for blacks and whites
- They enforced separate toilets and restrooms
- Some states made marriages between whites and blacks illegal
- Ensured that transport facilities – trains and buses – were segregated
- Supreme Court decision in 1896 Plessy case enshrined the "separate but equal" idea in law and made Jim Crow laws acceptable
- Some laws hindered blacks from voting
- Led to black Americans feeling humiliated/feeling like second citizens/feeling inferior
- Led to anger and demands for change

You can always get extra marks if you bring in more information to back up a point you are making. E.g. the Jim Crow laws enforced separate schools for blacks and whites (**1 mark**). Schools for black children were usually poorly equipped compared to white schools (**1 mark**).

5

2. *You need to make 5 clear points about the usefulness of the source.*

You would probably start by arguing that the source does provide useful evidence about the effects of the Birmingham protest. Comment on who wrote the source, when it was written and why it was written:

- The source was written by the President who had to deal with the events at Birmingham
- The source was written at the time of the events
- The source was written to describe the effects of what was happening in Birmingham

You should then comment on the information contained in the source:

- The source mentions events were damaging the reputation of the US
- The source also mentions that events in Birmingham increased the need for equality

You would gain marks by pointing out that in some ways the source is less useful because of important information that has not been mentioned. E.g. segregation was lifted in Birmingham and there were revenge killings of Civil Rights workers by the KKK.

5

3. *Start off by saying that the source partly explains the situation. This allows you to go on to show what is and what is not in the source.*

The source mentions:

- Thousands of buses and many trains were needed to bring the crowd into Washington
- 20% of the protesters were white
- The huge demonstration was peaceful and orderly

However the source does not mention:

- Martin Luther King's speech
- Coverage of the event was international
- Boosted support for a new Civil Rights Act

5

4. *You should try to make 5 separate points from recall.*

You could mention:

- Speeches against peaceful protest by Malcolm X and Stokely Carmichael
- Feeling that the Civil Rights Movement had done little to help black people in the North
- Long hot summers brought black youths on to the streets
- White police patrolled black areas
- Police harassment of black youths

You can always get extra marks if you add more information to back up a point you are making. E.g. police harassment of black youths (**1 mark**). For example the arrest and beating up of a black youth sparked the Watts Riot in LA (**1 mark**).

5

Section 3, Part H

1. *You need to make 5 clear points about the usefulness of the source.*

You would probably start by arguing that the source does provide useful evidence about Nazi ideas on race. Comment on who wrote the source, when it was written and why it was written:

- Source written by Nazis
- Source written in 1934 at the start of the Nazi regime
- Source written to put forward Nazi racial theory

You should then comment on the information contained in the source:

- The source mentions people of German blood had defended Europe in the past
- The source also mentions Aryan race is superior to others

You would gain marks by pointing out that in some ways the source is less useful because of important information that has not been mentioned. E.g. Jews were a target of Nazi ideas on race and Nazis believed in the notion of racial purity.

4

2. *Start off by saying that the source partly explains why Hitler wanted to rearm Germany. This allows you to go on to show what is and what is not in the source.*

The source mentions:

- Germany had been disarmed in 1919
- Hitler wanted to take every opportunity to attack the Treaty of Versailles
- Germany was surrounded by "hostile" enemies
- A strong Germany would safeguard European civilisation

However the source does not mention:

- Rearmament was a long term goal of Hitler's foreign policy
- Hitler interpreted the lack of disarmament by the allied powers as a breech of Versailles
- Hitler claimed that Europe was under threat from Communist USSR

5

3. *You should try to make 5 separate points from recall.*

You could mention:

- British public opinion favoured peace
- Memories of the horrors of the Great War
- Britain was weakened by economic depression
- British armed forces were over-stretched by the need to defend the empire
- Defence chiefs warned politicians against the war
- Britain lacked reliable allies

You can always get extra marks if you add more information to back up a point you are making. E.g. Britain lacked reliable allies (**1 mark**) as the USA was isolationist and France favoured defence (**1 mark**).

5

4. *You should try to make 5 separate points from recall.*

You could mention:

- Nazi agitation in Sudetenland organised by Henlein
- Runciman mission failed to persuade Czechs to hand over Sudetenland
- First meeting between Hitler and Chamberlain – agreement to transfer Sudetenland
- Second meeting – Hitler makes new demands
- Munich Conference – arranges for transfer of Sudetenland
- March 1939 – Hitler invades Czech territory

You can always get extra marks if you bring in more information to back up a point you are making. E.g. at the second meeting between Hitler and Chamberalain, Hitler made new demands (**1 mark**). He required the immediate hand over of the Sudetenland (**1 mark**).

5

Section 3, Part I

1. *You need to make 5 clear points about the usefulness of the source.*

You would probably start by arguing that the source does provide useful evidence about Blitzkrieg tactics. Comment on who wrote the source, when it was written and why it was written:

- The source was written by a German tank commander
- The source was written at the time of Blitzkrieg attacks
- The source was written to describe the effectiveness of Blitzkrieg

You might want to comment on ways in which the source is less useful:

- The source was written by a German soldier who may be biased

You should then comment on the information contained in the source:

- The source mentions terror caused to French soldiers and civilians
- The source also mentions the speed of the attack

You would gain marks by pointing out that in some ways the source is less useful because of important information that has not been mentioned. E.g. importance of air power and the use of Blitzkrieg in other campaigns during 1940 e.g. Denmark and the Netherlands.

5

2. *You should try to make 5 separate points from recall.*

You could mention:

- Shortages of food and fuel
- Presence of enemy soldiers
- Severe punishment for "crimes" committed against the occupying force
- Censorship of newspapers and radio
- Restrictions on travel

You can always get extra marks if you bring in more information to back up a point you are making. E.g. Shortages of food and fuel (**1 mark**). Fore example, the "hongerwinter" 1944 in the Netherlands (**1 mark**).

5

3. *Start off by saying that the source partly explains the situation. This allows you to go on to show what is and what is not in the source.*

The source mentions:

- Rescue and sheltering of Jews
- Manufacture of false papers
- Distribution of secret documents
- Involvement of over 50,000 individuals in the resistance

However the source does not mention:

- Rescuing and concealing allied airmen
- Sabotage of enemy installations
- Assassination of enemy officers

5

4. *You should try to make 5 separate points from recall.*

You could mention:

- Japan faced severe shortage of war materials
- Army and airforce had taken huge losses
- Destruction of the Japanese fleet
- Devastating air raids on Japanese cities
- US economy in full war production
- Atomic bombs dropped on Hiroshima and Nagasaki

You can always get extra marks if you add more information to back up a point you are making. E.g. Japan faced a severe shortage of war materials (**1 mark**) and was still involved in a costly war in China (**1 mark**).

5

Section 3, Part J

1. *Start off by saying that the source partly explains the situation. This allows you to go on to show what is and what is not in the source.*

The source mentions:

- A new labour law preventing strikes had caused unrest in the factories
- There were shortages of food and higher prices
- There had been a massive increase of refugees fleeing to the West
- In the six months up to June 1961, 103,000 East Germans had fled through Berlin

However the source does not mention:

- Many people living in East Berlin saw that West Berlin was wealthier and had a more democratic society
- Many East Germans were unhappy at being separated from friends and family in the West
- It was felt that Berlin was a centre for western spies
- The East German government took the decision to close the border between East and West Berlin and build a wall

5

2. *You should try to make 5 separate points from recall.*

You could mention:

- The Soviet Union had developed an alliance with Cuba following Castro's seizure of power
- With Castro's agreement, the Soviet Union constructed missile launch sites on Cuba

- Soviet cargo ships with missiles on board headed for Cuba, despite American protests
- U2 spy plane shot down by Soviet missile over Cuba
- Khrushchev thought he could take advantage of youth and inexperience of American President, Kennedy
- Khrushchev eventually backed down
- Soviet missiles were removed from Cuba in exchange for the removal of American ones in Europe

You can always get extra marks if you bring in more information to back up a point you are making. E.g. Khrushchev eventually backed down (**1 mark**) when Kennedy held firm to his blockade around Cuba (**1 mark**).

5

3. *You should try to make 5 separate points from recall.*

You could mention:

- US forces seemed to be making little progress in the war
- Thousands of American casualties
- War was widely reported on TV
- Disgust at the use of chemical weapons such as Napalm
- Student protests against the war
- Prominent figures such as Martin Luther King spoke out against the war

You can always get extra marks if you add more information to back up a point you are making. E.g. disgust at the use of chemical weapons such as Napalm (**1 mark**) and Agent Orange, which was shown to cause birth defects in Vietnamese children (**1 mark**).

5

4. *You need to make 5 clear points about the usefulness of the source.*

You would probably start by arguing that the source does provide useful evidence about why the process of détente had come to a halt by the early 1980s. Comment on who wrote the source, when it was written and why it was written:

- Source written by the President of the United States who dealt directly with the Soviet leadership
- Source written in 1983 when détente was collapsing
- Source written to explain why détente could no longer continue

You should then comment on the information contained in the source:

- The source mentions the build up of Soviet military might
- The source also mentions that the freeze on nuclear weapons made peace less secure

You would gain marks by pointing out that in some ways the source is less useful because of important information that has not been mentioned. E.g. the Soviet invasion of Afghanistan had increased tension and the USA boycott of Moscow Olympics increased tension.

5

NATIONAL 5 HISTORY
2014

Section 1, Context A, The Wars of Independence, 1286-1328

1. *Candidates can be credited in a number of ways up to a maximum of 5 marks.*

Candidates must show a causal relationship between events.

Up to a **maximum of 5 marks in total**, **1 mark** should be given for each accurate, relevant reason, and a **second mark** should be given for reasons that are developed. Candidates may achieve full marks by providing five straightforward reasons, three developed reasons, or a combination of these.

Possible reasons may include:
1. Alexander III had died without a surviving male heir/ Scots had agreed the infant Margaret was his heir, Edward approached for help
2. Edward had been Alexander's brother-in-law and a friend
3. Edward was a strong king who could use his authority to subdue Scottish troublemakers/there was a threat of civil war
4. Edward was Margaret's great uncle so could claim an interest as a relative
5. The Scots agreed to the Treaty of Birgham and the marriage of Margaret to Edward's infant son
6. Margaret died before she reached Scotland so there was now no direct heir – a further opportunity for Edward's involvement
7. Bishop Fraser invited Edward to help choose from the claimants to the throne
8. Edward insisted the claimants/competitors accepted him as their overlord before he would begin to judge the claims
9. Edward insisted the Scottish castles be handed over to him, to hold for the eventual king
10. All the competitors accepted that Edward was overlord
11. Edward judged that John Balliol had the best claim
12. Balliol paid homage to Edward for Scotland after his coronation, making Edward's superiority clear

2. *Candidates can be credited in a number of ways up to a maximum of 5 marks.*

They may take different perspectives on the events and may describe a variety of different aspects of the events.

1 mark should be given for each accurate relevant key point of knowledge. **A second mark** should be given for each point that is developed, up to a maximum of **5 marks**. Candidates may achieve full marks by providing five straightforward points, by making three developed points, or a combination of these.

Possible points of knowledge may include:
1. Wallace and Murray joined forces on the north side of the River Forth
2. The Scots were on the high ground of Abbey Craig/the English assembled on the south side of the river
3. The English delayed the start of the battle/Surrey slept in
4. The English could not decide whether to use the narrow bridge or travel further upstream and cross at the broader ford

5. Cressingham did not want any further expenses and wanted to get the battle over as quickly as possible in case the Scots escaped so opted for the bridge
6. The English partly crossed, turned back and then began again, making their plans clear to the Scots
7. The English crossed the bridge slowly/only three abreast
8. The Scots attacked before all the English were over
9. The Scots attacked the end of the bridge trapping the English who had crossed and preventing the rest from crossing to help them
10. English soldiers who attempted to escape across the river were drowned/weighed down by waterlogged tunics
11. Bridge collapsed and English fled
12. The English were defeated/Cressingham was killed

3. *Candidates can be credited in a number of ways up to a maximum of 5 marks.*

Candidates must make a judgement about the usefulness of the source and support this by making evaluative comments on identified aspects of the source.

1 mark should be given for each relevant comment made, up to a **maximum of 5 marks in total**.

- A maximum of **4 marks** can be given for evaluative comments relating to the author, type of source, purpose and timing.
- A maximum of **2 marks** may be given for comments relating to the content of the source.
- A maximum of **2 marks** may be given for comments relating to points of significant omission.

Examples of aspects of the source and relevant comments:

Aspect of the source	Possible comment
Author: Walter of Guisborough	Churchman in Guisborough Priory in Yorkshire, so not an eyewitness, so perhaps less useful
Type of Source: Chronicle	Contains details of events, generally thought to be reliable so more useful
Purpose: To record	Keep a record of events as a history, so may be more useful, but an English version so may be biased against Bruce
Timing: Early 14th century	Written during the Wars of Independence at the time of Bruce taking the throne, so more useful.

Content	Possible comment
He lured him to a meeting in Greyfriars Church	Suggests Bruce planned a deception so shows bias so less useful
Bruce accused Comyn of telling lies about him	May not be accurate so less useful
He struck him with his sword	Puts blame on Bruce so may be biased and less useful

Possible points of significant omission may include:
1. Comyn was his main rival so more useful
2. Comyn was killed by Bruce/Bruce's men
3. Comyn's body was left at the altar
4. Bruce was excommunicated for sacrilege
5. Bruce had himself crowned king

4. *Candidates can be credited in a number of ways up to a maximum of 5 marks.*

Candidates must make an overall judgement about how fully the source explains the events. **1 mark** may be given for each valid point interpreted from the source or each valid point of significant omission provided. The candidate can achieve **up to 3 marks** for their interpretation of the parts of the source they consider are relevant in terms of the proposed question where there is also at least one point of significant omission identified to imply a judgement has been made about the limitations of the source. For full marks to be given each point needs to be discretely mentioned in terms of the question.

A maximum of 2 marks may be given for answers which refer only to the source or in which no judgement has been made.

Possible points which may be identified in the source include:

1. Bruce's parliament agreed that Scots nobles who had not made peace with him would lose their lands in Scotland
2. Bruce gave this forfeited land to his own supporters
3. Scots nobles would no longer be allowed to have English estates so their loyalties would not be divided
4. Continued to raid the north of England to put pressure on Edward

Possible points of significant omission may include:

1. Defeated English army at Bannockburn
2. Secured release of his wife and daughter/Wishart, in exchange for ransomed English prisoners
3. Recaptured Berwick from English occupation
4. Added to Scottish exchequer by accepting protection money from northern English towns
5. Encouraged production of Declaration of Arbroath
6. Renewed Alliance with France
7. Agreed Treaty of Edinburgh with England in 1328
8. Made a marriage treaty for his son/heir

Section 1, Context B, Mary Queen of Scots, and the Scottish Reformation, 1542–1587

1. *Candidates can be credited in a number of ways up to a maximum of 5 marks.*

They may take different perspectives on the events and may describe a variety of different aspects of the events.

1 mark should be given for each accurate relevant key point of knowledge. **A second mark** should be given for each point that is developed, up to a maximum of **5 marks**. Candidates may achieve full marks by providing five straightforward points, by making three developed points, or a combination of these.

Possible points of knowledge may include:

1. English wanted Mary to marry Edward, son of Henry VIII, Treaty of Greenwich
2. Scots cancelled their agreement for Mary to marry Edward, this angered Henry
3. Henry VIII sent armies to destroy Scottish cities/punish the Scots – known as the 'Rough Wooing'
4. English armies tried to capture Mary
5. English armies burned Edinburgh/Borders Abbeys, St Andrews etc
6. English defeated the Scots at the Battle of Pinkie, 1547
7. Scots needed French help/French agreed if Mary married the French Dauphin (Treaty of Haddington)
8. Mary left for France from Dumbarton in August 1548

2. *Candidates can be credited in a number of ways up to a maximum of 5 marks.*

Candidates must make an overall judgement about how fully the source explains the events. **1 mark** may be given for each valid point interpreted from the source or each valid point of significant omission provided. The candidate can achieve **up to 3 marks** for their interpretation of the parts of the source they consider are relevant in terms of the proposed question where there is also at least one point of significant omission identified to imply a judgement has been made about the limitations of the source. For full marks to be given each point needs to be discretely mentioned in terms of the question.

A maximum of 2 marks may be given for answers which refer only to the source or in which no judgement has been made.

Possible points which may be identified in the source include:

1. The Protestant form of worship meant that people could participate much more in services.
2. The Bible was available in English, not Latin; therefore people who could not read Latin could still understand it
3. Some people began to criticise the Catholic Church because of its great wealth
4. Local priests were resented for charging people for christening their children.

Possible points of significant omission may include:

1. Some Scots began to resent the wealth of the Catholic Church eg excessive spending on decoration
2. Some priests & nuns attacked for setting bad example eg spent wealth on themselves not the poor/broke vow of chastity
3. Resentment at the way Protestant preachers had been treated led to more sympathy for Protestants eg Wishart burned as a heretic
4. Resentment at Catholic foreign influence at court (French)
5. Creation of the Lords of the Congregation/many favoured Protestantism
6. Scottish Parliament that met in 1560 was controlled by men who had sympathised with the Reformation
7. Scottish Parliament banned the celebration of mass in 1560/agreed to end the power of the Pope over the Church in Scotland
8. Lack of priests or poor quality of priests caused resentment

3. *Candidates can be credited in a number of ways up to a maximum of 5 marks.*

Candidates must make a judgement about the usefulness of the source and support this by making evaluative comments on identified aspects of the source.

1 mark should be given for each relevant comment made, up to a **maximum of 5 marks in total.**

- A maximum of 4 marks can be given for evaluative comments relating to the author, type of source, purpose and timing.
- A maximum of 2 marks may be given for comments relating to the content of the source.
- A maximum of 2 marks may be given for comments relating to points of significant omission.

Examples of aspects of the source and relevant comments:

Aspect of the source	Possible comment
Author: John Knox	Useful as he was an influential Protestant reformer/hated Mary as a Catholic ruler
Type of Source: Sermon	Useful as heard by Protestant followers/ public expression of Knox's views
Purpose: To persuade	Less useful as it is biased/ enthusiastically condemns Mary and her Catholic religion/to persuade people to turn against Mary
Timing: 1560s	Useful as it was delivered when the Protestant faith was growing in Scotland
Content	**Possible comment**
In the north of the country, where Mary had travelled before harvest time, the famine was hardest with great suffering. Many people died	Less useful as Knox blames Mary for causing famine – extreme and much exaggerated view/but perhaps useful as many Protestants also held these views
Thus did God punish the many sins of our wicked Queen and her followers	Less useful as he claims God is punishing Scotland for having a Catholic Queen – extreme and much exaggerated view/but perhaps useful as many Protestants also held these views
The excessive celebrations and huge feasts in the palace and in the country provoked God into this action	Less useful as he claims God punished Scotland because of Mary's behaviour – extreme and much exaggerated view/but perhaps useful as many Protestants also held these views

Possible points of significant omission may include:

1. John Knox denounced Mary for her whole way of life, she was an 'ungodly ruler', eg dancing criticised
2. Knox would often lecture Mary on religion, condemning Catholicism (Mary reduced to tears by him on one occasion)
3. Some Protestants were happy with Mary eg she tolerated their religion/ ensured the Protestant Church had an income

4. *Candidates can be credited in a number of ways up to a maximum of 5 marks.*

Candidates must show a causal relationship between events.

Up to a **maximum of 5 marks in total**, **1 mark** should be given for each accurate, relevant reason, and a **second mark** should be given for reasons that are developed. Candidates may achieve full marks by providing five straightforward reasons, three developed reasons, or a combination of these.

Possible reasons may include:

1. Nobles persuaded Darnley that Riccio was too friendly with Mary/implied they were having an affair
2. Riccio was humiliating the Scottish nobles by making them ask him to see Mary
3. Riccio was boasting about his influence over Mary
4. Riccio was dressing and behaving like a nobleman which angered the nobles as he was below them in status

5. Darnley thought Riccio had persuaded Mary not to give him the crown matrimonial, which angered Darnley
6. Some nobles thought Riccio was a spy sent by the Pope so were suspicious of Riccio

Section 1, Context C, The Treaty of Union, 1689-1715

1. *Candidates can be credited in a number of ways up to a maximum of 5 marks.*

They may take different perspectives on the events and may describe a variety of different aspects of the events.

1 mark should be given for each accurate relevant key point of knowledge. **A second mark** should be given for each point that is developed, up to a maximum of **5 marks**. Candidates may achieve full marks by providing five straightforward points, by making three developed points, or a combination of these.

Possible points of knowledge may include:

1. King William wanted to remain on good terms with the Spanish and so deliberately sabotaged the Darien colony
2. English officials prevented investment in the Darien scheme
3. There was a feeling that the English had not done enough to help Scotland during the Ill Years of the 1690s
4. William took little positive interest in Scotland eg Glencoe massacre
5. Anne had declared herself to be "entirely English"
6. The strength of Jacobitism in Scotland caused tension
7. Scots loyalties were suspect after the rebellion of 1689
8. The Scots were angry that the English Parliament passed the succession to Sophia of Hanover without consulting them
9. The English were angry when the Scots Parliament passed the Act of Security
10. Scottish trade badly affected by England's French wars (no Scottish gains in the peace treaties)
11. Worcester incident

2. *Candidates can be credited in a number of ways up to a maximum of 5 marks.*

Candidates must make a judgement about the usefulness of the source and support this by making evaluative comments on identified aspects of the source.

1 mark should be given for each relevant comment made, up to a **maximum of 5 marks in total**.

- A maximum of **4 marks** can be given for evaluative comments relating to the author, type of source, purpose and timing.
- A maximum of **2 marks** may be given for comments relating to the content of the source.
- A maximum of **2 marks** may be given for comments relating to points of significant omission.

Examples of aspects of the source and relevant comments:

Aspect of the source	Possible comment
Author: Andrew Fletcher	Useful as he was one of the leading opponents of the Union.
Type of Source: Leaflet	Useful as this was a common method of trying to communicate political ideas at this time.
Purpose: To persuade	Less useful as the writer is biased against the Union/designed to persuade the reader that the Union will be bad for Scotland

Timing: One year before Union was agreed	Useful as it is written when the Union was being debated in Scotland.
Content	**Possible comment**
Scotland needs to keep its own separate law and church	Useful as it was a commonly held view at the time.
If the Scots agree to these interests being controlled by a single Parliament they will surrender control to the English	Useful as it reflects the fears of many Scots.
The English will have a vast majority.	Useful as it is an accurate statement about the parliamentary arithmetic after Union.

Possible points of significant omission may include:

1. Scotland had always been an independent nation and its identity would be subsumed if there was a new united Parliament.
2. Public opinion in Scotland was against a union.
3. Some Scots would have preferred a Federal Union eg Andrew Fletcher.
4. Episcopalians in Scotland opposed union as it would secure the Hanoverian succession and only a return to the Stuart dynasty could restore episcopacy to the Scottish church.
5. Some Presbyterians feared over the position of the Church of Scotland. The English Parliament was dominated by the Episcopalian church with Bishops' seats in the House of Lords.

3. *Candidates can be credited in a number of ways **up to a maximum of 5 marks**.*

Candidates must make an overall judgement about how fully the source explains the events. **1 mark** may be given for each valid point interpreted from the source or each valid point of significant omission provided. The candidate can achieve **up to 3 marks** for their interpretation of the parts of the source they consider are relevant in terms of the proposed question where there is also at least one point of significant omission identified to imply a judgement has been made about the limitations of the source. For full marks to be given each point needs to be discretely mentioned in terms of the question.

A maximum of 2 marks may be given for answers which refer only to the source or in which no judgement has been made.

Possible points which may be identified in the source include:

1. By this union we will all have access to all the advantages of trade that the English enjoy at the moment
2. We will be able to improve our wealth
3. We will have our liberty, our property and our religion secured
4. Scotland will be under the protection of one sovereign and one Parliament of Great Britain.

Possible points of significant omission may include:

- If Scotland failed to accept Union voluntarily they might be forced to accept it on unfavourable terms after an English invasion.
- The Scots knew that Ireland had been conquered by England and wanted to avoid this fate.

- Presbyterians wanted to solve the problem of the succession and ensure that the exiled Stuarts did not return
- The Union guaranteed the position of the Presbyterian Church
- Fear of the reintroduction of the Alien Act if Union was not approved by the Scots
- Many Scots believed the Scottish economy would benefit from Union
- Scots attracted by guarantee of free trade with the UK and the colonies
- Some felt that failure of Darien proved that Scotland could no longer go it alone/some influential Scots saw it as only way to recover from the financial disaster of the Darian Scheme
- The position of Scots Law had been guaranteed

4. *Candidates can be credited in a number of ways up to a maximum of 5 marks.*

Candidates must show a causal relationship between events.

Up to a **maximum of 5 marks in total**, **1 mark** should be given for each accurate, relevant reason, and a **second mark** should be given for reasons that are developed. Candidates may achieve full marks by providing five straightforward reasons, three developed reasons, or a combination of these.

Possible reasons may include:

1. The 1707 Union was deeply unpopular. It had failed to bring economic prosperity to Scotland
2. Many participated as they were anti-Union. James VIII promised to end the Union
3. Dislike of the Campbells (especially in the Highlands)
4. Episcopalians offered support as the return of James seemed to provide the best prospect of an Episcopalian church settlement
5. Loyalty to the House of Stuart. Jacobites did not accept William, Anne or George. They believed James was the rightful King
6. Highland clansmen felt loyalty to the exiled King
7. Some participants were "forced out"
8. The Earl of Mar fought for selfish political reasons as he had lost his government position under George I
9. Dislike of new currency, weights etc
10. Disappointment at failure of payment of the Equivalent motivated some to participate

Section 1, Context D, Migration and Empire, 1830–1939

1. *Candidates can be credited in a number of ways up to a maximum of 5 marks.*

Candidates must show a causal relationship between events.

Up to a **maximum of 5 marks in total**, **1 mark** should be given for each accurate, relevant reason, and a **second mark** should be given for reasons that are developed. Candidates may achieve full marks by providing five straightforward reasons, three developed reasons, or a combination of these.

Possible reasons may include:

1. Scots accused them of taking Scots' jobs, so resented immigrants
2. Scots accused them of working for less money/lowering wages, so suspicious of immigrants
3. Immigrants were exploited as strike breakers/did not

join in with strikes so were unpopular

4. Some had a reputation for drunkenness, so many Scots were wary of immigrants
5. Some had a reputation for violence/fighting, so some Scots were afraid of immigrants
6. Accused them of causing overcrowding/pressure on limited housing stock/ putting up rents, which caused resentment
7. Immigrants were said to spread disease/unhygienic way of life/'brought down' the Scots, so viewed with suspicion
8. Accused some of claiming poor relief intended for Scots, so were resented
9. Some immigrants practised a different religion, which made Scots suspicious of them
10. Some immigrants failed to fit in/kept to themselves/ kept their own customs, so were viewed with suspicion

2. *Candidates can be credited in a number of ways up to a maximum of 5 marks.*

They may take different perspectives on the events and may describe a variety of different aspects of the events.

1 mark should be given for each accurate relevant key point of knowledge. **A second mark** should be given for each point that is developed, up to a maximum of **5 marks**. Candidates may achieve full marks by providing five straightforward points, by making three developed points, or a combination of these.

Possible points of knowledge may include:
1. Fares were paid by landlords in the Highlands
2. HIES – sent poor crofter families to Australia
3. Glasgow Emigration Society – gave assistance to settle in Canada
4. British Government/Colonial Land and Emigration Commissioners – 'Bounty' settlers to Australia
5. Emigrants' Information Office – gave advice and assistance on aspects of emigration
6. Empire Settlement Act 1922 – gave loans and grants to help with passages and training
7. Barnardos/Quarriers – sent orphan boys and girls to Australia and Canada
8. YMCA – helped young men to emigrate as farm workers/Big Brother scheme supported boys who emigrated/'Dreadnought' boys supported as farm workers
9. Personal loans from family paid for fares etc
10. Cheap rail/steamer fares offered by transport companies eg Anchor-Donaldson Line
11. Subsidised passages paid for by Australian and Canadian governments
12. Free passage for domestic servants to New Zealand, Lewis girls as servants to Canada etc

3. *Candidates can be credited in a number of ways up to a maximum of 5 marks.*

Candidates must make an overall judgement about how fully the source explains the events. **1 mark** may be given for each valid point interpreted from the source or each valid point of significant omission provided. The candidate can achieve **up to 3 marks** for their interpretation of the parts of the source they consider are relevant in terms of the proposed question where there is also at least one point of significant omission identified to imply a judgement has been made about the limitations of the source. For full marks to be given each point needs to be discretely mentioned in terms of the question.

A maximum of 2 marks may be given for answers which refer only to the source or in which no judgement has been made.

Possible points which may be identified in the source include:
1. Alexander Spark was a leading member of the business community/ prominent in banking
2. By 1840 owned £40,000 of land
3. Became the local agent for a variety of companies
4. Scottish Agents in Australia handled the interests of many Scots who invested money in Australian businesses without ever leaving Scotland.

Possible points of significant omission may include:
1. Scots introduced merino sheep to Australia/developed sheep farming in New Zealand
2. Scots developed shipping companies/developed refrigerated sea transport for meat
3. Scots pioneered the sugar industry in Australia/ introduced sugar mills/ refineries
4. Scots were involved in developing the wine industry/ brewing in Australia
5. Scots set up universities in Canada/New Zealand/ education systems variously
6. Scots developed engineering companies in Canada, Australia/developed shipbuilding in New Zealand
7. Scots developed Canadian Pacific railroad as engineers and financiers
8. Scots cleared and developed virgin land in Canada, Australia, New Zealand
9. Scots masons built prestigious public buildings in new cities
10. Scots developed the jute industry in India
11. Scots' were active in politics/reached high positions eg JA MacDonald, Prime Minister of Canada

4. *Candidates can be credited in a number of ways **up to a maximum of 5 marks.***

Candidates must make a judgement about the usefulness of the source and support this by making evaluative comments on identified aspects of the source.

1 mark should be given for each relevant comment made, up to a **maximum of 5 marks in total.**
- A maximum of **4 marks** can be given for evaluative comments relating to the author, type of source, purpose and timing.
- A maximum of **2 marks** may be given for comments relating to the content of the source.
- A maximum of **2 marks** may be given for comments relating to points of significant omission.

Examples of aspects of the source and relevant comments:

Aspect of the source	Possible comment
Author: Mary Contini	Personal recollection of her own family history so useful
Type of Source: Memoirs about her grandparents' experience	Not describing a first-hand experience so may be less accurate, so less useful
Purpose: Informs why they worked hard	Simple explanation, not exaggerated, so useful
Timing: Reflection on early 20th century	Grandparents arrived around time of peak Italian immigration to Scotland so fairly typical and more useful/looking back with the benefit of hindsight

Content	Possible comment
Many of them made their living selling fish and chips	Useful as true of many Italian immigrants
Debt worried them and made them work even harder	Useful as explains concerns of immigrants to succeed
Shops were open long hours/the whole family helped serve customers/shops became the focus of social life	Useful as explains why families had so much contact with new communities/useful as accurate

Possible points of significant omission may include:
1. Italian cafes became very stylish and fashionable eg Nardini's in Largs
2. Names changed to Scottish versions/nicknames were used to seem less foreign
3. Second generation immigrants spoke Scots English
4. Some intermarriage, especially Scots and Irish
5. Worked with Scots in Trade Union movement/ Temperance movement
6. Worked with Scots in politics/Women's suffrage movement
7. Scots and immigrants served together in the Great War

Section 1, Context E, The Era of the Great War, 1910–1928

1. *Candidates can be credited in a number of ways up to a maximum of 5 marks.*

They may take different perspectives on the events and may describe a variety of different aspects of the events.

1 mark should be given for each accurate relevant key point of knowledge. **A second mark** should be given for each point that is developed, up to a maximum of **5 marks**. Candidates may achieve full marks by providing five straightforward points, by making three developed points, or a combination of these.

Possible points of knowledge may include:
1. **Use of Tanks:**
   • Able to cross trenches/crush barbed wire
   • Use fascines to cross trenches
   • Scattered German infantry
   • Achieved some success/at Cambrai
   • Protected the infantry going forward
   • Were armoured/bullet proof/equipped with machine guns/six pound guns
   • However were easily bogged down/inefficient/ unreliable/dangerous or uncomfortable for the crew
2. **Use of Machine guns:**
   • Vickers was highly efficient/successful/accurate weapon
   • Could fire up to 600 bullets a minute
   • Killed thousands of men
   • Development of portable machine guns
3. **Use of Aircraft**
   • Used for reconnaissance, ascertain enemy actions
   • Used to photograph enemy lines
   • Used to protect troops in the trenches
   • Fighter planes built to shoot down enemy planes
   • Used to bomb enemy trenches
   • Used to strafe enemy trenches

4. **Use of Gas**
   • Germans were first to use gas at Ypres in 1915 British use of gas eg …
   • operation of gas canisters/shells; delivery; unreliability
   • different types of gas used (chlorine, mustard, phosgene, tear)
   • surprise/fear/panic factor of gas
   • importance of weather/wind direction
   • effects of gas (suffocating/choking, blinding, blisters/ burns)
   • use of gas masks; soldiers urinated on hankies
   • gas rarely used after 1917 as the Germans ran out of chemicals
   • (initially) killed thousands
   • (overall) more injuries than deaths
5. Development of range finding techniques for heavy artillery
6. Flamethrowers used to clear out enemy trenches

2. *Candidates can be credited in a number of ways **up to a maximum of 5 marks**.*

Candidates must make a judgement about the usefulness of the source and support this by making evaluative comments on identified aspects of the source.

1 mark should be given for each relevant comment made, up to a **maximum of 5 marks in total**.
• A maximum of 4 marks can be given for evaluative comments relating to the author, type of source, purpose and timing.
• A maximum of 2 marks may be given for comments relating to the content of the source.
• A maximum of 2 marks may be given for comments relating to points of significant omission.

Examples of aspects of the source and relevant comments:

Aspect of the source	Possible comment
Author: David Lloyd George	Useful as he is an eyewitness/a government minister soon to be Prime Minister so an expert on women's war effort
Type of Source: Memoir extract	Useful as based on Lloyd George's feelings/as a memoir could be less useful as could be coloured by subsequent events
Purpose: To record	Useful as it is an accurate account of the dangers faced by the women/ to record DLG's admiration of the women who worked in the munitions factories
Timing: Memoir from his time as Minister of Munitions (from 1915)	Useful as it is an account of his wartime experiences

Content	Possible comment
They had to work under conditions of real danger to life	Useful as it tells of the dangers of explosions which were common
One of the risks of shell filling factories was toxic jaundice resulting from the TNT poisoning/ The poor girls were nicknamed 'canaries'	Useful as it explains the dangers of the TNT poisoning
They were quite proud of this/They had earned it in the path of duty	Useful as it shows the women were proud of the jobs they were doing, despite the danger

Possible points of significant omission may include:
1. Details of other jobs done by women eg the Land Army, Nursing etc
2. Mourning for lost loved ones
3. Women became head of the family/struggled to juggle children, jobs, bills etc
4. Women got the vote as a result of contribution

3. *Candidates can be credited in a number of ways up to a maximum of 5 marks.*

Candidates must make an overall judgement about how fully the source explains the events. **1 mark** may be given for each valid point interpreted from the source or each valid point of significant omission provided. The candidate can achieve **up to 3 marks** for their interpretation of the parts of the source they consider are relevant in terms of the proposed question where there is also at least one point of significant omission identified to imply a judgement has been made about the limitations of the source. For full marks to be given each point needs to be discretely mentioned in terms of the question.

A maximum of 2 marks may be given for answers which refer only to the source or in which no judgement has been made.

Possible points which may be identified in the source include:
1. Men who refused to enlist in the army had to face military discipline
2. Some were sentenced to death for refusing orders although the sentence was always reduced if the 'conchie' still refused to give in
3. Special prisons and work camps were opened up in addition to the ordinary prisons to which many objectors were sent
4. Twenty four objectors died while detained at work camps

Possible points of significant omission may include:
1. In their communities conscientious objectors were often subject to a torrent of verbal and sometimes physical abuse
2. They were often ignored or refused service in shops
3. Women would give these men white feathers to signify cowardice

4. *Candidates can be credited in a number of ways up to a maximum of 5 marks.*

Candidates must show a causal relationship between events.

Up to a **maximum of 5 marks in total**, **1 mark** should be given for each accurate, relevant reason, and a **second mark** should be given for reasons that are developed. Candidates may achieve full marks by providing five straightforward reasons, three developed reasons, or a combination of these.

Possible reasons may include:
1. Post-war lack of demand/orders for shipbuilding eg 1921–23 tonnage of ships built on the Clyde declined/ from 510,000 to 170,000
2. Poor industrial relations (eg demarcation disputes) created difficulties
3. Failure to invest in new technology/lack of investment
4. Lack of demand led to iron and steel production declining/plants closing
5. Lack of orders led to decline in railway production eg by two-thirds at the North British Locomotive company
6. New fuels, so coal production also declined/pits closed
7. Foreign competition challenged Scottish industry
8. International markets lost during the war were not recovered
9. The jute factories in Dundee were in need of fresh investment and repair/lack of demand for sandbags reduced demand for jute
10. At the same time jute prices fell around the world
11. The management of Scottish industry suffered from disproportionate effect of losses of middle-class officers

Section 2, Context A, The Creation of the Medieval Kingdoms, 1066–1406

1. *Candidates can be credited in a number of ways up to a maximum of 8 marks.*

Candidates must use knowledge to present a balanced assessment of the influence of different possible factors and come to a reasoned conclusion.

Up to 5 marks are allocated for relevant points of knowledge used to address the question. **1 mark** should be given for each relevant, factual key point of knowledge used to support a factor. **If only one factor is presented, a maximum of 3 marks should be given for relevant points of knowledge.**

Possible factors may include:	Relevant, factual, key points of knowledge to support this factor may include:
William's leadership skills	1. William was experienced in battle and had previously defeated the French king
	2. William feigned retreat during the battle tricking the Anglo-Saxons
William's superior army	3. William's army was well trained and wore chain mail armour
	4. William's cavalry rode specially bred horses. The horses also had a saddle on them keeping the knights in position and allowing them to fight
	5. William had brought supplies with him from Normandy and so his army was well fed and rested

Harold's inferior army	6. Harold's army was a mixture of professional soldiers/bodyguards and ordinary men 7. The army was not as well trained as the Normans 8. Death of Harold and his brothers meant there was no clear leadership during the battle
Harold's army were tired	9. Harold's army had only just fought the Battle of Stamford Bridge 10. Harold's army had been forced to march quickly to the south to meet the Normans
Any other valid factor	

Up to 3 marks should be given for presenting the answer in a structured way, leading to a conclusion which addresses the question, as follows:

1 mark for the answer being presented in a structured way, with knowledge being organised in support of different factors.
1 mark given for a valid judgement or overall conclusion.
1 mark given for a reason being provided in support of the conclusion.

2. *Candidates can be credited in a number of ways up to a maximum of 6 marks.*

Candidates must make a judgement about the usefulness of the source and support this by making evaluative comments on identified aspects of the source.

1 mark should be given for each relevant comment made, up to a **maximum of 6 marks in total.**
- A maximum of 4 marks can be given for evaluative comments relating to the author, type of source, purpose and timing.
- A maximum of 2 marks may be given for comments relating to the content of the source.
- A maximum of 2 marks may be given for comments relating to points of significant omission.

Examples of aspects of the source and relevant comments:

Aspect of the source	Possible comment
Author: Royal clerk	Useful because he was well placed to gather information
Type of Source: Chronicle	Useful because it was an official record of events
Purpose: To describe	Less useful as clearly biased description of rebellions/author may have exaggerated when describing the actions of the Scots
Timing: 1174	At the time that Henry II was facing rebellion
Content	Possible comment
William rebelled and attacked Northumberland	Useful because it gives details of William's rebellion
Women and children were slaughtered/ priests murdered inside their own churches	Less useful because it could be exaggerating what happened.

His army besieged the castle/by cutting off their supplies/forced the English to make a treaty with the Scots.	Useful because it provides details on what William did next.

Possible points of significant omission may include:
1. Henry II's sons rebelled against him/the Great Rebellion 1173
2. Further rebellions by Henry's sons in 1183 and 1187

3. *Candidates can be credited in a number of ways up to a maximum of 6 marks.*

Candidates must show a causal relationship between events.

Up to a **maximum of 6 marks in total**, **1 mark** should be given for each accurate, relevant reason, and a **second mark** should be given for reasons that are developed. Candidates may achieve full marks by providing five straightforward reasons, three developed reasons, or a combination of these.

Possible reasons may include:
1. Effects of the Black Death eg some peasants were free some were not
2. Peasants prevented from earning higher wages than they had before the Black Death eg 1351 Statute of Labour (ie wages were cut), so unhappy
3. Peasants' discontent with war with France
4. Peasants had been taxed in 1377, 1379 and 1381, so unhappy
5. 1381 tax targeted new groups eg over 15s/craftsmen/ women taxed whether they worked or not, which was resented
6. Peasants unhappy as wanted an end to forced labour/ greater access to forests
7. Lack of faith in King Richard II who was a boy
8. Hatred of the King's advisor/allegations of corruption
9. Inspired by speakers who criticised the Church and monarchy eg John Ball/ Waldergrave

Section 2, Context B, War of the Three Kingdoms, 1603-1651

1. *Candidates can be credited in a number of ways up to a maximum of 8 marks.*

Candidates must use knowledge to present a balanced assessment of the influence of different possible factors and come to a reasoned conclusion.

Up to 5 marks are allocated for relevant points of knowledge used to address the question. **1 mark** should be given for each relevant, factual key point of knowledge used to support a factor. **If only one factor is presented, a maximum of 3 marks should be given for relevant points of knowledge.**

Possible factors may include:	Relevant, factual, key points of knowledge to support this factor may include:
Religious differences	1. Some in Parliament were offended by James' belief in the Divine Right of Kings 2. Millenary Petition 1603 demanded changes to church practices – rejected by James VI and I

Religious differences (continued)	3. Archbishops Canons – clergy had to subscribe to 39 articles and Prayer Book, James licensed the Canons, which provoked the clergy
	4. 1622 – Direction of Preachers issued, gave Bishops more control, which worried Puritans
	5. Demands of Presbyterians for the removal of Bishops
	6. Demands from Catholics for more lenient treatment
	7. Gunpowder plot
Financial grievances	8. Extravagant spending and debts built up by James eg clothing banquets
	9. Gave money and power to his favourites at court
	10. Bates Case 1606 – judges agreed that impositions (new source of revenue of additional tax on imports and exports) were legal
	11. Failure of Great Contract 1610 – reciprocal distrust
	12. Monopolies caused anger and resentment
Political factors	13. James dismissed Parliament in 1610
	14. Failure of 'Addled Parliament' in 1614
	15. James' insistence on creating a legal and administrative Union with Scotland caused suspicions in England
Any other relevant factor	

Up to 3 marks should be given for presenting the answer in a structured way, leading to a conclusion which addresses the question, as follows:
1 mark for the answer being presented in a structured way, with knowledge being organised in support of different factors.
1 mark given for a valid judgement or overall conclusion.
1 mark given for a reason being provided in support of the conclusion.

2. *Candidates can be credited in a number of ways **up to a maximum of 6 marks**.*

Candidates must show a causal relationship between events.

Up to a **maximum of 6 marks in total**, **1 mark** should be given for each accurate, relevant reason, and a **second mark** should be given for reasons that are developed. Candidates may achieve full marks by providing six straightforward reasons, three developed reasons, or a combination of these.

Possible reasons may include:
1. Believed in the Divine Right of Kings, which was resented
2. Married to Henrietta Maria – a Catholic, unpopular with Protestants
3. Spending habits eg paintings and expensive clothes were resented

4. 1629-1640 – ruled without Parliament (Personal Rule), so was unpopular
5. Forced Ship Money, those who refused went to prison, created resentment
6. Appointed Laud as Archbishop of Canterbury, who was unpopular
7. Laud changed Church of England services (statues, music and candles introduced) – offended some Protestants
8. Introduced New Prayer Book – in Scotland this caused riots
9. Scots attacked English because of religious changes (Bishops' Wars)
10. Charles called Parliament to get money to fight the Scots, which was resented
11. Earl of Strafford ruled Ireland for Charles – Strafford unpopular with the Irish and the Long Parliament

3. *Candidates can be credited in a number of ways **up to a maximum of 6 marks**.*

Candidates must make a judgement about the usefulness of the source and support this by making evaluative comments on identified aspects of the source.

1 mark should be given for each relevant comment made, up to a **maximum of 6 marks in total**.
• A maximum of 4 marks can be given for evaluative comments relating to the author, type of source, purpose and timing.
• A maximum of 2 marks may be given for comments relating to the content of the source.
• A maximum of 2 marks may be given for comments relating to points of significant omission.

Examples of aspects of the source and relevant comments:

Aspect of the source	Possible comment
Author: Oliver Cromwell	Useful as he was the leader of the Parliamentary forces (who was an extreme Puritan and who hated the Irish Catholics)
Type of Source: Letter (to the House of Commons)	Useful as an official account of the events of the battle, so should be accurate/less useful as may be biased based on Cromwell's actions
Purpose: To inform	Useful as provides reasons for victory at Drogheda/ Cromwell justifying his actions
Timing: September 1649	Useful as written soon after the battle took place
Content	**Possible comment**
On Monday 9th the battering guns began/Our guns then beat down the corner tower, and made gaps in the east and south walls	Useful as it provides accurate details of when the battle began/weapons used
I sent Sir Arthur Aston a request to surrender the town but received no satisfactory answer	Useful as Sir Arthur Aston ignored Cromwell's order to surrender
On the following day, after some fierce fighting, we entered the town/several of the enemy, including Sir Arthur Aston, retreated into Mill Mount	Useful as it describes the successful storming of the city by Cromwell's forces

Possible points of significant omission may include:
1. Cromwell ordered his men to kill everyone remaining in the town who had weapons
2. Cromwell's men killed approximately 2000 men after the surrender
3. The Church of St. Peters was set on fire, burning alive a group of defenders who had barricaded themselves in
4. Parliamentarian losses are regarded to be around 150
5. Sir Arthur Aston reported to have been beaten to death with his own wooden leg

Section 2, Context C, The Atlantic Slave Trade, 1770-1807

1. *Candidates can be credited in a number of ways up to a maximum of 8 marks.*

Candidates must use knowledge to present a balanced assessment of the influence of different possible factors and come to a reasoned conclusion.
Up to 5 marks are allocated for relevant points of knowledge used to address the question. **1 mark** should be given for each relevant, factual key point of knowledge used to support a factor. **If only one factor is presented, a maximum of 3 marks should be given for relevant points of knowledge.**

Possible factors may include:	Relevant, factual, key points of knowledge to support this factor may include:
Role of Thomas Clarkson	1. Visited ports such as Liverpool to collect evidence about the cruelties of the slave trade 2. Interviewed sailors who were involved in the slave trade 3. Risked his life to campaign for the abolition of slavery 4. Clarkson published his evidence about the slave trade 5. Clarkson's influence on Wilberforce and others
Role of other campaigners	6. William Wilberforce led the campaign against the slave trade in parliament. 7. Wilberforce presented bills to abolish the slave trade 8. Wilberforce used his friendship with the prime minister and the monarchy to win support for abolition 9. Wilberforce became leader of the Society for the Abolition of the Slave Trade 10. Former slave ship captain, John Newton, preached against the evils of the trade/wrote the hymn, Amazing Grace 11. Freed slaves such as Olaudah Equiano published personal accounts about the terrible nature of the slave trade 12. Granville Sharp campaigned against slavery in British courts 13. Many people across Britain signed petitions against the slave trade.
Role of other campaigners *(continued)*	14. Pamphlets, posters, newspaper adverts were used to campaign against the slave trade 15. Slogans such as 'Am I not a man and a brother' were used/appeared on Wedgwood crockery 16. Boycotts of slave produced goods such as sugar
Changing attitudes	17. Christian teaching led people to change their attitudes to the slave trade 18. People began to think of Africans as fellow human beings 19. Plantation agriculture became less important to the British economy 20. People began to regard slave labour as an inefficient way to produce goods
Any other relevant factor	

Up to 3 marks should be given for presenting the answer in a structured way, leading to a conclusion which addresses the question, as follows:

1 mark for the answer being presented in a structured way, with knowledge being organised in support of different factors.
1 mark given for a valid judgement or overall conclusion.
1 mark given for a reason being provided in support of the conclusion.

2. *Candidates can be credited in a number of ways **up to a maximum of 6 marks**.*

Candidates must show a causal relationship between events.

Up to a **maximum of 6 marks in total**, **1 mark** should be given for each accurate, relevant reason, and a **second mark** should be given for reasons that are developed. Candidates may achieve full marks by providing six straightforward reasons, three developed reasons, or a combination of these.

Possible reasons may include:
1. The slave trade brought wealth to Britain, so was popular with those who became wealthy
2. The slave trade brought employment to Britain in areas such as shipyards, ports, mills, manufacturing, so was supported by many involved in these industries
3. Cities profited from the slave trade (eg Bristol, Liverpool and Glasgow), so many in these cities wished to see slavery continue
4. The products of the slave trade were in great demand (eg cotton, tobacco and sugar) and many believed that slavery was needed in order to meet demand for these products
5. Involvement in the slave trade helped Britain to remain a world power, so many continued to support slavery
6. The slave trade was seen as a valuable training ground for the Royal Navy, so it was supported
7. Many MPs had financial interests in the slave trade, so wished to see it continue
8. Many MPs were being bribed to ensure that they continued to give their support for the continuation of the trade

9. The slave trade still enjoyed the support of the King
10. Profits from the trade were essential to fund the war with France

3. *Candidates can be credited in a number of ways* **up to a maximum of 6 marks.**

Candidates must make a judgement about the usefulness of the source and support this by making evaluative comments on identified aspects of the source.

1 mark should be given for each relevant comment made, up to a **maximum of 6 marks in total.**
- A maximum of **4 marks** can be given for evaluative comments relating to the author, type of source, purpose and timing.
- A maximum of **2 marks** may be given for comments relating to the content of the source.
- A maximum of **2 marks** may be given for comments relating to points of significant omission.

Examples of aspects of the source and relevant comments:

Aspect of the source	Possible comment
Author: Historian	Useful as modern historians are likely to be experts on the issue and have carried out research
Type of Source: Textbook	Factual account of the treatment of slaves on the plantations
Purpose: To inform	Useful as evidence of harsh treatment of slaves on the plantations
Timing: 1995	A secondary source written with the benefit of hindsight
Content	**Possible comment**
They followed a policy of control through fear	Useful as this shows how harsh the treatment of slaves was
Slaves had no rights. They were seen as possessions rather than human beings	Useful as this shows slaves were not treated equally
There was no punishment for owners who worked their slaves to death/ no one questioned owners burning or torturing their slaves	Useful as this shows how cruel plantation owners were/not answerable for their actions towards their slaves

Possible points of significant omission may include:
1. Slaves were forced to work long hours
2. Slaves were often whipped for not working hard enough
3. Slave families were often broken up when slaves were bought and sold from plantations

Section 2, Context D, Changing Britain, 1760–1900

1. *Candidates can be credited in a number of ways up to a maximum of 6 marks.*

Candidates must make a judgement about the usefulness of the source and support this by making evaluative comments on identified aspects of the source.

1 mark should be given for each relevant comment made, up to a **maximum of 6 marks** in total.
- A maximum of **4 marks** can be given for evaluative comments relating to the author, type of source, purpose and timing.
- A maximum of **2 marks** may be given for comments relating to the content of the source.
- A maximum of **2 marks** may be given for comments relating to points of significant omission.

Examples of aspects of the source and relevant comments:

Aspect of the source	Possible comment
Author: Doctor	Useful as it was written by an eyewitness to poor housing conditions in Manchester
Type of Source: Report	Useful as it was part of an official document by someone with medical expertise/reports tend to be factual
Purpose: To record	May be less useful, as report only focuses on one area of Manchester/ but useful because factual record of poor housing conditions in Manchester
Timing: 1832	Useful as it was written at the time of urbanisation/growth of cities/ industrial revolution/time when there was a lot of poor housing in British cities
Content	**Possible comment**
The houses that the mill workers live in are poorly ventilated and do not have toilets	Useful as fairly typical of urban housing in poorer areas at this time
The streets are narrow, unpaved and worn into deep ruts, which become the resting place of mud, refuse and rubbish	Useful as typical of cities at this time with poor sanitation
In Parliament Street there is only one toilet for 380 inhabitants. The flow of muck from this toilet infests close-by houses and must be a source of disease	May be less useful as may have been exaggerated for effect but could also say useful as fairly typical of concerns about dirt and disease at this time

Possible points of significant omission may include:
1. Lack of clean water
2. Overcrowding
3. Poorly constructed homes
4. Impact of these living conditions on health – eg rickets/ cholera/TB, vermin spread other diseases

2. *Candidates can be credited in a number of ways up to a maximum of 8 marks.*

Candidates must use knowledge to present a balanced assessment of the influence of different possible factors and come to a reasoned conclusion.

Up to 5 marks are allocated for relevant points of knowledge used to address the question. **1 mark** should be given for each relevant, factual key point of knowledge used to support a factor. **If only one factor is presented, a maximum of 3 marks should be given for relevant points of knowledge.**

Possible factors may include:	Relevant, factual, key points of knowledge to support this factor may include:
Technology	1. Iron rails underground made it easier to transport coal 2. Steam power to raise cages 3. Wire rope to raise cages 4. Steam-powered drainage pumps 5. Davy safety lamp 6. Metal pit props 7. Gunpowder used to loosen rock 8. Technology enabled deeper shafts to be dug, reaching into seams of coal below water-bearing ground 9. Chain coal-cutting machines from the 1880s 10. Better ventilation systems 11. Electric lighting from the 1890s 12. Electric hauling from the 1890s
Legislation	13. 1842 – banned women and children under 10 from working underground/fatalities reduced as fewer children employed 14. 1850 – Mine Inspectors appointed, which improved safety 15. 1860 – boys under 12 forbidden to go underground 16. 1862 – mines must have at least two exits 17. 1872 – mine managers required a certificate, which improved safety 18. from 1894 – minimum wage for miners
Animals	19. Canaries used to detect pockets of suffocating gas (Choke Damp) 20. Ponies used (instead of putters) to move wagons of coal
Pressure groups	21. Trade unions campaigned for shorter working hours/better conditions
Any other valid factor	

Up to 3 marks should be given for presenting the answer in a structured way, leading to a conclusion which addresses the question, as follows:

1 mark for the answer being presented in a structured way, with knowledge being organised in support of different factors.

1 mark given for a valid judgement or overall conclusion.
1 mark given for a reason being provided in support of the conclusion.

3. *Candidates can be credited in a number of ways up to a maximum of 6 marks.*

Candidates must show a causal relationship between events.

Up to a **maximum of 6 marks in total**, **1 mark** should be given for each accurate, relevant reason, and a **second mark** should be given for reasons that are developed. Candidates may achieve full marks by providing six straightforward reasons, three developed reasons, or a combination of these.

Possible reasons may include:
1. Canals very slow means of transport – railways much faster
2. Canals could not go everywhere, especially in hilly country
3. A more extensive network of railways developed
4. Canals often different widths and depths, so goods had to be transferred from one size of boat to another
5. Even short journeys involved several canal companies/inconvenient paperwork/expensive
6. Locks slowed up movement considerably
7. Canal transport more expensive than railways/railways carried more goods so more cost effective
8. Factories could have their own railway sidings – more convenient than canals
9. Canal companies failed to invest their profits back into widening and deepening canals/Investment needed to widen canals was diverted to railways

Section 2, Context E, The Making of Modern Britain, 1880-1951

1. *Candidates can be credited in a number of ways up to a maximum of 8 marks.*

Candidates must use knowledge to present a balanced assessment of the influence of different possible factors and come to a reasoned conclusion.

Up to 5 marks are allocated for relevant points of knowledge used to address the question. **1 mark** should be given for each relevant, factual key point of knowledge used to support a factor. **If only one factor is presented, a maximum of 3 marks should be given for relevant points of knowledge.**

Possible factors may include:	Relevant, factual, key points of knowledge to support this factor may include:
Poor health	1. Absence from work due to sickness could lead to loss of job/earnings 2. Poor could not afford doctors/medicine 3. Many occupations dangerous/few safety precautions eg miners/shipyards so greater chance of accidents/injury

Old age	4. Those on low wages unable to save, so when too old to work, fell into poverty 5. Limited poor relief 6. Caring for elderly relatives was an added burden on poor households
Death of wage-earner	7. Death of the main wage-earner would cause families to fall into poverty 8. Only limited compensation available for illness or accidents caused through work
Family size	9. Large families often lived below poverty-line, especially when children were very young 10. No easily available child-care, so mother often prevented from working
Irregular/ low earnings/ unemployment	11. Work was often cyclical/ irregular or seasonal – causing temporary poverty 12. Wages were often below subsistence-level 13. Considerable time often had to be spent looking for work/ queuing outside factory gates 14. Women were particularly low paid half or even less of male wages 15. Unemployment meant a lack of income
Other causes	16. Secondary poverty caused when earnings spent/wasted on other things – eg drinking or gambling 17. High rents used up a lot of family income 18. Discrimination could add to unemployment eg Irish in Scotland

Up to 3 marks should be given for presenting the answer in a structured way, leading to a conclusion which addresses the question, as follows:

1 mark for the answer being presented in a structured way, with knowledge being organised in support of different factors.
1 mark given for a valid judgement or overall conclusion.
1 mark given for a reason being provided in support of the conclusion.

2. *Candidates can be credited in a number of ways **up to a maximum of 6 marks.***

Candidates must make a judgement about the usefulness of the source and support this by making evaluative comments on identified aspects of the source.

1 mark should be given for each relevant comment made, up to a **maximum of 6 marks in total.**
- A maximum of **4 marks** can be given for evaluative comments relating to the author, type of source, purpose and timing.
- A maximum of **2 marks** may be given for comments relating to the content of the source.
- A maximum of **2 marks** may be given for comments relating to points of significant omission.

Examples of aspects of the source and relevant comments:

Aspect of the source	Possible comment
Author: Historians	Useful because they would have researched the subject thoroughly
Type of Source: Modern history book	Useful as published sources tend to be factual
Purpose: To inform	Useful as will be a balanced/ comprehensive account of reasons for Liberals passing reforms to help the young
Timing: Published in 2002	Useful as written with the benefit of hindsight

Content	Possible comment
The Boer War and the condition of many recruits led politicians to act	Useful as the Boer War did raise concern about the fitness of recruits/national stock/efficiency
The children would be the soldiers of the future	Useful as this was a typical/ important concern at the time of international tensions
Healthy children would grow up to be healthy soldiers and workers and the British Empire would be stronger as a result	Useful as there was great concern about Britain's status in the world

Possible points of significant omission may include:
1. Rowntree's report in particular revealed that families with young children often fell below the poverty line.
2. Children regarded as 'deserving' poor.
3. Report of the 1904 Inter-departmental Committee on Physical Deterioration recommended reforms to improve the health of children/ free school meals and medical inspections.
4. School leaving age 13/desire to improve access to free secondary education for some.
5. High levels of juvenile crime/often caused by poverty.
6. Desire to alter justice system which treated juvenile criminals in the same way as adult criminals.
7. Work of Margaret McMillan in pushing for school meals and medical inspections.

3. *Candidates can be credited in a number of ways **up to a maximum of 6 marks.***

Candidates must show a causal relationship between events.

Up to a maximum of **6 marks** in total, **1 mark** should be given for each accurate, relevant reason, and a **second mark** should be given for reasons that are developed. Candidates may achieve full marks by providing six straightforward reasons, three developed reasons, or a combination of these.

Possible reasons may include:
1. Sense of determination/will to 'build a better Britain' after the war.
2. Evacuation highlighted the poor health/physical condition of children and the problem of poverty, so opened eyes/changed attitudes
3. Rich and poor subject to bombing/created need for reform
4. Rationing ensured a fair supply of food for all – rich and poor alike, levelled classes/created expectation of further government intervention

5. Social classes mixed more than ever before during the war – raised awareness of social problems and need for welfare reform
6. Government had been forced to intervene more during the war – eg Ministry of Food, rationing, and free health care for war-wounded/War forced government to change laissez-faire attitudes
7. Greater acceptance of government control during wartime was accepted to tackle post-war problems
8. War highlighted social problems that only the state could tackle – eg poverty, housing, people accepted this
9. Beveridge Report of 1942 highlighted social problems/ Beveridge Report popular and created an expectation of government action

Section 3, Context A, The Cross and the Crescent; the Crusades, 1071-1192

1. *Candidates can be credited in a number of ways up to a maximum of 5 marks.*
They may take different perspectives on the events and may describe a variety of different aspects of the events.

1 mark should be given for each accurate relevant key point of knowledge.

A second mark should be given for each point that is developed, up to a maximum of **5 marks**. Candidates may achieve full marks by providing five straightforward points, by making three developed points, or a combination of these.

Possible points of knowledge may include:
1. Castles used as a home
2. Castles used for protection/defence against an enemy eg control of river crossings
3. Castles were used as barracks for knights
4. Castles were a symbol of power/wealth
5. Castles were administrative centres
6. Castles were used to hold courts
7. Castles were used to store food
8. Castles held feasts

2. *Candidates can be credited in a number of ways up to a maximum of 5 marks.*

Candidates must show a causal relationship between events.

Up to a **maximum of 5 marks in total**, **1 mark** should be given for each accurate, relevant reason, and a **second mark** should be given for reasons that are developed. Candidates may achieve full marks by providing five straightforward reasons, three developed reasons, or a combination of these.

Possible reasons may include:
1. Inspired by the Pope's speech/preachers such as Peter the Hermit
2. To recapture Jerusalem/free eastern Christians from Muslim rule
3. Religious motives/desire to fulfil Christian duty to God eg Raymond of Toulouse
4. To have sins forgiven/to be able to enter heaven in the afterlife
5. To gain land eg younger sons or those disinherited eg Bohemond of Taranto/Baldwin of Boulogne
6. Peer pressure/to represent a family eg Hugh of Vermandois/Stephen of Blois
7. Military skills/to fight in battle with the Church's blessing eg Tancred wanted to escape the limitations of the Peace of God movement

8. Social mobility eg peasants wanted better life/"land of milk and honey"

3. *Candidates can be credited in a number of ways up to a maximum of 6 marks.*

Candidates must make an overall judgement about how fully the source explains the events. **1 mark** may be given for each valid point interpreted from the source or each valid point of significant omission provided. The candidate can achieve **up to 3 marks** for their interpretation of the parts of the source they consider are relevant in terms of the proposed question where there is also at least one point of significant omission identified to imply a judgement has been made about the limitations of the source. For full marks to be given each point needs to be discretely mentioned in terms of the question.

A maximum of 2 marks may be given for answers which refer only to the source or in which no judgement has been made.

Possible points which may be identified in the source include:
1. Alexius feared they would attack his city/made them camp outside the city and only allowed them to enter in small groups
2. Offered treasure and supplies to Crusaders who agreed to fight for him
3. Any Crusader who refused was attacked and forced to surrender
4. Alexius did not trust the Crusaders/made plans to remove them from Constantinople

Possible points of significant omission may include:
1. Crusaders blamed Alexius for the failure of the People's Crusade
2. Made Crusaders take an oath of loyalty/made Crusaders take an oath they would capture land for him
3. Provided the Crusaders with a guide/troops/supplies
4. Provided the Crusaders with boats to blockade Nicaea
5. Negotiated with the Muslims inside Nicaea/took the city behind the Crusaders' back
6. Baldwin broke his oath and captured Edessa
7. Alexius did not arrive at Antioch to help the Crusaders
8. Bohemond broke his oath and claimed Antioch

4. *Candidates can be credited in a number of ways up to a maximum of 4 marks.*

Candidates must make direct comparisons of the two sources, either overall or in detail. A simple comparison will indicate what points of detail or overall viewpoint they agree or disagree about and should be given **1 mark**.

A developed comparison of the points of detail or overall viewpoint should be given **2 marks**. Candidates may achieve full marks by making four simple comparisons, two developed comparisons or by a combination of these.

Possible points of comparison may include:

Overall: The sources agree about the character of Richard I	
Source B	**Source C**
Vowed to fulfil his Christian duty	Promised he would keep his oath to God
Excellent military commander who used clever tactics to win key battles	Used his experience and leadership to force the city to surrender
Always fought alongside his men, courageously attacking the enemy	Richard showed great bravery by defending his men and killing the enemy

Section 3, Context B, "Tea and Freedom,": the American Revolution, 1774-83

1. *Candidates can be credited in a number of ways **up to a maximum of 6 marks**.*

Candidates must make an overall judgement about how fully the source explains the events. **1 mark** may be given for each valid point interpreted from the source or each valid point of significant omission provided. The candidate can achieve **up to 3 marks** for their interpretation of the parts of the source they consider are relevant in terms of the proposed question where there is also at least one point of significant omission identified to imply a judgement has been made about the limitations of the source. For full marks to be given each point needs to be discretely mentioned in terms of the question.

A maximum of 2 marks may be given for answers which refer only to the source or in which no judgement has been made.

Possible points which may be identified in the source include:
1. The decision to increase taxes was very unpopular
2. The decision to maintain a standing army alarmed colonists
3. The Stamp Act provoked a furious reaction
4. Colonists organised a boycott of British goods

Possible points of significant omission may include:
1. Colonists felt that actions of the British government were damaging trade
2. The colonists were unhappy that the British were stopping them from moving West
3. There was anger among the colonists about the Quartering Act which allowed British soldiers to invade private property
4. There was anger among the colonists about a lack of representation in the British parliament
5. Events such as the Boston Massacre increased tension

2. *Candidates can be credited in a number of ways **up to a maximum of 5 marks**.*

They may take different perspectives on the events and may describe a variety of different aspects of the events.

1 mark should be given for each accurate relevant key point of knowledge. **A second mark** should be given for each point that is developed, up to a maximum of **5 marks**. Candidates may achieve full marks by providing five straightforward points, by making three developed points, or a combination of these.

Possible points of knowledge may include:
1. Colonists were angered by the passing of the Tea Act in 1773 which allowed the East India Company to undercut colonial merchants and smugglers
2. Bostonians disguised themselves as Mohawk Indians and boarded the three tea ships
3. Tea was emptied into the water of Boston harbour
4. Some of the tea was stolen
5. King George III and Parliament were outraged when they heard of these events
6. Lord North rejected the offer of compensation from some of the colonial merchants
7. Led to the passing of the 'Intolerable Acts' eg Massachusetts Act/ Administration of Justice Act/ Quartering Act/Quebec Act
8. Port of Boston closed

3. *Candidates can be credited in a number of ways **up to a maximum of 5 marks**.*

Candidates must show a causal relationship between events.

Up to a **maximum of 5 marks in total**, **1 mark** should be given for each accurate, relevant reason, and a **second mark** should be given for reasons that are developed. Candidates may achieve full marks by providing five straightforward reasons, three developed reasons, or a combination of these.

Possible reasons may include:
1. The British forces were poorly led so poorer tactics/ communication
2. There were tactical errors by Britain eg at Yorktown, so battles were lost
3. British army had to rely on mercenary forces, so less loyalty
4. British soldiers were not properly trained, so less effective
5. Colonial army was effectively led by George Washington, strong leader
6. British generals underestimated the bravery of the Americans
7. Rebel tactics also made life very difficult/rebels often used guerrilla tactics against British which were successful
8. Colonists had greater forces/able to call on minutemen when required, so more effective
9. Fighting a war so far from home made it difficult to supply British forces
10. Attacks by French and Spanish weakened/distracted British forces
11. Assistance from French and Spanish navies gave colonists control of the seas

4. *Candidates can be credited in a number of ways **up to a maximum of 4 marks**.*

Candidates must make direct comparisons of the two sources, either overall or in detail. A simple comparison will indicate what points of detail or overall viewpoint they agree or disagree about and should be given **1 mark**.

A developed comparison of the points of detail or overall viewpoint should be given **2 marks**. Candidates may achieve full marks by making four simple comparisons, two developed comparisons or by a combination of these.

Possible points of comparison may include:

| Overall: The sources agree that there were a number of reasons for the British defeat at Saratoga ||
Source B	Source C
Progress was then slowed by mountains and dense forest	Progress was slowed by the difficult terrain
Burgoyne had no reinforcements	Burgoyne's army was left on its own
Army was trapped against the Hudson River	British found themselves trapped at the little community of Saratoga

Section 3, Context C, USA 1850–1880

1. *Candidates can be credited in a number of ways **up to a maximum of 5 marks**.*

They may take different perspectives on the events and may describe a variety of different aspects of the events.

1 mark should be given for each accurate relevant key point of knowledge.

A second mark should be given for each point that is developed, up to a maximum of **5 marks**. Candidates may achieve full marks by providing five straightforward points, by making three developed points, or a combination of these.

Possible points of knowledge may include:
 1. Many subject to strict rules and regulations/had no freedom
 2. Slaves could be bought and sold/seen as property
 3. Worked long hours at hard work with only short breaks
 4. Subject to harsh/inhuman discipline eg whipping common
 5. Runaway slaves were beaten/maimed: use of dogs to hunt runaways
 6. Slaves needed permission to get married
 7. Slave marriages had no legal status
 8. Slave owners often named slave children
 9. Slave families often broken up/separated
 10. Slaves unable to visit family/relatives on other plantations
 11. Female slaves sometimes sexually abused by owners/overseers
 12. Children born to a slave, fathered by white owner, were still slaves
 13. Pregnant slaves were expected to work until the child was born.

2. *Candidates can be credited in a number of ways **up to a maximum of 5 marks**.*

Candidates must show a causal relationship between events.

Up to a **maximum of 5 marks in total**, **1 mark** should be given for each accurate, relevant reason, and a **second mark** should be given for reasons that are developed. Candidates may achieve full marks by providing five straightforward reasons, three developed reasons, or a combination of these.

Possible reasons may include:
 1. Kansas – Nebraska Act allowed States to decide if slave state or free state, which caused tension.
 2. Violence in Kansas (Bleeding Kansas) had led to a number of deaths, which increased tension
 3. Dred Scott Case caused unhappiness among abolitionists and Northern States
 4. Attack on Harpers Ferry by John Brown heightened tension
 5. Growth of Republican Party which favoured Northern Interests upset South
 6. Election of Lincoln upset South
 7. South felt North was infringing on states' rights, caused resentment
 8. Growth of militant abolitionism in North increased tension
 9. Southern planters resented Northern trade tariffs which affected their trade
 10. Expansion of Northern cities and immigration worried the South

3. *Candidates can be credited in a number of ways **up to a maximum of 6 marks**.*

Candidates must make an overall judgement about how fully the source explains the events. **1 mark** may be given for each valid point interpreted from the source or each valid point of significant omission provided. The candidate can achieve **up to 3 marks** for their interpretation of the parts of the source they consider are relevant in terms of the proposed question where there is also at least one point of significant omission identified to imply a judgement has been made about the limitations of the source. For full marks to be given each point needs to be discretely mentioned in terms of the question.

A maximum of 2 marks may be given for answers which refer only to the source or in which no judgement has been made.

Possible points which may be identified in the source include:
 1. Attracted by the promise of a better life
 2. Attracted by the warmer weather in California
 3. Went west because they thought the land would be more fertile
 4. Ranch owners realised that the plains could be used to feed their huge herds of cattle

Possible points of significant omission may include:
 1. Gold in California attracted many. Later gold discoveries in Black Hills also attracted prospectors
 2. Cheap land available in the west for farmers
 3. Belief in Manifest Destiny eg many Americans saw it as a duty to spread their way of life
 4. Mormons wished to find new lands to settle away from other people
 5. Railways encouraged many settlers west
 6. Government Acts offered land to settlers
 7. The Homestead Act of 1862/Timber and Culture Act of 1875 each offered cheap/free land to settlers
 8. Railroad companies sold land cheaply to settlers
 9. Freed slaves headed west after 1865 to escape persecution
 10. Shopkeepers and hotel owners travelled west to exploit the demand of the settlers
 11. Overcrowding of cities in East
 12. Sense of adventure

4. *Candidates can be credited in a number of ways **up to a maximum of 4 marks**.*

Candidates must make direct comparisons of the two sources, either overall or in detail. A simple comparison will indicate what points of detail or overall viewpoint they agree or disagree about and should be given **1 mark**.

A developed comparison of the points of detail or overall viewpoint should be given **2 marks**. Candidates may achieve full marks by making four simple comparisons, two developed comparisons or by a combination of these.

Possible points of comparison may include:

Overall: The sources disagree about the events which took place during the Sand Creek massacre of 1864.	
Source B	**Source C**
In the village there were 500 people	In the Cheyenne camp there were about 1200 people
Two-thirds of whom were women and children.	700 were warriors
Counted from 60 to 70 dead bodies, a large majority of whom were women and children.	I estimate there were 500 or 600 people killed/I saw only one woman who had been killed and I saw no dead children

Section 3, Context D, Hitler and Nazi Germany, 1919–1939

1. *Candidates can be credited in a number of ways* **up to a maximum of 5 marks.**

They may take different perspectives on the events and may describe a variety of different aspects of the events.
1 mark should be given for each accurate relevant key point of knowledge.

A second mark should be given for each point that is developed, up to a maximum of **5 marks.** Candidates may achieve full marks by providing five straightforward points, by making three developed points, or a combination of these.

Possible points of knowledge may include:
1. All men and women over 20 had the vote/over 35 in Presidential elections
2. All Germans were equal before the law
3. People had the right to vote by secret ballot
4. Everyone had the right of freedom of speech/to express opinions freely and openly
5. Freedom of association/people had the right to hold peaceful meetings
6. Freedom of press
7. Everyone had the right of freedom of religion
8. Letters and correspondence could not be opened and read
9. No one could be arrested without good reason/unless they broke the law
10. People had the right to join trade unions and societies
11. No one could be imprisoned without trial
12. Rights of privacy/people had the right of privacy in their own homes
13. People had the right to form political parties.

2. *Candidates can be credited in a number of ways* **up to a maximum of 4 marks.**

Candidates must make direct comparisons of the two sources, either overall or in detail. A simple comparison will indicate what points of detail or overall viewpoint they agree or disagree about and should be given **1 mark.**

A developed comparison of the points of detail or overall viewpoint should be given **2 marks.** Candidates may achieve full marks by making four simple comparisons, two developed comparisons or by a combination of these.

Possible points of comparison may include:

Overall: The sources agree that hyperinflation caused people difficulties	
Source B	**Source C**
Workers were paid twice a day/ rushed to shops before prices went up	Some workers were paid twice a day/could spend their wages instantly.
Millions of people faced starvation due to hyperinflation	They faced homelessness and starvation.
Pensioners who were living on fixed incomes found that prices rose much faster than their earnings	Pensioners lived on fixed incomes and received the same amount each week; these incomes were now worth nothing

3. *Candidates can be credited in a number of ways* **up to a maximum of 5 marks.**

Candidates must show a causal relationship between events.

Up to a **maximum of 5 marks in total**, **1 mark** should be given for each accurate, relevant reason, and a **second mark** should be given for reasons that are developed. Candidates may achieve full marks by providing five straightforward reasons, three developed reasons, or a combination of these.

Possible reasons may include:
1. Hitler appeared to offer Germany strong leadership, which was appealing
2. Offered solutions to Germany's economic problems, so popular
3. Promised to provide jobs for the unemployed , which was popular
4. Promised to overthrow the Treaty of Versailles, which was welcomed
5. Nazi rallies, eg Nuremberg, impressed people
6. Hitler was a superb speaker
7. Effective use of propaganda to get over his message
8. Hitler had a clear, simple message which appealed to many people
9. Promised support for the farmers, shopkeepers, etc, which was popular
10. Businessmen were attracted by Hitler's promise to destroy trade unions
11. Young people were attracted to the Hitler Youth
12. Promised to restore Germany as a world power, which was welcomed
13. Germany's best defence against Communism/support from middle classes
14. Discipline/uniforms of the SA impressed people
15. Widespread support from nationalists for his racial theories/anti-Semitism
16. Tired of the chaos of the Weimar Government and wanted a change/belief that democracy weak

4. *Candidates can be credited in a number of ways* **up to a maximum of 6 marks.**

Candidates must make an overall judgement about how fully the source explains the events. **1 mark** may be given for each valid point interpreted from the source or each valid point of significant omission provided. The candidate can achieve **up to 3 marks** for their interpretation of the parts of the source they consider are relevant in terms of the proposed question where there is also at least one point of significant omission identified to imply a judgement has been made about the limitations of the source. For full marks to be given each point needs to be discretely mentioned in terms of the question.

A maximum of 2 marks may be given for answers which refer only to the source or in which no judgement has been made.

Possible points which may be identified in the source include:
1. The KDF (Strength through Joy Organisation) controlled most forms of entertainment
2. Each year around seven million people took part in KDF sports matches
3. Mass outings to the theatre and the opera were arranged
4. Workers were also provided with affordable holidays including cruises and walking or skiing holidays

Possible points of significant omission may include:
1. Other Strength through Joy programmes such as: Evening classes for adults
The Peoples Car (Volkswagen) hire purchase scheme which turned out to be a swindle
2. Nuremberg Laws
3. Hitler Youth later made compulsory
4. Role of Gestapo
5. Propaganda (examples of)
6. Censorship of newspapers/films/books/films
7. Books considered unacceptable were burned
8. Complaining about the Nazis against the law
9. Penalty for anti-Hitler jokes was death
10. National Labour Service
11. Compulsory Military Service

Section 3, Context E, Red Flag: Lenin and the Russian Revolution, 1894-1921

1. *Candidates can be credited in a number of ways up to a maximum of 5 marks.*

They may take different perspectives on the events and may describe a variety of different aspects of the events.

1 mark should be given for each accurate relevant key point of knowledge.

A second mark should be given for each point that is developed, up to a maximum of **5 marks**. Candidates may achieve full marks by providing five straightforward points, by making three developed points, or a combination of these.

Possible points of knowledge may include:
1. The Pillars of Autocracy controlled the Russian people
2. The Civil Service controlled everyday life eg censorship of newspapers
3. Use of secret police the Okhrana to spy on opponents
4. Support from church who taught peasants that Tsar should be obeyed
5. Use of army/Cossacks to crush uprisings or opponents
6. Use of exile to get rid of opponents

2. *Candidates can be credited in a number of ways up to a maximum of 5 marks.*

Candidates must show a causal relationship between events.

Up to a **maximum of 5 marks in total**, **1 mark** should be given for each accurate, relevant reason, and a **second mark** should be given for reasons that are developed. Candidates may achieve full marks by providing five straightforward reasons, three developed reasons, or a combination of these.

Possible reasons may include:
1. Peasants unhappy due to redemption payments and high taxes (bad harvests made situation worse)
2. Peasant 'land hunger' caused discontent
3. Workers unhappy with poor wages and working conditions
4. Violent strikes due to long hours and low wages (government reaction made situation worse eg by arresting leaders)
5. Radical politics among university students caused further discontent
6. Defeat in the Russo – Japanese War led to unrest
7. Policy of Russification caused discontent amongst nationalities eg Poles
8. Some sections of military become discontented – Potemkin Mutiny.
9. Events of Bloody Sunday in January 1905 led to discontent and strikes
10. Set up of St Petersburg & Moscow Soviets
11. October Manifesto split middle classes from workers and socialists

3. *Candidates can be credited in a number of ways up to a maximum of 6 marks.*

Candidates must make an overall judgement about how fully the source explains the events. **1 mark** may be given for each valid point interpreted from the source or each valid point of significant omission provided. The candidate can achieve **up to 3 marks** for their interpretation of the parts of the source they consider are relevant in terms of the proposed question where there is also at least one point of significant omission identified to imply a judgement has been made about the limitations of the source. For full marks to be given each point needs to be discretely mentioned in terms of the question.

A maximum of 2 marks may be given for answers which refer only to the source or in which no judgement has been made.

Possible points which may be identified in the source include:
1. First World War was to have a terrible impact on Russia
2. Heart-breaking losses were suffered by the Tsars armies
3. Thousands of wounded soldiers were left lying untreated on the ground for days
4. Not even quarter enough bandages

Possible points of significant omission may include:
1. Military defeat at Tannenburg and Masurian lakes
2. Collapse of the economy
3. Inflation affected prices
4. Population suffered shortages of food and fuel
5. Tsar took control of the armies and was then blamed for defeats
6. Tsarina took charge and was unpopular as she was German-born/thought to be under the influence of Rasputin
7. Political instability – regular changes to both Prime Ministers and Ministers/ministerial 'leapfrog'
8. Allegations of government corruption eg Rasputin weakened Tsar's authority
9. Conscripting millions of peasants led to shortage of grain
10. Inability of the government to organise procurement/movement of supplies to civilians or war production for the military

4. *Candidates can be credited in a number of ways **up to a maximum of 4 marks**.*

Candidates must make direct comparisons of the two sources, either overall or in detail. A simple comparison will indicate what points of detail or overall viewpoint they agree or disagree about and should be given **1 mark**.

A developed comparison of the points of detail or overall viewpoint should be given **2 marks**. Candidates may achieve full marks by making four simple comparisons, two developed comparisons or by a combination of these.

Possible points of comparison may include:

Overall: The sources agree the situation was serious with shortages and unrest	
Source B	**Source C**
Disturbances...are becoming more serious	The situation was already very serious
Shortages of bread	They wanted bread but... many had been unable to get any
Workers are without jobs	Several thousand workmen unemployed

Section 3, Context F, Mussolini and Fascist Italy, 1919-1939

1. *Candidates can be credited in a number of ways **up to a maximum of 5 marks**.*

They may take different perspectives on the events and may describe a variety of different aspects of the events.

1 mark should be given for each accurate relevant key point of knowledge.

A second mark should be given for each point that is developed, up to a maximum of **5 marks**. Candidates may achieve full marks by providing five straightforward points, by making three developed points, or a combination of these.

Possible points of knowledge may include:
1. Mussolini aimed to make Italy a great power/wanted control of Mediterranean
2. Mussolini wanted to expand Italy's colonial empire in Africa/increase Italian influence in the Balkans
3. In 1924 Mussolini took control of the Yugoslavian port of Fiume
4. Wished to appear as a statesman in early years eg Locarno 1925
5. Mussolini supported King Zog in Albania (by signing a Treaty of Friendship in 1926 Mussolini made Albania into an Italian satellite state)
6. Mussolini funded Croat nationalists in order to create trouble for Yugoslavia
7. Mussolini settled the border dispute with Britain over Libya and Egypt
8. Mussolini aided Dolfuss in order to provide a bulwark against Nazi aggression
9. In 1935 concluded Stresa Front with France and Britain (wished to be recognised as a great power)
10. Launched attack on Ethiopia
11. Intervened in Spanish Civil War
12. Agreed Anti-Comintern Pact with Japan and Germany in 1937
13. Posed as mediator at Munich Conference Sept 1938
14. Invaded Albania in 1939
15. Pact of Steel with Germany concluded May 1939

2. *Candidates can be credited in a number of ways **up to a maximum of 5 marks**.*

Candidates must show a causal relationship between events.

Up to a **maximum of 5 marks in total**, **1 mark** should be given for each accurate, relevant reason, and a **second mark** should be given for reasons that are developed. Candidates may achieve full marks by providing five straightforward reasons, three developed reasons, or a combination of these.

Possible reasons may include:
1. Many were unhappy when trade unions were outlawed
2. Revaluation of the lira in 1927 led to decline in exports, causing discontent
3. Increase in unemployment 1926-28. By 1933 unemployment had reached 2 million, causing unpopularity
4. High tariffs restricted imports, so people unhappy
5. Real wages fell, so people unhappy
6. Sick pay and paid holidays were not introduced until 1938, so people were unhappy
7. The failure to make Italy self-sufficient – embarrassment/unpopularity
8. As part of the Battle For Grain land in central and southern regions was turned over to wheat production despite being unsuitable (traditional agricultural exports declined), unpopular in these areas
9. Increasing government control of industry was resented

3. *Candidates can be credited in a number of ways **up to a maximum of 6 marks**.*

Candidates must make an overall judgement about how fully the source explains the events. **1 mark** may be given for each valid point interpreted from the source or each valid point of significant omission provided. The candidate can achieve **up to 3 marks** for their interpretation of the parts of the source they consider are relevant in terms of the proposed question where there is also at least one point of significant omission identified to imply a judgement has been made about the limitations of the source. For full marks to be given each point needs to be discretely mentioned in terms of the question.

A maximum of 2 marks may be given for answers which refer only to the source or in which no judgement has been made.

Possible points which may be identified in the source include:
1. Mussolini's press office issued official versions of events which all the newspapers were expected to publish without question
2. The radio and the cinema were also used to broadcast Fascist propaganda
3. News bulletins broadcast a daily diet of Mussolini's speeches and praised him as the saviour of Italy
4. The media played a crucial role in the cult of "Il Duce"

Possible points of significant omission may include:
1. Mussolini started a new calendar with Year 1 beginning in 1922
2. The regime made propagandist feature films
3. The Duce was shown as a great athlete and musician (cult of personality)
4. Brainwashing/indoctrination of young at school/ textbooks or youth groups
5. The newspapers suggested that Mussolini was infallible
6. An image of youthfulness was portrayed by not referring to Mussolini's age or the fact he wore glasses/usually seen in uniform
7. It was said that Mussolini worked 16 hour days – his light was left on after he had gone to bed to maintain this fiction

8. Use of RC church to support Fascists policies eg against communism at home or in Spain

4. *Candidates can be credited in a number of ways **up to a maximum of 4 marks**.*

Candidates must make direct comparisons of the two sources, either overall or in detail. A simple comparison will indicate what points of detail or overall viewpoint they agree or disagree about and should be given **1 mark**.

A developed comparison of the points of detail or overall viewpoint should be given **2 marks**. Candidates may achieve full marks by making four simple comparisons, two developed comparisons or by a combination of these.

Possible points of comparison may include:

Overall: The sources agree that there was a limited opposition to the regime	
Source A	Source B
Fascist policies benefited the rich to ensure their support.	Big businessmen and landowners supported a regime which always seemed to be on their side.
The signing of the Lateran agreement in 1929 was important in winning the support of Catholics.	This new close relationship with the church reduced the threat of opposition from Catholics.
There was some opposition in the army, but this was never carried out in a coordinated way	While some army generals opposed Mussolini others liked his aggressive attitude.

Section 3, Context G, Free at Last? Civil Rights in the USA, 1918–1968

1. *Candidates can be credited in a number of ways **up to a maximum of 4 marks**.*

Candidates must make direct comparisons of the two sources, either overall or in detail. A simple comparison will indicate what points of detail or overall viewpoint they agree or disagree about and should be given **1 mark**.

A developed comparison of the points of detail or overall viewpoint should be given **2 marks**. Candidates may achieve full marks by making four simple comparisons, two developed comparisons or by a combination of these.

Possible points of comparison may include:

Overall: The sources agree about the poor living and working conditions of immigrants	
Source A	Source B
Immigrants from the same country usually lived in the same areas of the city	Immigrants tended to live in their own communities: in New York there was a Polish district, a Jewish district and an Italian district
These areas contained tenement slums which were damp, dark and filthy with no water supply, toilets or drains	Tenements buildings in these areas were often five or six storeys high with rooms which lacked light or sanitation
Immigrants had to take any work they could get, usually low paid jobs such as labourers or servants	Finding a well-paid, skilled job was a common problem for poorly educated immigrants

2. *Candidates can be credited in a number of ways **up to a maximum of 5 marks**.*

They may take different perspectives on the events and may describe a variety of different aspects of the events.

1 mark should be given for each accurate relevant key point of knowledge.

A second mark should be given for each point that is developed, up to a maximum of **5 marks**. Candidates may achieve full marks by providing five straightforward points, by making three developed points, or a combination of these.

Possible points of knowledge may include:
1. Legal action leading to the decision of the Supreme Court in 1954 to declare segregation in schools unconstitutional
2. Bus boycott in Montgomery
3. Little Rock, Arkansas – attempt by black students to enter Central High School
4. Sit-downs/Sit-ins eg deliberately holding up traffic/ the occupation of lunch counters and other segregated places
5. Freedom rides – travel on buses through southern states using segregated facilities at bus stations
6. Project C – sit-ins and marches in Birmingham, Alabama led by Martin Luther King
7. March on Washington

3. *Candidates can be credited in a number of ways **up to a maximum of 6 marks**.*

Candidates must make an overall judgement about how fully the source explains the events. **1 mark** may be given for each valid point interpreted from the source or each valid point of significant omission provided. The candidate can achieve **up to 3 marks** for their interpretation of the parts of the source they consider are relevant in terms of the proposed question where there is also at least one point of significant omission identified to imply a judgement has been made about the limitations of the source. For full marks to be given each point needs to be discretely mentioned in terms of the question.

A maximum of 2 marks may be given for answers which refer only to the source or in which no judgement has been made.

Possible points which may be identified in the source include:
1. President Truman issued orders to desegregate the US military
2. He also set up a President's Committee on civil rights in 1946 to report to him on how progress towards black civil rights could be made
3. In 1960 Congress passed a Civil Rights Act which established penalties for obstructing black voting.
4. The assassination of President Kennedy in November 1963 came at the time he was preparing a Civil Rights Bill

Possible points of significant omission may include:
1. Supreme Court decision declared that schools could no longer be segregated
2. In 1957 President Eisenhower sent in federal troops to Little Rock in Arkansas to ensure that nine black children could safely enter a recently desegregated high school
3. Federal Marshalls were sent to escort James Meredith through the gates of Mississippi University
4. Civil Rights Act passed in 1964

4. *Candidates can be credited in a number of ways up to a maximum of 5 marks.*

Candidates must show a causal relationship between events.

Up to a maximum of **5 marks in total**, **1 mark** should be given for each accurate, relevant reason, and a **second mark** should be given for reasons that are developed. Candidates may achieve full marks by providing five straightforward reasons, three developed reasons, or a combination of these.

Possible reasons may include:
1. Black Panthers gained support for their demand for the release of black prisoners
2. Black Panthers gained support due to their efforts to give practical help to poor blacks eg breakfast clubs in schools
3. Black Panthers had charismatic leaders who gained attention and popularity
4. The Black Panthers encouraged blacks to be proud of the colour of their skin and their African American culture. This appealed to many
5. Black Panthers condoned violence and this appealed to many blacks who were frustrated by the non-violent methods of the Civil Rights Movement
6. Black Panthers attracted further support after gaining the much publicised support of athletes at the Olympic Games in 1968

Section 3, Context H, Appeasement and the Road to War, 1918-1939

1. *Candidates can be credited in a number of ways up to a maximum of 5 marks.*

They may take different perspectives on the events and may describe a variety of different aspects of the events.

1 mark should be given for each accurate relevant key point of knowledge.

A second mark should be given for each point that is developed, up to a maximum of 5 marks. Candidates may achieve full marks by providing five straightforward points, by making three developed points, or a combination of these.

Possible points of knowledge may include:
1. The German army was limited to 100,000 men
2. The German army was forbidden from having tanks
3. The German army was forbidden from being situated in the Rhineland
4. The German navy was forbidden from having submarines
5. The German navy was limited to six battleships
6. Germany was forbidden from having an air force

2. *Candidates can be credited in a number of ways up to a maximum of 6 marks.*

Candidates must make an overall judgement about how fully the source explains the events. **1 mark** may be given for each valid point interpreted from the source or each valid point of significant omission provided. The candidate can achieve **up to 3 marks** for their interpretation of the parts of the source they consider are relevant in terms of the proposed question where there is also at least one point of significant omission identified to imply a judgement has been made about the limitations of the source. For full marks to be given each point needs to be discretely mentioned in terms of the question.

A maximum of 2 marks may be given for answers which refer only to the source or in which no judgement has been made.

Possible points which may be identified in the source include:
1. The USA refused to join as they were not interested in getting involved in the problems of other countries
2. Initially Russia was not invited to join, so another great country of the world was absent
3. Taking decisions was difficult as the Assembly had to be unanimous and member states often could not agree
4. A further problem was that the League did not have its own army to back up its decisions

Possible points of significant omission may include:
1. Germany was not allowed to join until 1926, so another major power was absent
2. Member countries were reluctant to agree to economic sanctions for fear of damaging their own economies
3. Member countries were reluctant to take action against a powerful member state
4. The two most powerful member countries Britain and France were reluctant to commit troops to fight for the League
5. Countries lost faith in the League with each failure

3. *Candidates can be credited in a number of ways up to a maximum of 5 marks.*

Candidates must show a causal relationship between events.

Up to a **maximum of 5 marks in total**, **1 mark** should be given for each accurate, relevant reason, and a **second mark** should be given for reasons that are developed. Candidates may achieve full marks by providing five straightforward reasons, three developed reasons, or a combination of these.

Possible reasons may include:
1. There was a belief that although Germany had broken the Treaty, they had been too severely punished at Versailles
2. It was argued that Germany had done little more than liberate her own territory
3. Many believed that the Franco-Soviet Pact had unduly provoked Hitler
4. Many within Britain saw a stronger Germany as a useful barrier against the spread of communism
5. It was hoped that a conciliatory approach might persuade Germany to re-enter the League and resume disarmament talks
6. It was felt that the relative weakness of the British armed forces restricted the opportunity for direct action
7. There was little sign that public opinion would have supported military action against Hitler

4. *Candidates can be credited in a number of ways up to a maximum of 4 marks.*

Candidates must make direct comparisons of the two sources, either overall or in detail. A simple comparison will indicate what points of detail or overall viewpoint they agree or disagree about and should be given **1 mark**.

A developed comparison of the points of detail or overall viewpoint should be given **2 marks**. Candidates may achieve full marks by making four simple comparisons, two developed comparisons or by a combination of these.

Possible points of comparison may include:

Overall: The sources agree that Anschluss was a positive event which should be welcomed	
Source B	Source C
The population of Austria comprised ethnic Germans, a majority of whom are enthusiastic about the Anschluss/The Austrians will not only feel at home as part of Germany/Their German brothers	That there has been no fighting is proof of the desire of the Austrian people to belong to Germany
It was a mistake of the peacemakers at Versailles to forbid the union of Austria and Germany	The union of these two countries should never have been forbidden at Versailles
They will benefit financially too from an increase in trade	Austrians will also benefit from greater markets for their raw materials and manufactured goods

Section 3, Context I, World War II, 1939-1945

1. *Candidates can be credited in a number of ways **up to a maximum of 4 marks**.*

Candidates must make direct comparisons of the two sources, either overall or in detail. A simple comparison will indicate what points of detail or overall viewpoint they agree or disagree about and should be given **1 mark**.

A developed comparison of the points of detail or overall viewpoint should be given **2 marks**. Candidates may achieve full marks by making four simple comparisons, two developed comparisons or by a combination of these.

Possible points of comparison may include:

Overall: The sources agree that the tactic of Blitzkrieg was effective at the beginning of the war.	
Source A	Source B
Blitzkrieg was a tactic based on speed and surprise	Hitler was very excited by a plan of attack that was based purely on speed and movement
It required the effective use of Stuka dive bombers	Stuka dive bombers were sent in to 'soften' up the enemy
These were supported by light tank units and infantry	Then the tanks attacked, supported by infantry

2. *Candidates can be credited in a number of ways **up to a maximum of 5 marks**.*

They may take different perspectives on the events and may describe a variety of different aspects of the events.

1 mark should be given for each accurate relevant key point of knowledge.

A second mark should be given for each point that is developed, up to a maximum of **5 marks**. Candidates may achieve full marks by providing five straightforward points, by making three developed points, or a combination of these.

Possible points of knowledge may include:
1. Citizens in the west placed under German military rule
2. Eastern European civilians more brutally governed under German civil administrations
3. Vichy regime set up in southern France where citizens lived under German controlled French Government
4. Economies controlled: industry and agriculture supervised and the people often left to go hungry
5. Workers issued with work cards and free deployment of labour was prohibited
6. In western Europe workers pressured to 'volunteer' for work in Germany/ pressure on young men to join 'crusade' against communism in East
7. Almost all food was rationed
8. Curfews in place
9. All citizens had to carry an identity card
10. Gestapo operated under Night and Fog Decree of 1941, giving them powers to seize anyone endangering German security
11. Media censorship
12. SS brutality and the Police State ruled over occupied citizens
13. Jews and other 'undesirables' deported to concentration camps mostly in the east/willing collaboration in deportation Jews eg Vichy
14. Jewish Poles dispossessed, property and belongings confiscated
15. Jews in Poland forced to live in ghettos then deported to camps in the east/examples of life in the ghettos
16. Special forces in Eastern Europe killed Jews and other undesirables in mass killings eg gypsies

3. *Candidates can be credited in a number of ways **up to a maximum of 6 marks**.*

Candidates must make an overall judgement about how fully the source explains the events. **1 mark** may be given for each valid point interpreted from the source or each valid point of significant omission provided. The candidate can achieve **up to 3 marks** for their interpretation of the parts of the source they consider are relevant in terms of the proposed question where there is also at least one point of significant omission identified to imply a judgement has been made about the limitations of the source. For full marks to be given each point needs to be discretely mentioned in terms of the question.

A maximum of 2 marks may be given for answers which refer only to the source.

Possible points which may be identified in the source include:
1. It helped Jews or Allied airmen who had crash landed in France, to escape
2. School children were recruited to help smuggle people across the borders of northern and southern France
3. The Resistance movement produced anti-German propaganda which was crucial in undermining Nazi rule
4. Nazi control was further challenged by the Resistance who worked to punish any French collaboration

Possible points of significant omission may include:
1. Key intelligence link for Allied spy networks
2. Sabotaged German military operations eg blowing up trains, convoys, ships etc
3. Targeted and killed many high ranking Nazi officials
4. Carried out acts of sabotage prior to and during the D-Day landings to help Allied establish a foothold in Normandy/pinned down vital German forces
5. Radio operators (pianists) to send messages of German activities and other communications back to Britain

6. Telephone workers sabotaged telephone lines and intercepted German military messages
7. Postal workers intercepted important military communications
8. Rail workers diverted freight shipments/caused derailments/destroyed tracks/blew up bridges
9. Created labs to manufacture explosives/stole explosives and other resources from German army

4. *Candidates can be credited in a number of ways* **up to a maximum of 5 marks.**

Candidates must show a causal relationship between events.

Up to a **maximum of 5 marks in total**, **1 mark** should be given for each accurate, relevant reason, and a **second mark** should be given for reasons that are developed. Candidates may achieve full marks by providing five straightforward reasons, three developed reasons, or a combination of these.

Possible reasons may include:
1. Russian army encircled the city by mid-April due to their success in previous battles
2. Stalin had prioritised capturing Berlin before the Allies
3. Russians advanced easily against poor German defences at the Oder River/German units chose to concentrate fighting to the west of the city so they could surrender to Allied forces rather than Russian
4. Defence of the city of Berlin relied upon disorganised/poorly armed units from the German army and Hitler Youth members/elderly men or boys
5. City of Berlin defences in panic and disarray, so easier
6. Allied aerial bombing of the city assisted the Russian army
7. Artillery barrage into the city began on April 16th and pushed back the German defences further
8. Hitler sacked commanders, created confusion
9. Loss of morale after Hitler committed suicide

Section 3, Context J, The Cold War, 1945-1989

1. *Candidates can be credited in a number of ways* **up to a maximum of 5 marks.**

Candidates must show a causal relationship between events.

Up to a **maximum of 5 marks in total**, **1 mark** should be given for each accurate, relevant reason, and a **second mark** should be given for reasons that are developed. Candidates may achieve full marks by providing five straightforward reasons, three developed reasons, or a combination of these.

Possible reasons may include:
1. The only thing that kept them together was over – the Second World War
2. Disagreements at Potsdam eg over Poland
3. The Americans had developed the atomic bomb and this angered/ worried the Soviet Union
4. Soviet troops were occupying most of Eastern Europe and this caused tension
5. Truman, the new American President was more anti-communist than Roosevelt
6. An arms race developed causing further tension
7. Different ideas – capitalism versus communism
8. The Soviets saw Marshall Aid as an American attempt to dominate Europe/Soviet satellites prevented from accepting Marshall Aid
9. Berlin Blockade, 1948-1949, deepened the divisions between East and West

10. The establishment of NATO by America and its allies in 1949 caused further division
11. Establishment of Warsaw Pact 1955 heightened tensions
12. The Soviets and the Americans involved on different sides in proxy wars eg Korea

2. *Candidates can be credited in a number of ways* **up to a maximum of 6 marks.**

Candidates must make an overall judgement about how fully the source explains the events. **1 mark** may be given for each valid point interpreted from the source or each valid point of significant omission provided. The candidate can achieve **up to 3 marks** for their interpretation of the parts of the source they consider are relevant in terms of the proposed question where there is also at least one point of significant omission identified to imply a judgement has been made about the limitations of the source. For full marks to be given each point needs to be discretely mentioned in terms of the question.

A maximum of 2 marks may be given for answers which refer only to the source or in which no judgement has been made.

Possible points which may be identified in the source include:
1. President Truman explained that America would resist the spread of Communism
2. The Americans had responded to French requests for assistance in Vietnam
3. It was clear that South Vietnam could not resist Communism without the support of American troops
4. Many in America believed war was necessary to stop the spread of Soviet influence

Possible points of significant omission may include:
1. America feared that a civil war was developing in South Vietnam.
2. America was increasingly concerned about the influence of China in south-east Asia
3. There was a widespread belief in the Domino Theory eg Thailand, Laos, Burma, Cambodia even New Zealand and Australia could fall to communism
4. There was a general concern that America was falling behind in the Cold War at this time
5. Gulf of Tonkin incident led America to become involved in a full scale war in Vietnam.

3. *Candidates can be credited in a number of ways* **up to a maximum of 4 marks.**

Candidates must make direct comparisons of the two sources, either overall or in detail. A simple comparison will indicate what points of detail or overall viewpoint they agree or disagree about and should be given **1 mark**.

A developed comparison of the points of detail or overall viewpoint should be given **2 marks**. Candidates may achieve full marks by making four simple comparisons, two developed comparisons or by a combination of these.

Possible points of comparison may include:

Overall: The sources agree that the Soviets were at fault	
Source A	**Source B**
The source of world trouble and tension is Moscow	We now say with confidence that this crisis was caused by Moscow.
They have rejected an all-German peace treaty	The Soviets rejected an American proposal for a peace treaty
It is they who have rejected … the rule of international law.	The Soviet domination of East Germany was a clear breach of international law

4. *Candidates can be credited in a number of ways **up to a maximum of 5 marks**.*

They may take different perspectives on the events and may describe a variety of different aspects of the events.

1 mark should be given for each accurate relevant key point of knowledge.

A second mark should be given for each point that is developed, up to a maximum of **5 marks**. Candidates may achieve full marks by providing five straightforward points, by making three developed points, or a combination of these.

Possible points of knowledge may include:
1. Cuba stayed Communist/Castro's position strengthened as Kennedy promised not to invade
2. American missiles withdrawn from Turkey/Italy
3. Kennedy greatly improved his reputation in America and the West
4. Khrushchev was able to claim he prevented America from taking over Cuba, a useful ally so close to America
5. Krushchev seemed weak as American missiles removed in secret/led directly to Krushchev's fall 2 years later
6. Led to a thaw in the Cold War
7. 'Hot line' set up between the White House and the Kremlin
8. Nuclear Test Ban Treaty signed in 1963

Acknowledgements

Permission has been sought from all relevant copyright holders and Hodder Gibson is grateful for the use of the following:

Source B: An extract from the "Inverness Courier", 30 May 1838 (public domain) (SQP page 6);

Source A: An extract from "Forgotten Voices of the Great War" by Max Arthur, published by Ebury Press 2002 © The Random House Group Ltd. (SQP page 7);

Source B: An extract from http://www.spartacus.schoolnet.co.uk/FWWdora.htm © Spartacus Educational (SQP page 7);

Source A: An extract from "The Bitter Cry of Outcast London, An Enquiry into the Conditions of the Abject Poor" by Andrew Mearns, 1883 (public domain) (SQP page 12);

Source C: An extract from www.middle-ages.org.uk/saladin.htm © Linda Alchin, www.middle-ages.org.uk (SQP page 13);

Source A: An extract from http://americanhistory.about.com/od/civilwarmenu/a/cause_civil_war.htm © About, Inc. (SQP page 15);

Source C: An extract from "Civil Rights in the USA, 1863-1890" by David Paterson, Susan and Doug Willoughby, published by Heinemann © Pearson Education (SQP page 15);

Source C: An extract from "Hitler's Domestic Policy" published by HarperCollins Publishers Ltd. © 1997 Andrew Boxer (SQP page 16);

Source C: An extract from "Europe's Changing Economy in the Second Half of the Nineteenth Century" by Sidney Pollard © Sempringham; www.ehistory.org.uk (SQP page 18);

Source C: An extract from "Laughter Wasn't Rationed: Remembering the War Years in Germany" by Dorothea (von Schwanenfluegel) Lawson, 1999 © Tricor Press (SQP page 21);

Source A: An extract from "History of the Reformation in Scotland" by John Knox (public domain) (Model Paper 1 page 4);

Source A: An extract from "History of the Union" by Daniel Defoe, 1709 (public domain) (Model Paper 1 page 5);

Source A: An extract from "The Glasgow Reporter", 4 March 1846 (public domain) (Model Paper 1 page 6);

Source B: An extract from "Modern World History" by Ben Walsh, published by John Murray 1996 © Hodder Education (Model Paper 1 page 7);

Source A: An extract from "The History of Mary, Queen of Scots" by F. Mignet (public domain) (Model Paper 2 page 4);

Source B: An extract from "The Emperor's New Kilt" by Jan-Andrew Henderson, published by Mainstream, 2000 © The Random House Group Ltd. (Model Paper 2 page 6);

Source A: An extract from "Scotland: A New History" by Michael Lynch, published by Pimlico, 1992 © The Random House Group Ltd. (Model Paper 2 page 7);

Source B: An extract from "Women's Suffrage a Short History of a Great Movement" by Millicent Fawcet, 1912 (public domain) (Model Paper 2 page 7);

Source A: An extract from "Waterloo to the Great Exhibition" by Colin McNab and Robert MacKenzie, published by Longman, 1982 © Pearson Education (Model Paper 2 page 9);

Source C: An extract from "Race Relations in the USA 1863–1980" by Vivienne Sanders, published by Hodder Murray, 2006 © Hodder Education (Model Paper 2 page 12);

Source A: An extract from "Inside The Third Reich" by Albert Speer, 1970 © The Macmillan Company, New York (Model Paper 2 page 13);

Source B: An extract from "Turning Points in History – The Abolition of Slavery 1863" by Janet Riehecky, published by Heinemann, 2002 © Capstone Global Library Ltd. (Model Paper 3 page 12);

Source A: An extract from "People and Power: Germany" by Ian Matheson, published by Hodder & Stoughton, 1999 © Hodder Education (Model Paper 3 page 13);

Source B: An extract from "Weimar Germany and the Third Reich" by J.F. Corkery and R.C.F. Stone, published by Heinemann, 1982 © J.F. Corkery and R.C.F. Stone (Model Paper 3 page 13);

Source A: An extract from "History of the Russian Revolution" by Leon Trotsky, published by Pathfinder Press, 1932 (public domain) (Model Paper 3 page 14);

Source B: An extract from 'Dear Francesca' by Mary Contini, published by Ebury Press © The Random House Group Ltd. 2003 (2014 page 6);

Source A: The War Memoirs of David Lloyd George, 1938, published by Odhams (public domain) (2014 page 7);

Source A: An extract from 'Black Peoples of the Americas', by Nigel Smith published by Oxford University Press, 1995 (2014 page 10);

Source A: An extract from a report on housing in Manchester, written by a doctor in 1832. Taken from 'The Report from the Poor Law Commissioners on an Inquiry into the Sanitary Conditions of the Labouring Population of Great Britain, London, 1842' by Edwin Chadwick. (2014 page 11);

Source A: An extract from 'From The Cradle to the Grave: Social Welfare in Britain 1890s–1951' by Simon Wood & Claire Wood, published by Hodder & Stoughton Educational 2002 (2014 page 12).

Hodder Gibson would like to thank SQA for use of any past exam questions that may have been used in model papers, whether amended or in original form.